# EX AUDITU

An International Journal for the Theological Interpretation of Scripture

**VOL. 24**  **2008**

Ex Auditu is published annually by
Wipf and Stock Publishers, 199 West 8th Avenue, Suite 3, Eugene, Oregon 97401, USA

---

**SUBSCRIPTIONS**

*Individuals:*
U.S.A. and all other countries (in U.S. funds): $20.00
Students: $12.00

*Institutions:*
U.S.A. and all other countries (in U.S. funds): $30.00

---

This periodical is indexed in the ATLA Religion Database, published by the American Theological Library Association, 300 S. Wacker Dr., Suite 2100, Chicago, IL 60606, Email: atla@atla.com, WWW: http://www.atla.com/; *Internationale Zeitschriftenshau für Bibelwissenschaft; Religious and Theological Abstracts; and Old Testament Abstracts.*

Please address all subscription correspondence
and change of address information to Wipf & Stock Publishers.

©2009 by Wipf and Stock Publishers
ISSN: 0883-0053
ISBN: 978-1-60608-740-4

# EX AUDITU

An International Journal for the Theological Interpretation of Scripture

**Klyne R. Snodgrass**, Editor
**Stephen Chester**, Associate Editor
**D. Christopher Spinks**, Associate Editor

North Park Theological Seminary
3225 West Foster Avenue
Chicago, Illinois 60625-4987
USA

Tel: (773) 244-6243
Fax: (773) 244-6244
email: ksnodgrass@northpark.edu
Web site: http://wipfandstock.com/journals/ex_auditu

**EDITORIAL BOARD**

**Terence E. Fretheim**, Luther Seminary, St. Paul, MN
**Richard B. Hays**, The Divinity School, Duke University, Durham, NC
**John E. Phelan, Jr.**, President of North Park Theological Seminary, Chicago, IL
**Jon R. Stock**, Wipf & Stock Publishers, Eugene, OR
**Miroslav Volf**, Yale Divinity School, New Haven, CT
**John Wipf**, Wipf & Stock Publishers, Eugene, OR

THE EDITORIAL BOARD MEMBERS AND CONSULTANTS represent various disciplines and denominations. Theological Interpretation of Scripture is a task to be taken seriously by scholars who are committed to the Christian faith and tradition. However, as one editorial consultant stated: "let people gradually get used to the idea that a sane hermeneutics is both oriented in advance toward agreement/consent and is simultaneously exigent, discriminating, critical."

## EDITORIAL CONSULTANTS

**Richard Bauckham**
University of St. Andrews, Emeritus
St. Andrews, Scotland

**M. Daniel Carroll R.**
Denver Seminary
Denver, Colorado

**Jan Du Rand**
Rand Afrikaans University
Johannesburg, South Africa

**Willie Jennings**
The Divinity School
Duke University
Durham, N. Carolina

**Robert Johnston**
Fuller Theological Seminary
Pasadena, California

**R. Walter L. Moberly**
University of Durham
Durham, England

**Kathleen M. O'connor**
Columbia Theological Seminary
Decatur, Georgia

**Iain Provan**
Regent College
Vancouver, B.C.

**Graham Stanton**
University of Cambridge, Emeritus
Cambridge, England

**Anthony Thiselton**
University of Nottingham
Nottingham, England

**Augustine Thompson**
University of Virginia
Charlottesville, Virginia

**Marianne Meye Thompson**
Fuller Theological Seminary
Pasadena, California

**Kevin J. Vanhoozer**
Trinity Evangelical Divinity School
Deerfield, Illinois

**Geoffrey Wainwright**
The Divinity School
Duke University
Durham, N. Carolina

**Sondra Wheeler**
Wesley Theological Seminary
Washington, D.C.

**William H. Willimon**
Bishop of the North Alabama Conference
the United Methodist Church
Birmingham, Alabama

**N. T. Wright**
Bishop of Durham
Durham, England

# EX AUDITU

## CONTENTS

Announcement of the 2009 Symposium — v

Abbreviations — vi

Introduction — vii
*Klyne Snodgrass*

Fear in the Garden: The State of Emergency and the Politics of Blessing — 1
*Scott Bader-Saye*

Response to Bader-Saye — 14
*Amy E. Black*

"In God We Trust"? The Challenge of the Prophets — 18
*R. W. L. Moberly*

Response to Moberly — 34
*Robert L. Hubbard, Jr.*

Imagining the Unthinkable:
Exposing the Idolatry of National Security in Amos — 37
*M. Daniel Carroll R.*

Response to Carroll — 55
*Robert D. Haak*

Security and Self-Sufficiency: A Comparison of Paul and Epictetus — 60
*John M. G. Barclay*

Response to Barclay — 73
*Joel Willitts*

Martin Luther's Teachings on Security in the Psalms
and Their Significance for the Art of Reading Scripture — 78
*G. Sujin Pak*

| | |
|---|---|
| Response to Pak<br>*Jo Ann Deasy* | 97 |
| "One Who Trusts Will Not Panic":<br>Providence and the Prophet of Desecuritization<br>*Jill Carson Colwell* | 101 |
| Response to Colwell<br>*Darrell Cosden* | 122 |
| The Radical Insecurity of Idolatry? Or of Faith?<br>*Randall C. Zachman* | 127 |
| Response to Zachmann<br>*Kyle J. A. Small* | 145 |
| Homeland Insecurity: The Spiritual Lust for an Escape Clause<br>*Ben Witherington III* | 150 |
| Response to Witherington<br>*Andy Johnson* | 176 |
| Hoofbeats Full of Grace?<br>*Andy Johnson* | 181 |
| Security<br>*William H. Willimon* | 185 |
| Protecting God: Psalm 91, Luke 4:1–14<br>*Brent Laytham* | 192 |
| Annotated Bibliography on the Idolatry of Security | 197 |
| Presenters and Respondents | 207 |
| *Ex Auditu* – Volumes Available | 209 |

# ANNOUNCEMENT OF THE 2009 SYMPOSIUM

North Park Theological Seminary in Chicago, Illinois, is pleased to announce that the twenty-fifth Symposium on the Theological Interpretation of Scripture will take place September 24–26, 2009. The symposium will start at 7:00 p.m. on September 24 in Nyvall Hall and will extend through a Saturday afternoon worship service on September 26. The theme in 2009 will be Conversion. The following persons have agreed to make presentations:

> Markus Bockmuehl, Oxford University, New Testament
> Stephen Chester, North Park Theological Seminary, New Testament
> Andrew Dearman, Austin Presbyterian Theological Seminary, Old Testament
> Eric James Greaux, Winston-Salem State University, Preaching
> Frank Macchia, Vanguard University, Theology
> Scot McKnight, North Park University, New Testament
> Lewis Rambo, San Francisco Theological Seminary, Pastoral Psychology
> Wyndy Corbin Reuschling, Ashland Theological Seminary, Theology
> Warren Smith, Duke Divinity School, History

Persons interested in attending the sessions should write before September 1 to:

> Ms. Guylla Brown
> North Park Theological Seminary
> 3225 W. Foster Avenue
> Chicago, Illinois 60625

Meals may be taken at North Park and assistance can be provided in finding nearby lodging.

# ABBREVIATIONS

| | |
|---|---|
| *BibInt* | *Biblical Interpretation* |
| CHANE | Culture and History of the Ancient Near East |
| *DDD* | *Dictionary of Deities and Demons in the Bible* |
| ET | English Translation |
| ICC | International Critical Commentary |
| *IG* | *Inscriptiones graecae.* Editio Minor, Berlin, 1924– |
| *Inst.* | *Institutes of the Christian Religion*, Jean Calvin |
| JSOTSup | Journal for the Study of the Old Testament: Supplement Series |
| LHB/OTS | Library of Hebrew Bible/Old Testament Studies |
| LXX | Septuagint |
| LW | *Luther's Works*, ed. Jaroslav Pelikan |
| MT | Masoretic Text |
| NAC | New American Commentary |
| NICOT | New International Commentary on the Old Testament |
| NRSV | New Revised Standard Version |
| *NTS* | *New Testament Studies* |
| OTL | Old Testament Library |
| *P. Oxy.* | *Oxyrhynchus Papyri* |
| *R & T* | *Religion and Theology* |
| RLT | *Revista latinoamericana de teología* |
| SCHANE | Studies in the History and Culture of the Ancient Near East |
| SIG | *Sylloge inscriptionum graecarum,* ed. W. Dittenberger |
| SP | Sacra pagina |
| TDOT | *Theological Dictionary of the Old Testament* |
| ZNW | *Zeitschrift für die neutestamentliche Wissenschaft und die Kunde der älteren Kirche* |

# INTRODUCTION

The quest for security may well be the premium human drive, for which people are willing to sacrifice all else, which also allows security easily to be turned into an idol. Nowhere is it clearer than with the idolatry of security that idols demand sacrifices, for we have sacrificed freedom, money, common sense, and any semblance of normal life.

By coincidence just before the symposium I encountered, perhaps, the largest window into the idolatry of security—Leni Riefenstahl's movie "Triumph des Willens," which documents the 1934 Nürnburg rally of the Nazi party. The language used of Hitler, the Nazis, and Germany is at times blasphemous. Reading Elie Wiesel's *Night* in the same context as watching the movie was unnerving. Also revealing is the title of a Czech movie dealing with residents in Prague during the Nazi occupation: "The Fifth Horseman is Fear."

No one questions that security is important, but in addition to finding that it quickly becomes an idol, it is also clear that security is unattainable, a mirage. To use the words of the prophet, when we have been rescued from the lion, we are attacked by a bear, and when we are rescued from the bear and safe at home, a snake bites us in our own home (Amos 5:19). In the end, especially the end, we are vulnerable. Even when we say God is our only security, which we must, we are still vulnerable. This is a life of faith, not security.

Given our idolatrous quest for security, it is surprising that so little theological discussion focuses on the idolatry of security. Both from looking at ourselves in the mirror and from looking at the mirror of Scripture, this is a theme demanding our attention. Security and the lack of security are frequent themes, especially in the psalms and the prophets. Jesus cared about security and especially in texts like Luke 12–14 tried to redirect thinking about security, about whom to fear, about the false security of assuming one will be at the eschatological banquet (14:15–24), and about how antithetical security and discipleship are (14:25–33). Paul and other NT writers focus on the same themes, notably in texts like Rom 8 or 2 Cor 11–12.

We should ask as well, as several papers do by implication, why many of our doctrines are the result of our desire for security. Is the inordinate focus by some Christians on ideas such as eternal security, inerrancy, or an unbalanced sovereignty of God a result of our quest for security?

Still, none of us should think the issues here are easy. All of us seek security, even those at the symposium who decried bowing before this idol, but how are we to deal with the need for security and the realities of human depravity and human vulnerability at the same time? I cannot help thinking the discussion at the symposium would have been different if less secure people had been present—say my friend who lives in Johannesburg, one of the most violent cities in the world, and whose wife has breast cancer.

Appreciation is expressed once again to all the presenters and respondents who made a significant investment in the life of North Park. The friendship of these people is a privilege. Special gratitude is expressed to Jill Carlson Colwell for her contributions regarding security theory and to the bibliography. The authors of papers were given a chance to edit their contributions after the symposium, but the responses are essentially as they were presented. As is obvious, the views expressed are those of the authors and not necessarily those of the journal or of North Park. We also thank all those in attendance for their interest and contribution to the discussions and especially to Guylla Brown from North Park's staff, without whom the symposium would be impossible.

In addition to the papers and responses from the symposium two other relevant contributions are included: a lecture by William Willimon given originally at Bluffton University and a sermon delivered shortly after 9/11 by Brent Laytham. Gratitude is expressed to both.

The annotated bibliography is shorter than usual for an obvious reason. Relatively little is written that focuses specifically on this theme, so the subject was not conducive to the usual kinds of searches. Hopefully the material here will be helpful. Most of it was submitted by the participants and supplemented and arranged by Kirsten Kronberg and Erin McDermott, to whom thanks is expressed.

Klyne Snodgrass<br>The Editor

# FEAR IN THE GARDEN
## The State of Emergency and the Politics of Blessing

## *Scott Bader-Saye*

In the history of Christian interpretation, much has been made of the "two gardens" that frame the story of redemption in the Bible—in Eden, the first Adam sins through disobedience and pride; in Gethsemane, the second Adam redeems the world from sin through obedience and humility. In the first garden humankind falls and receives the curse; in the second garden humankind is redeemed and receives blessing. The tree in the first story that occasions sin is replaced by the tree in the second upon which Christ dies for sin. The figurative connections are striking and fruitful. John Donne imagined the human soul as the meeting place of these two gardens:

> We thinke that *Paradise* and *Calvarie,*
> *Christs* Crosse, and *Adams* tree, stood in one place; Looke,
> Lord, and finde both *Adams* met in me; As the first *Adams*
> sweat surrounds my face, May the last *Adams* blood my soule
> embrace.[1]

Yet one connection has, as far as I know, never been commented upon. That is, in the first garden, humankind knows fear for the first time and hides from God. In the second Jesus knows fear for the first time and remains faithful to God. Each knows fear, but they offer us alternative paths for responding to that fear.

In what follows I explore the ways in which fear, left unchecked, provokes the twin impulses of hiding and sacrifice—desperate attempts to cut off community and secure life at the expense of another. Fear thus interrupts the flow of blessing, invites a state of emergency, and perpetuates an economy of curse. In contrast, when we deny fear the power to determine our actions and acknowledge that security is not our highest good, a new politics becomes possible, based not on the friend/enemy distinction, nor on the exceptional state of emergency, but on the true exception which is the gift of blessing.

---

1. John Donne, "Hymn to God, my God, in My Sickness," *Poems of John Donne*, vol. I (ed. E. K. Chambers; London: Lawrence & Bullen, 1896), 211-12.

## Eden: The Economy of Blessing

The creation stories of Genesis situate the created order in an economy of blessing.[2] God blesses the animals and humankind with the power of fertility—"be fruitful and multiply" (Gen 1:22, 28)—thus granting the ability to fulfill life by extending life and creating the opportunity for blessing to flow between generations. In his extensive study of blessing, Keith Grüneberg concludes that "the content of blessing is... prosperity, i.e., everything required for a good life."[3] Grüneberg takes "prosperity" to mean something like "flourishing" and even suggests a parallel to the Greek concept of *eudaimonia* (happiness).[4] As Kendall Soulen describes it, God's blessing communicates "life, wholeness, well-being, and joy to that which is other than God."[5] Blessing involves the provision of those things, spiritual and material, necessary for human beings to reach our highest end. These benefits are received first and foremost as gifts from God, but are then passed on between persons to create an ongoing exchange of blessing which is the origin and the *telos* of creation as well as the fundamental economy of the heavenly city.

The pattern of blessing narrated in the early chapters of Genesis suggests that blessing thrives in relationships constituted by difference and mutual dependence.[6] Blessing does not circulate within the same but between those whose difference makes possible a sharing of good that neither would possess on his or her own. Thus blessing passes between creator and creature, between man and woman, between parent and child. Human dominion over the earth, insofar as it constitutes one aspect of the human imaging of God (Gen 1:26), involves the ordering of blessing among creatures and between the earth and its inhabitants. In Gen 12 the natural economy of blessing is supplemented by a political economy of blessing. Abraham and Sarah are chosen to parent a nation, a people who will be blessed and who will be a blessing to others.[7] The gift bestowed on this people is not simply to be

---

2. R. Kendall Soulen, *The God of Israel and Christian Theology* (Minneapolis: Fortress Press, 1996), 114–19.

3. Keith Grüneberg, *Abraham, Blessing and the Nations* (New York: Walter de Gruyter, 2003), 101.

4. Ibid., 101–2.

5. Soulen, *The God of Israel and Christian Theology*, 115.

6. Soulen, *The God of Israel and Christian Theology*, 115–17.

7. The translation of Gen 12:3 is difficult, given that the niphal in 3b can be read as passive or reflexive, thus altering the meaning of the text. Abraham can be seen as either the mediator of blessing (passive voice, i.e., the nations will "be blessed" by Abraham and his offspring) or as example of blessing (reflexive voice, i.e., the nations will "bless themselves" using Abraham's name). Here I follow

returned to God in the form of thankfulness or good works, for such a direct return threatens to nullify the gift by turning it into a contractual exchange constituted by debt. Rather the blessing is to be passed on, extended, allowed to flow through God's people and beyond them. The logic of blessing is not to pay it back but to pay it forward, to disseminate it.

In Genesis God's blessing extends beyond creatures to include time as well. The blessing of the seventh day opens the possibility that we can take time to rest, to enter the slow rhythms of the divine gift that require waiting, patience, and receptivity. A frenetic posture toward time, the fear that there is not enough time or the fear created by "emergency time," defeats blessing because it turns us into those who grasp and hoard rather than those who receive and release. The sabbatical year and the Jubilee year formally structure Israel's economy according to the logic of the blessed time of Sabbath. In the seventh year debt is cancelled and slaves are freed. In the Jubilee year, the seventh seventh year, land that has been sold is returned to its original owners. These measures are intended as ways to keep blessing flowing through the community, to reduce the possibility that the material goods that make human flourishing possible will be hoarded in the hands of a few to the exclusion of others. For those whose misfortune or bad choices have left them in debt or enslaved, there is a fresh start. God refuses to underwrite a polity in which a permanent underclass remains excluded from the goods necessary for human fulfillment.

When slaves are released in the sabbatical year, God commands that they not be sent out "empty-handed." Rather the slave holder is commanded to "provide liberally out of your flock, your threshing floor, and your wine press, thus giving to him some of the bounty with which the Lord your God has blessed you" (Deut 15:13–14). With the giving of blessing comes the expectation that it will be passed on, even, or perhaps especially, to those who in conventional terms have not earned it.

The story of the gift of manna in Exod 16 displays quite nicely the logic of blessing as well as the results of the refusal to allow blessing to flow in excess beyond one's grasp. In response to Israel's cries of hunger in the wilderness, God provides manna, bread for the day (16:14). Each is told to gather only what is needed for the household, no more and no less, so that "those who gathered much had nothing left over, and those who gathered little had no shortage" (16:18). Those Israelites who

---

Grüneberg, who has persuasively argued for the passive voice reading in *Abraham, Blessing and the Nations*, 2–3, 176–90. Acts 3:5 and Gal 3:8 support this reading as well, interpreting the extension of blessing to the nations in a christological sense. The reading is also reflected clearly in the Vulgate of Gen 12:3.

took more than they needed for their daily bread learned the next day that blessing hoarded turns it into curse, leaving a spoiled gift of worm-infested fare.

### Spoiling the Gift, Consuming the Blessing: Sin, Fear, and Curse

This spoiling of gift, which is the refusal to participate in the economy of blessing, echoes the paradigmatic story of curse in the Bible, the fall of humankind in Gen 3. Simone Weil gives a fascinating reading of this story, construing it as an attempt to consume beauty. She writes,

> It may be that vice, depravity, and crime are nearly always, or even perhaps always, in their essence, attempts to eat beauty, to eat what we should only look at. Eve began it. If she caused humanity to be lost by eating the fruit, the opposite attitude, looking at the fruit without eating it, should be what is required to save it.[8]

Weil refuses to let us read this story through a Gnostic lens. When the text tells us that the tree was a "delight to the eyes" (3:6), it is neither denigrating such delight nor equating beauty with temptation. Quite the contrary. The beautiful is meant to be gazed upon, to be delighted in, but it is not meant to be plucked and consumed. A proper response to blessing allows the beauty of another—another person, another object—to exist outside of oneself in such a way that its integrity is maintained and its gifts can be extended. As Augustine reads Gen 3, even the beauty of God becomes an object of human grasping. He observes,

> ... instead of staying still and enjoying [God's beauty and excellence] as it ought to do, [the soul] wants to claim them for itself, and rather than be like [God] by his gift it wants to be what he is by its own right. So it turns away from him and slithers and slides down into less and less which is imagined to be more and more.[9]

Humankind refuses the gift by seeking to grasp and possess it, to consume the beauty that is God rather than patiently receive a blessing that cannot finally come under human control.

Here we begin to see the connections between blessing, curse, and fear. For it is in the story of the first garden, just following the act of consuming the beautiful, that fear enters the story in two forms—the fear of the other and the fear of death,

---

8. Simone Weil, *Waiting for God* (trans. Emma Craufurd; New York: Harper and Row, 1951), 166.
9. St. Augustine, *The Trinity* (trans. Edmund Hill; Hyde Park, NY: New City, 1991), 10, 5, 7.

each fear symbolized by an act of hiding. The first act of hiding occurs as soon as the couple's "eyes are opened" and they see that they are naked. They are suddenly aware that they are laid bare, transparent to one another and to God and they are no longer comfortable with the vulnerability of their exposed bodies. Once the human beings have shown themselves willing to transgress the boundaries of God, nakedness becomes frightening, since even the boundaries of their bodies no longer seem secure. So they make clothes and hide from each other.

The second act of hiding occurs when God enters the garden looking for them. God has stated that if the human beings eat of this tree they will die. So when God approaches, the human beings hide as if from death itself. Both Adam and Eve seek to deflect the punishment, each offering up another to be sacrificed, to bear the punishment of death. It was *her* fault, Adam says; it was the *serpent's* fault, Eve says. In some ways this story in the garden narrates for us all of our fears, for they all return in one way or another to the fear of death, the fear of the other, and our willingness to sacrifice the other to make ourselves safe.

God responds to these attempts to deflect death onto the other by pronouncing a curse on all three of the creatures. For the woman and man the curse strikes at the point of their own creating, bringing forth children and bringing forth food from the earth. Those who would sacrifice another for their own security are fated now to struggle for goods, and those things that should have come as blessing—offspring and sustenance—are now brought forth in pain. Curse constitutes the reversal, the dark underside, of the blessing for which humankind was created. As Soulen writes, "God's curse is simply God's blessing as seen from the backside, that is, as seen from the perspective of the creature who has repudiated it."[10] To echo Barth, curse is God's refusal of our refusal to participate in the economy of blessing. In the wake of the exile from Eden fear becomes an enemy of blessing and thus an enemy of human happiness. The impulse to hide or to sacrifice the other for one's own sake—i.e., the tendency to contract or attack in the face of danger—makes human beings that much less able or willing to extend themselves in blessing to another.

As the biblical story moves forward, it is disordered fear as much as anything that keeps humankind trapped in sin and curse, for insofar as self-preservation becomes the highest good, humans find themselves unwilling to risk the release of blessing to another and all the more willing to destroy even potential threats to their safety. Further, fear tempts humankind to trap blessing in an unending parody of gift. Goods remain safely managed in a circle of exchange between those who have

---

10. Soulen, *The God of Israel and Christian Theology*, 142.

and so can give. Jesus' parable of the great feast challenges this tendency by calling his hearers to host those who cannot repay, to break the gift free from the mannerly exchanges of the well-off and to continue its flow among those whose need makes direct return impossible. Fear tempts us to control and contain. Fear tempts us to withhold blessing from those who cannot repay. In this way, fear perpetuates curse, and it does this, at least in part, through the logic of emergency.

## The State of Emergency

Emergency names a particular quality of time that underwrites exceptions to ordinary practice. In an emergency, for instance, we assume that an ambulance will not follow ordinary traffic laws. Thomas Aquinas argued that in an emergency the poor person is justified in taking from the superabundance of the wealthy.[11] Emergency time changes the rules we live by. The state of emergency is the state in which laws, rights, and liberties are set aside or curtailed in order to engage a pressing threat. It is a sovereign consolidation of power. There is a pragmatic logic to setting aside normal rules and expectations in an emergency, but as philosophers such as Walter Benjamin, Giorgio Agamben, and Slavoj Žižek have argued, the logic of emergency can lead quite easily to the normalizing and exploitation of the exception.[12]

Consider three examples of how the logic of emergency functions today. First, and most obviously, there is 9/11 and the war on terror. Just after 9/11 Dick Cheney, being interviewed by Tim Russert on "Meet the Press," said that America was going to have to "work the dark side." Russert followed up, "There have been restrictions placed on the United States intelligence gathering, reluctance to use unsavory characters, those who violated human rights, to assist in intelligence gathering. Will we lift some of those restrictions?" Cheney responded, "Oh, I think so. I think the—one of the by-products, if you will, of this tragic set of circumstances is that we'll see a very thorough sort of reassessment of how we operate and the kinds of people we deal with."[13] Clearly, we have here an example of the state of emergency being used

---

11. Aquinas, *Summa Theologica*, II–II, Q. 66, art. 7

12. See Walter Benjamin, "Theses on the Philosophy of History," in *Illuminations* (trans. Harry Zohn; New York: Schocken, 1968); Giorgio Agamben, *Homo Sacer: Sovereign Power and Bare Life* (Stanford: Stanford University Press, 1998) and his *State of Exception* (trans. Kevin Attell; Chicago: University of Chicago, 2004); Slavoj Žižek, "Are we in a war? Do we have an enemy?" *London Review of Books* (May 23, 2002).

13. Dick Cheney, Interview with Tim Russet, "Meet the Press" (Sept. 16, 2001) transcript, "The Vice President Appears on Meet the Press with Tim Russert," URL: http://www.whitehouse.gov/vicepresident/news-speeches/speeches/vp20010916.html, accessed: June 28, 2006.

to justify activities that, under other circumstances, would have been ruled out of bounds as acceptable tactics. There are many for whom Abu Ghraib, Guantanamo Bay, and even the Iraq war itself stand as prime examples of the exploitation of emergency to consolidate power, throw off moral restraint, and pursue interests that press well beyond a specific response to the actual emergency of 9/11.

George Bush's decision to describe 9/11 as a "war" rather than a "crime" created an ongoing state of emergency in which it has become unclear how we would even know when the "war on terror" is over and when emergency powers should be relinquished. Giorgio Agamben reminds us that "because the sovereign power of the [American] president is essentially grounded in the emergency linked to a state of war, over the course of the twentieth century the metaphor of war becomes an integral part of the presidential political vocabulary whenever decisions considered to be of vital importance are being imposed."[14] Richard Nixon's "war on drugs" and Lyndon Johnson's "war on poverty" preceded Bush's "war on terror" in calling for an exceptional response to a crisis, thus requiring a consolidation of powers and decision making which would otherwise be extended across a larger web of conversation and deliberation. While emergency measures may at times be necessary, the questions of which measures and for how long are questions that are rarely asked or answered with much clarity. Part of the problem is that these questions require the kind of deliberation that is precluded by the posture of emergency. Because it demands immediate action, emergency shuts down ordinary processes of deliberation, reflection, and conversation in favor of quick and decisive measures. A state of emergency is a state produced by fear but also productive of fear. We are reminded, for instance, via the Homeland Security Threat Advisory System just how fearful we need to be on a given day.

A second example of the logic of emergency can be found in some of the rhetoric regarding climate change. In recent years the environmental lobby has been more than willing to create a sense of emergency in order to convince people to take seriously issues of climate change. In an article in *Vanity Fair* in 2006 Al Gore wrote,

> The climate crisis may at times appear to be happening slowly, but in fact it is a true planetary emergency.... unless we act boldly and quickly to deal with the causes of global warming, our world will likely experience a string of catastrophes.... All of this, incredibly, could be set in motion in the lifetime of the children already living—unless we act boldly and quickly. Even more incredibly, some of the leading scientific experts are

---

14. Agamben, *State of Exception*, 11–22.

now telling us that without dramatic changes we are in grave danger of crossing a point of no return within the next 10 years! So the message is unmistakable. This crisis means danger! . . . Today, there are dire warnings that the worst catastrophe in the history of human civilization is bearing down on us, gathering strength as it comes.[15]

In a time marked by fear, the language of emergency has become our lingua franca—the standard rhetorical form for all political or activist appeals. The assumption seems to be that if it is not an emergency, we do not have time to think about it. Emergency time drives out precisely the kind of patient reflection needed to respond to something like climate change.

So Gore, while deploying the rhetoric of the age, may also be diminishing the possibility that this issue will receive the kind of sober and sustained analysis it needs. Jérôme Bindé calls this the "tyranny of emergency," which he says, "leaves no time for either analysis, forecasting, or prevention." We sacrifice the "sober quest for long-term solutions" in favor of an "immediate protective reflex." Bindé argues that "Devising any durable response to human problems such as environmental ones requires looking at a situation from a distance and thinking in terms of the future. Conversely, the logic of emergency responds to a need for immediate results and for the direct viability of the efforts made."[16] The central point here is that responding to something like climate change is going to require a thoroughgoing rethinking of our habits and patterns of living that cannot be properly addressed if we allow fear and emergency to drive us to seek quick solutions.

A third example of the tyranny of emergency has arisen in the last few months as we have watched the meltdown of the financial industries on Wall Street. In response to what is by all counts a real moment of crisis, the Bush administration sought to consolidate unprecedented power in the hands of the treasury secretary. The original proposal that was sent to Congress stated that "Decisions by the Secretary [Treasury Secretary Henry Paulson] pursuant to the authority of this Act are non-reviewable and committed to agency discretion, and may not be reviewed by any court of law or any administrative agency." It went on, "The Secretary is authorized to take such actions as the Secretary deems necessary to carry out the authorities in this act, without regard to any other provision of law regarding public contracts." The funding of this proposal would be entirely at the discretion of the Treasury

---

15. Al Gore, "The Moment of Truth," *Vanity Fair* (April 17, 2006), URL: http://www.climateark.org/shared/reader/welcome.aspx?linkid=55267.

16. Jérôme Bindé, "Toward an Ethics of the Future," *Public Culture*, 12:1 (2000): 51–72.

secretary: "Any funds expended for actions authorized by this Act, including the payment of administrative expenses, shall be deemed appropriated at the time of such expenditure." The mere fact of spending the money constitutes it having been appropriated to be spent—except that no actual appropriation would be going on, because there would be no oversight of the Secretary's actions. As one reporter put it, "[The proposed bill] is the financial equivalent of the Patriot Act."[17]

A perpetual state of emergency functions to make our security against some impending evil more important than the goods that we ordinarily hold to constitute our goals as a people, whether those are the democratic goods of public debate and government accountability or the Christian goods of loving God and neighbor. We take refuge in the fantasy that "there is no alternative," that we are driven to these responses by circumstances beyond our control, and that we are victims whose self-protective reflexes cannot and should not be questioned.[18]

Part of the church's role in a time like this is to call us back to the critical work of analyzing and judging these reflexes in the light of the gospel. We must ask what sorts of concessions to fear are *pragmatically* warranted? What concessions are *morally* acceptable? Perhaps most importantly, when is the emergency over? At what point do we return life to normal, knowing that even normal life poses risks that cannot be entirely repelled or avoided but which are accepted because they constitute the unavoidable vulnerability of living well as human beings, i.e., living in relations of mutual self-giving and radical reciprocity.

## Courage and Patience

That emergency time is a threat to the virtue of patience should be a clear and rather straightforward claim. But, I want to argue that it is also a threat to courage, precisely because true courage, as opposed to rashness or recklessness, requires patience. In his discussion of courage (or "fortitude") in the *Summa Theologica*, Aquinas argues that "*Fortitude is more concerned to allay fear, than to moderate daring. For it is more difficult to allay fear than to moderate daring, since the danger which is the object of daring and fear, tends by its very nature to check daring, but to increase fear.*" Daring and fear, for Aquinas, correspond to the fight and flight impulses we have in the face of danger. Daring he defines as our tendency to move out against a threat

---

17. Andrew Ross Sorkin, "A Bailout Above the Law," *New York Times* (Sept. 22, 2008), URL: http://www.nytimes.com/2008/09/23/business/23sorkin.html?em.

18. See Rowan Williams, *The Truce of God* (2d ed.; Grand Rapids: Eerdmans, 2005).

while fear is our tendency to withdraw from it. Aquinas continues, "Now to attack belongs to fortitude in so far as the latter moderates daring, whereas to endure follows the repression of fear. Therefore the principal act of fortitude is endurance, i.e., to stand immovable in the midst of dangers rather than to attack them. Endurance is more difficult that aggression" (*Summa Theologica*, II–II, Q. 123, Art. 6). Since fear naturally moderates our tendency to become rash, that is to be inordinately daring, courage is most needed to moderate fear, which is our tendency to retreat or contract. Thus, real courage is shown primarily in our ability to endure, to stand with fortitude, rather than in our willingness to attack. It is no accident that immediately following his discussion of courage in the *Summa* Thomas takes up the topic of martyrdom, since Thomas sees the martyr, not the soldier, as the paradigm case of Christian courage. Emergency time is the enemy of courage in so far as it tempts us to think that courage is the same thing as daring, that acting quickly is the same thing as acting wisely, suggesting, in fact, that courage and recklessness are indistinguishable.

Courage not only helps us face our fears with faith, it helps us fend off the temptation to make security our highest good, that is, to make security an idol. This temptation is arguably at the center of the state of emergency, since it suggests that security can be justifiably pursued by any and all means, sacrificing all other goods to this one necessary thing. Yet the gospel calls us away from this logic. Security cannot be the highest good because Christians are not called to pursue existence for its own sake. In the biblical story human beings are created to image God, and if God is the self-giving love of the Trinity, then we only achieve our full humanity by mirroring that vulnerable self-giving love in our own lives and in our communities. As human beings our highest calling is not to be safe but to be good. As Christians, we understand goodness to be a participation in the reign of God which mirrors the trinitarian exchange of blessing.

## Gethsemane: Dethroning the Idol of Security

Having begun our reflections in Eden, the first garden that images for us both the peaceful harmony of the Sabbath and the disruption of sin which introduces the fearful temptation to secure ourselves at the expense of the other, we now turn to the second garden, Gethsemane, which marks the starting point of Jesus' road to the cross. Here we have the only time in the Gospels when Jesus is said to be afraid (*ekthambeō*). Yet he neither hides nor offers up the other to save himself. Unlike Adam and Eve he moves toward God in his fear; he seeks relief, but his prayer is not "save me at any cost." He subordinates his desire for safety—"remove this cup from me"—to his desire to be faithful—"not my will but yours be done" (Luke 22:42). Even here, or especially here, Jesus lives out his own command to "love your enemies, do good to those who hate you, bless those who curse you" (Luke 6:47–48). Jesus continues to participate in the economy of blessing despite the fact that his own life is threatened by those who live the way of curse. So when Peter seeks to defend Jesus with a preemptive strike, Jesus rebukes him and heals the slave who was wounded (Luke 22:50–51). Jesus refuses to allow fear to keep him from doing the good, which is to say, he refuses the idolatry of security. He goes to the cross in an act that extends blessing in the face of curse, and he pronounces forgiveness upon those who put him to death.

If the world construes sovereignty in Carl Schmitt's terms that the sovereign is the one "who decides on the state of exception," then Jesus is clearly the anti-sovereign king. He tells Pilate in John's Gospel, "If my kingdom were from this world, my followers would be fighting to keep me from being handed over to the Jews. But as it is, my kingdom is not from here" (John 18:36; cf. Luke 22:25–27). The distinctiveness of Jesus' kingdom, and thus of his rule, is that he refuses the violence of the sovereign exception, even to save his own life. In so doing he refuses the logic of emergency, though not simply for the sake of a return to normalcy. Rather, Jesus provokes a different kind of crisis through his excess of gift. We might say this excessive gift provokes the true emergency and embodies the true exception, which is the excess of charity.

Writing in Paris in 1940 the German, Jewish philosopher Walter Benjamin observed, "The tradition of the oppressed teaches us that the 'state of emergency' in which we live is not the exception but the rule. We must attain to a conception of history that is in keeping with this insight. Then we shall clearly realize that it is our task to bring about a real state of emergency."[19] Just a few months after he wrote these words, the German army took Paris and Benjamin died trying to flee to America. Many philosophers and political theorists have wrestled with the idea of a "true state of emergency," one that does not foreclose options through coercive power but which offers up new possibilities by breaking open oppressive structures. Slavoj Žižek writes, "When a state institution proclaims a state of emergency, it does so by definition as part of a desperate strategy to avoid the true emergency and return to the 'normal course of things'. . . . In short, reactionary proclamations of a state of

---

19. Benjamin, "Theses on the Philosophy of History," 257.

emergency are a desperate defense against the true state of emergency itself."[20] Žižek, among others, has turned to the apostle Paul as one who gives voice to the apocalyptic urgency of a revolutionary messianism—in other words, as one who gestures toward a Christ who exceeds emergency through gift and grace and thus invites us into the risky business of inaugurating the reign of God that is always yet to come.

Christians, then, insofar as we live beyond the constraints of fear, embody a kind of patient and peaceful revolution that is characterized by Paul's injunction to "bless those who persecute you; bless and do not curse them" (Rom 12:14). This determination to extend blessing in a world marked by fearful refusal of the gift means that Christians are called to embrace and enact the "true emergency" the true unbalancing of all false economies. There are few cultural voices helping us imagine what it would look like to enter into this kind of risk, but, interestingly, the *Harry Potter* series has done just that. The children in these stories are allowed to take real risks and face real dangers in a world where goodness is more important than safety. Alan Jacobs observes,

> Our culture is so deeply risk-averse, so determined to punish anyone who might cause injury to us or our children, or even might fail to take precautions to prevent us from being injured, that we can scarcely imagine an environment in which risk is so blithely accepted and injuries dealt with so matter-of-factly. But it is just because Hogwarts is a place which allows young people to take such risks—and therefore to test themselves and grow in capability and confidence—that its students and graduates love it so much.[21]

J. K. Rowling has recognized that young people are hungry for the risk from which we work so hard to protect them. They have latched onto the world of Hogwarts because they sense that they are being told the truth, i.e., that risk is unavoidable if we are to be people who love and make friends and keep commitments in a transient and vulnerable world.

We might go further and say that risk is not just unavoidable, but that it brings with it a certain kind of good. Martha Nussbaum helpfully reminds us of the beauty that is made possible by the fragility of goodness. She argues:

> There is in fact a loss in value whenever the risks involved in specifically human virtue are closed off. There is a beauty in the willingness to love

---

20. Žižek, "Are we in a war?"

21. Alan Jacobs, "The Youngest Brother's Tale: Harry Potter's Grand Finale," *Books and Culture*, URL: http://www.christianitytoday.com/bc/2007/005/1.47.html.

someone in the face of love's instability and worldliness that is absent from a completely trustworthy love. There is a certain valuable quality in social virtue that is lost when social virtue is removed from the domain of uncontrolled happenings.[22]

So, as vulnerable creatures, we can embrace risk, embrace a properly ordered fear, as a gift that helps us seize the moment to love, to rejoice, and to embrace the good.

Jesus calls his followers to renounce the false security of violence and power and so to risk everything in order to gain everything—or, as he puts it, to lose life in order to find it. Jesus calls his followers to embrace an ethic of risk even as the culture of fear views risk-taking as morally questionable. Jesus calls his followers to participate in God's economy in such a way that the blessings poured out upon them continue to circulate, not only across the differences of gender, race, tribe, and nation, but across chasms of fear and through walls of hate. We are left with two gardens and two choices in the face of fear. One is to hide and sacrifice the other for our own safety, making security our highest good; the other is to embrace a cruciform ethic of risk, losing our lives to find them, extending blessing in the face of curse because we trust that our true flourishing comes not from controlling or consuming the good but from extending it.

---

22. Martha Nussbaum, *The Fragility of Goodness* (New York: Cambridge University Press, 1986), 420.

# RESPONSE TO BADER-SAYE

## *Amy E. Black*

We have all likely heard the adage that civilized folk should avoid two topics in polite dinner conversation: religion and politics. Since I am a professor of political science married to a systematic theologian, the joke in our household is that we are always unwelcome at dinner parties. All too often our respective academic fields seem a dangerous, indeed combustible, mix.

When I first received the invitation to participate in this symposium, two immediate thoughts went through my head: for a theology conference, the subject sounds quite interesting; and I think the invitation was intended to reach the other professor in my household. I forwarded the message to my husband, adding the line "is this meant for you?"

Imagine my surprise when he assured me that the invitation was sent to the right person. The idea, indeed one of the purposes of the gathering, was to bring together people from *both* inside and outside of academic theology to wrestle with important issues facing the church and to inform one another's work. The folks at North Park, it seems, want to bring religion and politics to the conversation table; if they seek my perspective as a political scientist, then that is what I hope to provide in my response.

I should start by saying how much I enjoyed reading Professor Bader-Saye's paper. I found it creative, reflective, and at times even elegant in its call for a politics of blessing. In large part I agree with his central arguments and want to echo his clarion call toward a politics unafraid to "embrace a cruciform ethic of risk, losing our lives to find them, extending blessing in the face of curse . . ."

At the same time, I would be remiss in my role as the political scientist in the room if I did not do my best to throw at least a few curve balls to complicate the discussion with some practical concerns. The politics of blessing has great appeal, but what hope have we of living out such an ethic in the day-to-day, often gritty, world of American politics?

## The State of Emergency as Rhetorical Tool

Bader-Saye argues, "In a time marked by fear, the language of emergency has become a lingua franca—the standard rhetorical form for all political or activist appeals." Although I agree in large part, I would temper that statement with a few comments. The language of emergency and rhetoric of fear is not something new or distinctive to our current age; all too often it is the rhetoric of representative democracy.

First, it is a central rhetorical device in American campaigns. Throughout history Americans have responded to inflammatory rhetoric, ominous warnings, and statements of dire need. We see this kind of rhetoric in political campaigns going back to the earliest contested elections. Scholars describe the election of 1800, for example, as "one of the nastiest in U.S. history." In 1828 the politics of fear reached a high tide: "Attack dogs for incumbent John Quincy Adams accused Andrew Jackson of being a dictator who was determined to subvert the presidency into a tyranny. Jackson, they claimed, was so ambitious for empire that he would become the American Napoleon."[1]

The language of emergency and fear permeates modern political campaigns as well. Fundraising appeals are often stated in emergency terms. Consider the following: after raising twenty-seven million dollars in July, a John McCain fundraising appeal from this August begged, "I would not ask for your help if circumstances were not so dire."

In addition, campaigns craft advertisements designed specifically to play on fear. Why do they do this? The data show that it works. A recent content analysis of decades' worth of advertising concluded that ads designed to evoke enthusiasm do little to change voter behavior, but fear-based advertisements move voters' positions, increase voter turnout, and are most persuasive.[2]

Second, the rhetoric of emergency can hinder effective governing. As Bader-Saye demonstrated persuasively with his discussion of Al Gore's rhetoric on the issue of climate change, many politicians and interest group leaders use the rhetoric of emergency and crisis to raise awareness and concern about policy issues, polarizing voters and frustrating opportunities for "sober and sustained analysis." Voters and

---

1. Grand Valley State University, Hauenstein Center for Presidential Studies, *Modern Campaigning Origins* (2006). Retrieved from http://www.gvsu.edu/hauenstein/index.cfm?id=60B6 A52B-0D63-CBBE-491EA598355F6241.

2. Ted Brader, *Campaigning for Hearts and Minds: How Emotional Appeals in Political Ads Work* (Chicago: University of Chicago Press, 2006).

donors are much more likely to respond to an impending "crisis" than to a more nuanced, and perhaps more factual, appeal.

Consider the example of an e-mail message from MoveOn.org: "This week, Bush proposed a new budget with devastating cuts to public broadcasting. 'Sesame Street' and other ad-free kids' shows are under the knife. So is the independent journalism our country needs." Why worry if the rhetoric is misleading if it leads to tens of thousands of phone calls to Congress?[3]

Our political system is slow and deliberative by design, but political actors have learned that appeals to fear can provide the momentum needed to move legislation, even at the expense of deliberation. It is no accident that fifty-three of the 344 bills that have passed both the House and Senate during the 110th Congress include the word "emergency."[4] Some of these bills seek to address genuine crises, but most are merely escalating the rhetoric by renaming normal public policy issues "emergencies." I would argue there is a significant difference between the "Emergency Assistance for Secure Elections Act of 2008" and the "Disaster Relief and Emergency Assistance Act," which brings us to my second major point.

## When an Emergency Is an Emergency

We have seen throughout American history that political leaders have used and will use states of emergency (real and contrived) to justify a wider breadth of government power. Bader-Saye offers us several examples of this dangerous trajectory and we would do well to heed the warning.

However, it is also important to remember that real emergencies *do* arise. Many emergency situations demand emergency responses, and such responses do not necessarily lead to abuses of power. Put another way, a state of emergency need not automatically be connected to a politics of fear.

Right now in Washington, congressional leaders are on the verge of completing what they are calling an emergency plan to deal with a burgeoning series of economic events that seem rightly called a "crisis." We have seen all too clearly how much our domestic economy and markets worldwide are affected by fallout from the collapse of investment banks and major insurance companies. Some, to be sure, are using the situation to evoke more fear in the American public; others more so-

---

3. Amy E. Black, *Beyond Left and Right: Helping Christians Make Sense of American Politics* (Grand Rapids: Baker, 2008), 160–61.

4. Author's analysis of legislation introduced in the 110th Congress as of September 20, 2008.

berly are recognizing that this is a time for quick and decisive action. We can debate the merits of the policy route Congress ultimately chooses, but few will disagree that government action of some sort is necessary to stabilize the domestic and international economy.

Unfortunately, in a political climate within which everyday policy differences are all too often framed in terms of doom and gloom, state-of-emergency rhetoric designed to evoke fear, we risk becoming numb to real crises that will come and legitimately cry out for an immediate response.

## So What Is the Christian to Do?

How then should we respond as individuals, and how should we encourage the church to respond? First, we should reserve emergency language for the real emergencies, recapturing control of our language and authenticity in our political discourse.

In addition, we must stop rewarding the rhetoric of fear. If we respond to fear-based appeals, we only perpetuate the cycle. We cannot control the behavior of others, but we can control our own responses, and we can model more measured and informed political behavior.

Third, we should do our part as followers of Christ to extend blessing and not get caught up in the rhetoric of fear, even as we recognize that such actions run counter to many of the established norms of American political behavior. Our goal is faithfulness, not political expediency.

Finally and most importantly, we can model an alternative way. It may not win elections or change public policy, but that is not our ultimate calling. As Bader-Saye reminds us, security is not our end goal. Both as Christian individuals and working collectively as the church, we need to demonstrate courage, patience, and, I would add, love. We are promised that perfect love casts out fear (1 John 4:18); we are promised that the way of God's love is the "most excellent way" (1 Cor 12:31). As such, we are called to the radical life of discipleship, to extend Christ's love to a broken and needy world. What better way to be agents of divine love than to embrace the politics of blessing?

# "IN GOD WE TRUST"?
## The Challenge of the Prophets

## R. W. L. Moberly

Security is perhaps the most basic of human longings and needs. Nations, communities, families, and individuals all in their various ways seek security—safety, protection, confidence, stability. Negatively, security means a context in which people are free or protected from dangers and threats, while positively it means a context in which people are able to flourish together, ideally also with the existential awareness that this is so.

If one wants to put "being secure" into biblical Hebrew, the root that most readily springs to mind is *bṭḥ*; there is a common verb *bāṭaḥ* ("trust"), and a related noun *beṭaḥ*, which standard lexicons render as "security."[1] Another Hebrew root is *yšʿ*, whose common verb and noun forms (*hôšîaʿ*, *yešûʿāh*), generally rendered "deliver/deliverance" and "save/salvation," cover related conceptual ground.[2] Of the numerous other roots that might be mentioned, the noun *šālôm* ("peace") should perhaps be singled out as belonging in this context.[3] These are prime terms within the OT for depiction of the divine-human relationship as it should be. Of course the concept and reality may be present with no particular terminology to depict them.

Yet the more important the human need the greater both the potential for, and the seriousness of, its misunderstanding and misuse: *corruptio optimi pessima*. Unsurprisingly, it is the prophetic corpus within the OT which most obviously and extensively addresses misdirection and malpractice in the whole area of the long-

---

1. So e.g., F. Brown, S. R. Driver, and Charles A. Briggs, *A Hebrew and English Lexicon of the Old Testament* (Oxford: Clarendon, 1957), 105; and David J. A. Clines (ed.), *The Dictionary of Classical Hebrew*, Vol. II (Sheffield Academic, 1995), 141.

2. For example, when it is said of the "strong city" which YHWH provides that "salvation will he set as walls" (*yešûʿāh yāšît ḥômôt*), the sense is that the city's defences, its walls, are entirely secure (Isa 26:1).

3. For example, the message of those prophets whom Jeremiah sees as irresponsible, who say "'Peace, peace,' when there is no peace" (Jer 6:14, 8:11), would appear in context to be a message of national security.

ing for security.⁴ Indeed, this is one of the prime reasons why the prophets have been valued down the ages; their highlighting of the ways in which the heart of life under God can be perverted makes the prophets an enduring existential challenge to groups and individuals alike.⁵

Within the OT the temple in Jerusalem is the prime place of the presence of YHWH with His people,⁶ a place of enormous symbolic significance.⁷ The Psalms in particular often celebrate Zion as the focus of YHWH's good pleasure, and the place where His people can expect to meet with Him and receive His blessing. In many ways the temple symbolizes security. Here Israel can sing: "God is in the midst of the city; it shall not be moved. . . . The Lord of hosts is with us; the God of Jacob is our refuge" (Ps 46:6, 8 [ET 5, 7]).⁸

However, where much is given, there much is expected.⁹ A recurrent failure on the part of Israel/Judah to live up to those expectations and conduct themselves in a way commensurate with the presence of God in their midst is a prime concern in the prophetic literature. So I propose to look at three famous prophetic "temple sermons," passages that focus on the mismatch between the priorities of YHWH and those of Israel/Judah.¹⁰

---

4. Hence also Danny Carroll's paper on Amos in this symposium. I note Bob Hubbard's interesting proposal, in his response to my paper, to consider the whole issue from a wisdom perspective. Such an approach would, I think, be less straightforward, and so harder—but by no means less worthwhile.

5. Other passages which might fruitfully be considered in this context include Gen 22 (the need to relinquish to God the apparent guarantee of the future, even when received in fulfilment of God's promises after long waiting), Deut 8 (the double-edged nature of God's good gift of the land of Israel, because of the danger that when times are easy in the land Israel may neglect the foundational truth they learned when life was hard in the desert) and 1 Sam 8–12 (the complexly problematic nature of Israel's request for a king).

6. I use masculine pronouns for God in continuity with biblical usage. I capitalize such pronouns partly to indicate that gendered terms do not apply to God in the way they do to humans and partly for traditional reverential reasons.

7. Jon D. Levenson, *Sinai and Zion: An Entry into the Jewish Bible* (Minneapolis: Winston, 1985), 89–184 remains one of the most suggestive accounts of the significance of Zion and the temple.

8. Comparable sentiments can be found in many other psalms, e.g. Pss 2, 48, 76, 84, 87, 132. Throughout this paper the translations are from NRSV; where I disagree I discuss the reason.

9. This foundational principle, most famously articulated by Jesus (Luke 12:48), is classically enunciated in Amos 3:2.

10. My reading strategy in all three temple sermons is to focus on the biblical text in its received form and to attend to the speaking voice as it is presented in the text, without prejudice to questions of authorship and redaction.

## Amos's Temple Sermon: Amos 5:18–27

It must be admitted that it is not self-evident that my initial "temple sermon" is a temple sermon. I propose this, however, as a reading strategy, because the ten verses read well as a unit,[11] and there is direct address to people engaged in the practices of temple worship. Within the context of the book one can imagine the temple in Bethel as its location, with the hostility of Amaziah as its response (Amos 7:10–13).[12]

Amos says:

> [18] Alas for you who desire the day of the LORD!
>> Why do you want the day of the LORD?
>> It is darkness, not light;
>
> [19] as if someone fled from a lion,
>> and was met by a bear;
>> or[13] went into the house and rested a hand against the wall,
>> and was bitten by a snake.
>
> [20] Is not the day of the LORD darkness, not light,
>> and gloom with no brightness in it?

The people Amos addresses have a confident expectation associated with God, an expectation depicted as "the day of YHWH." The precise nature of this day is assumed to be known, and unfortunately this assumption no longer holds for Amos's readers.[14] Nonetheless, one main point is clear, that this is a time which can be depicted as "light," which would mean a time when in some special sense God's will is done, and God's people could expect to rejoice in it. Amos inverts this: "darkness, not light" is how the day of YHWH will be. This is illustrated by a picture of a man vainly

---

11. So, e.g., J. Lindblom, *Prophecy in Ancient Israel* (Blackwell: Oxford, 1962), 352 ("This passage [5:18–27] must be treated as a whole"). There is, to be sure, an introduction of first-person divine address in 5:21–27, but shifts between third and first person are common in prophetic speech. One might also note that within 5:18–20 the only third person reference to YHWH is in the formulaic "day of YHWH," so the shift, if such it is, is not striking.

12. Bob Hubbard, in his helpful response, points out that other possible locations might be envisaged. I should clarify that my point is not a historical claim as to location (which is unresolvable), but rather an imaginative issue of how readers might appropriately envisage Amos.

13. Preferable is "and"; cf. n. 15.

14. Commentators generally suggest either a day of victory over Israel's enemies (cf. "day of Midian," Isa 9:3 [ET 4] and Judg 7) or a major liturgical celebration within the temple. Since the temple would be the natural context for celebrating any victory, it may be that there is little at stake in the uncertainty—whatever the nature of the "day of YHWH" the temple would be the locus of its celebration.

trying to escape deadly animals[15]—he escapes from a lion (intrinsically a remarkable feat) only to be confronted by a bear, and when he escapes from the bear into a house, presumably imagining himself safe at last, an unnoticed snake bites him. The inexorability of disaster is reminiscent of the covenant curses of Deuteronomy 28. Moreover, at the risk of overreading the text, I would at least note that the imagery has strong canonical resonances:[16] the lion is an image of YHWH's judgment in Kings,[17] and YHWH's roar like a lion introduces Amos's whole message (Amos 1:2, cf. 3:8); while "the house" (*habbayit*) is the most common term for the Jerusalem temple.[18] So one could perhaps read the man's fleeing from a lion as an image of Israel's fleeing from YHWH, with the suggestion that there is nowhere safe to hide and even (or, rather, especially) the temple offers no refuge. In any case, the day of YHWH is that which utterly confounds hopeful expectation (v. 20).

Why should this be? A reason (additional to those earlier in the text of Amos) is directly given in 5:21–24:

> [21] I hate, I despise your festivals,
> 
> >  and I take no delight in your solemn assemblies.
> 
> [22] Even though you offer me your burnt-offerings and grain-offerings,
> 
> >  I will not accept them;
> 
> and the offerings of well-being of your fatted animals
> 
> >  I will not look upon.
> 
> [23] Take away from me the noise of your songs;
> 
> >  I will not listen to the melody of your harps.

---

15. NRSV, with many translations and interpreters, sees two images here ("the *coming home* has no connection with the lion and bear episodes . . . it is rather the sudden coming of misfortune when and where it would be least expected" [William Rainey Harper, *Amos and Hosea* (ICC; Edinburgh: T. & T. Clark, 1936), 132]). But the text is more potent if there is a single sequence; I find myself in full agreement with Hans Walter Wolff, "The chain of consecutive perfects and the single reference to 'someone' ('*iš*, literally 'a man') speak unequivocally in favor of there being here one single story" (*Joel and Amos* [Hermeneia; Philadelphia: Fortress, 1977; ET by Waldemar Janzen et al. from 2nd German edition of 1975], 256).

16. Rabbinic tradition identifies the hostile animals as Israel's historic enemies, from Babylonia onwards (e.g. Esther Rabbah I:3, conveniently available in Jacob Neusner, *Amos in Talmud and Midrash* [Lanham: University Press of America, 2007], 67–68). However, such an imaginative move is not developing resonances of the imagery so much as reading the sequence of constant threat as a picture of Israel's biblical history in the light of animals symbolizing Israel's enemies in Dan 7.

17. 1 Kgs 13:24, 20:36, 2 Kgs 17:25; cf. Hos. 13:7–8 where YHWH is likened to both lion and bear.

18. Interestingly, LXX at 5:19 reads "into his house" (*eis ton oikon autou*), which might suggest a *Vorlage* of *bêtô*. MT leaves open the resonance I am suggesting in a way that LXX does not.

> **24** But let justice roll down like waters,
>   and righteousness like an ever-flowing stream.

The text focuses on what YHWH rejects and on what He seeks[19] and concentrates on what the people do (the many activities of temple worship) rather than on what they do not do. Yet the point is clear and emphatic: worship without concomitant practice of justice and righteousness is not merely worthless but actively affronts YHWH and is an object of loathing to Him.[20] The imagery of rolling, flowing waters suggests that the practice of justice and righteousness should be both strong and constant,[21] an integral aspect of Israel's life.[22] Integrity in public life is the *sine qua non* of true worship.

> **25** Did you bring to me sacrifices and offerings the forty years in the wilderness, O house of Israel? **26** You shall take up Sakkuth your king, and Kaiwan your star-god, your images that you made for yourselves; **27** therefore I will take you into exile beyond Damascus, says the LORD, whose name is the God of hosts.

This is a difficult section.[23] Here we may simply note that Israel's worship not only lacks the necessary accompaniment of integrity but also is directed to recipients other than YHWH, such that YHWH is not the "one and only" focus of Israel's acts of devotion (cf. Deut 6:4–5). As a consequence, Israel will not only lose temple

---

19. Although there is a conceptual contrast between what the people want (5:18) and what YHWH wants (5:24), there is no parallel terminology to point to the contrast.

20. This is not the place to discuss the interpretation that Amos (or other prophets when they sound comparable notes) wants to abolish sacrificial practice and replace it with moral practice, other than to say that it seems to me wholly implausible in general historical terms and to depend on too wooden a construal of the prophetic rhetoric.

21. There is dispute as to whether the adjective 'êtān means either "lasting" or "strong" (see Erling Hammershaimb, *The Book of Amos* [Oxford: Blackwell, 1970; ET by John Sturdy from 3rd Danish ed.], 90). I incline to the former: "The adjective 'eythan carries the basic meaning of 'flowing voluminously' and thus serves to distinguish the 'stream [-bed]' (nḥl) which carries water throughout the year, even in the dry months, from the winter brooks that dry up easily" (Wolff, *Amos*, 264).

22. Cf. Jer 22:15 where the portrayal of Josiah's practice of justice and righteousness as set alongside his eating and drinking most likely means that active care for others was as natural and regular to him as his taking daily sustenance (cf. my *Prophecy and Discernment* [Cambridge: Cambridge University Press, 2006], 66).

23. For example, I am doubtful about the separation of 5:25 from 5:24 (NRSV represents a general consensus in its separation), since the negative rhetorical question about sacrifices best belongs integrally with 5:21-24, despite the fine interim climax that is made by the summons for justice and righteousness.

and land by going into exile, but YHWH himself will be the instigator of that loss (no doubt through the agency of one of Israel's enemies). The "day of YHWH" will be darkness, and the form that darkness will take will be the loss of all security through defeat and deportation. YHWH becomes, as it were, the enemy of his chosen people.

## Micah's Temple Sermon: Micah 3:9-12

No narrative context is given for the passage from Micah which follows, yet its content qualifies it as a "temple sermon." Moreover, the appeal to these words of Micah as a precedent for Jeremiah in the narrative account of Jeremiah's "temple sermon" (Jer 26, esp. vv.17-19) implicitly locates Micah within Jerusalem, and the text of Micah also imaginatively invites such a location.

Micah says:

> ⁹ Hear this, you rulers of the house of Jacob
> and chiefs of the house of Israel,
> who abhor justice
> and pervert all equity,
> ¹⁰ who build Zion with blood[24]
> and Jerusalem with wrong!
> ¹¹ Its rulers give judgment for a bribe,
> its priests teach for a price,
> its prophets give oracles for money;
> yet they lean upon the LORD and say,
> "Surely the LORD is with us!"[25]
> No harm[26] shall come upon us."

---

24. Better is "bloodshed," which is the regular sense of the plural form *dâmîm*, e.g., Gen 4:10, 1 Kgs 2:5 (cf. *Gesenius' Hebrew Grammar* [ed. E. Kautzsch; trans. A. E. Cowley; Oxford: Clarendon, 1910], 124n). The sense of the text is presumably that labourers are exploited and overworked, and their lives disposable. The rhetoric may involve a degree of hyperbole.

25. Preferable is "in our midst," which better captures the spatial temple-oriented implications of *běqirbēnû*, and preserves the differentiation of Micah's language from the "with us" (*'immānû*) of Ps 46:8, 12 [ET 7, 11].

26. Better perhaps is "disaster." The sense of the phrase is not "We shall not be hurt" but "We shall not be overthrown/defeated." The Hebrew term *rā'āh* is the standard term for the overthrow of a city by its enemies, cf. Amos 3:6; Jer 18:8.

Micah's address is direct and blunt. He speaks to the leaders of Israel,[27] those with responsibility for its common life (3:9a), and portrays them as corrupt, failing in their obligations for just dealings in public (3:9b), and maltreating those labouring on public and/or private building projects with a harshness that is careless of life (3:10).[28] The leadership in its various forms—both "secular" (rulers) and "spiritual" (priests, prophets)—is venal; the justice and guidance that should enable healthy communal life have become commodities, to be had only for a price (3:11a).[29] Yet apparently these leaders do not see their conduct as incompatible with strong religious claims; they acknowledge their dependence upon YHWH;[30] they claim YHWH's presence "in our midst," which is clearly a reference to the Jerusalem temple as the focal point of YHWH's presence with Israel/Judah; and they regard YHWH's presence in the temple as a guarantee of security from their enemies (as celebrated in, for example, Pss 46 and 48).

Micah continues:

> <sup>12</sup> Therefore because of you
>> Zion shall be ploughed as a field;
>
> Jerusalem shall become a heap of ruins,
>> and the mountain of the house a wooded height.

Micah brusquely draws out the implications of the mismatch between the leaders' practice and their religious claims, and "connect[s] fault with fate."[31] It is precisely because of their complacent corruption that the disaster they are confident cannot happen will happen: city and temple together will be reduced to ruins overgrown by

---

27. Interestingly, Micah does not specify or single out the king, yet Jer 26:19 depicts king Hezekiah as a responsive recipient of Micah's message.

28. William McKane has a strange comment here: "He [Micah] does not have in mind building operations which were careless of the human cost and treated fatal accidents to workers lightly. Rather it is the megalomania of those who build or acquire property ruthlessly without regard to the social damage which they inflict and the trail of human suffering which they leave in their wake" (*Micah* [Edinburgh: T. & T. Clark, 1998], 112). On what grounds within the text McKane considers it possible to make this distinction and this judgment it would be interesting to know.

29. The point of the rhetoric is not, of course, to deny that in appropriate contexts there might be legitimate questions about how best to provide financial support for those whose responsibilities as leaders may prevent them from being able to provide for their own upkeep.

30. The verb *nišʿan* characteristically expresses trusting dependence, as notably displayed by the servant of YHWH (Isa 50:10, where *nišʿan* is parallel to *bāṭaḥ*).

31. Leslie C. Allen, *The Books of Joel, Obadiah, Jonah and Micah* (NICOT; Grand Rapids: Eerdmans, 1976), 316.

vegetation. What will happen to the people is not specified; though insofar as the site of city and temple returns to the wild, the implication is that its inhabitants will not be there to rebuild, and so will either be dead or deported into exile.

## Jeremiah's Temple Sermon: Jeremiah 7:1-15

Jeremiah's well-known temple sermon is perhaps the only one of our three passages that would be generally recognized under this nomenclature. Although it is lengthier than the other two, and is provided with a clear narrative setting, there is, as will be seen, a striking commonality of content and understanding between all three. Jeremiah 7 begins:

> **1** The word that came to Jeremiah from the LORD: **2** Stand in the gate of the LORD's house, and proclaim there this word, and say, Hear the word of the LORD, all you people of Judah, you that enter these gates to worship the LORD. **3** Thus says the LORD of hosts, the God of Israel: Amend your ways and your doings, and I will let you dwell in this place.[32] **4** Do not trust in these deceptive words: "This is the temple of the LORD, the temple of the LORD, the temple of the LORD."

Jeremiah is to position himself in a place of maximal exposure to temple worshippers and initially say three things. First (v. 3a), he challenges temple worshippers to "amend their ways"; in other words, as Jeremiah puts it elsewhere, they are to "turn"/"repent" (3:12, 14; 4:1; 18:7-8); change of conduct is necessary. Secondly (v. 3b), he holds out a positive consequence of such turning, which is that YHWH will let the people of Judah stay in their land and not (by implication) be defeated by their enemies with consequent deportation for the survivors. Thirdly (v. 4), he warns against a deceptive thought, a false presumption, that is the (implicit) assumption that YHWH's presence in the temple means security for Judah from its enemies.

The rest of Jeremiah's address expands these three points.

> **5** For if you truly amend your ways and your doings, if you truly act justly one with another, **6** if you do not oppress the alien, the orphan, and the widow, or shed innocent blood in this place, and if you do not go after

---

32. I adopt the NRSV margin, which follows the MT vocalization, because the threat of exile is the note on which the primary text of the sermon ends (v. 15), and so the possibility of averting exile is appropriate to the introduction of the message. The issue of whether YHWH will continue to dwell with Judah, as in the NRSV text, is indeed an issue in Ezekiel (Ezek 8–11), but Jeremiah should not be conflated with Ezekiel.

other gods to your own hurt, ⁷ then I will let you dwell[33] in this place, in the land that I gave to your ancestors for ever and ever.

First, Jeremiah gives fuller content to the initial challenge to amendment and spells out what is involved. The basic requirement is to practise justice (*mišpāṭ*, v. 5b)—a key term as also in Amos (5:24) and Micah (3:9). This is specified in terms of not taking advantage of those of whom advantage might most easily be taken—the resident foreigner, the orphan, the widow—because they lacked normal social security as embodied in kin or head of the house. As so often in the OT, the assumption is that if justice is given to those who are most easily denied it, then justice will (in principle) be practised elsewhere too. Shedding of innocent blood could envisage either the oppressive maltreatment of labourers (as in Mic 3:10) or the manipulation of legal procedure (as against Naboth, 1 Kgs 21) or possibly some other malpractice; in all cases exploitation and violence are seen as the denial of justice. Going after other gods represents fundamental disloyalty to YHWH (a denial of the first of the Ten Commandments and of the Shema) and would also entail Judah's undoing ("to your own hurt").[34] In all these ways the Judahites are challenged to change for the better.

Also, YHWH's gift to Israel/Judah of its land in perpetuity ("for ever and ever") is implied to be no guarantee against YHWH's depriving them of that gift. The prophetic understanding is that gift implies expectation, so failure to live up to expectation can imperil the gift, and amendment is needed to retain it. Jeremiah's account of what that expectation entails now leads into his speaking further about how the people of Judah's belief in their security with YHWH, because of His presence in the temple, has in fact become false and, therefore, idolatrous.

> ⁸ Here you are, trusting in deceptive words to no avail. ⁹ Will you steal, murder, commit adultery, swear falsely, make offerings to Baal, and go after other gods that you have not known, ¹⁰ and then come and stand before me in this house, which is called by my name, and say "We are safe!"—only to go on doing all these abominations? ¹¹ Has this house, which is called by my name, become a den of robbers in your sight? You know, I too am watching, says the LORD.

---

33. The Hebrew verb is identical to that in v. 3. Again I stay with MT and follow the NRSV margin in v. 3, though inexplicably the NRSV fails to repeat its marginal note here.

34. The Hebrew (*leraʿ lākem*) is non-specific. It could envisage Judah's moral and social disintegration from within as a consequence of denying their identity as the people of YHWH, or else abandonment to their enemies as a consequence of faithlessness, or both.

Just as vv. 5–7 expanded v. 3, so now vv. 8–10 expand v. 4. The people's mantra, their "deceptive words" that "This is the temple of the Lord," is now resumed and clarified by the claim "We are safe," which makes more specific the belief that YHWH's presence in the temple means the deliverance of Jerusalem from its enemies. Yet Jeremiah sees self-contradiction here. In essence, Jeremiah's point is that the claim to YHWH's presence and protection is self-involving language, language that implies a human way of living commensurate with the divine presence that is invoked. But Judah is living in flagrant disregard of YHWH's priorities, and their specified transgressions read like a summary of disobedience to the Ten Commandments.[35] To suppose that one can use the language of YHWH's presence and protection and yet detach oneself from the intrinsic moral and spiritual dimensions of YHWH's will is to misunderstand one's language, to empty it of content, and to abuse it. This is what turns claims about YHWH's temple, which on one level are factually true—the building *was* the temple of YHWH—into something deceptive, a falsehood.

Jeremiah next develops further the issue mentioned in v. 3b, only casting it now not as hopeful possibility but as pure warning of disaster, where the possibility of hope can only be realized if the warning is heeded and acted upon:

> **12** Go now to my place that was in Shiloh, where I made my name dwell at first, and see what I did to it for the wickedness of my people Israel. **13** And now, because you have done all these things, says the LORD, and when I spoke to you persistently, you did not listen, and when I called you, you did not answer, **14** therefore I will do to the house that is called by my name, in which you trust, and to the place that I gave to you and to your ancestors, just what I did to Shiloh. **15** And I will cast you out of my sight, just as I cast out all your kinsfolk, all the offspring of Ephraim.

The warning is backed by appeal to a precedent—the temple of YHWH at Shiloh which by Jeremiah's time had been reduced to ruins and had been abandoned (i.e., Shiloh exemplified Micah's depiction of Jerusalem, Mic 3:12). If the corruption of Israel led to the overthrow of Shiloh,[36] then the heedless and unresponsive

---

35. Whether or not the Ten Commandments had been formulated as such, and were known, in the context of the formation of the book of Jeremiah is a historical issue on which I am agnostic (as the date of the Decalogue can be argued any which way). Within a canonical context, however, it is a natural reading strategy to read Jer 7 against the background of the Commandments in Exod 20 and Deut 5.

36. One thinks of the Philistine victory over Israel in 1 Sam 4. Indeed, there are strong theological affinities between Jer 7 and 1 Sam 4. The complacent, effectively superstitious, attitude of the Israelites, who suppose that the presence of the ark of YHWH will guarantee victory over the Philistines, is confounded by the presence of the ark leading to a defeat more crushing than that suffered previously. The

corruption of Judah can similarly lead to Jerusalem's overthrow at the hands of an enemy, operating at YHWH's behest. The consequence will be the familiar fate of the vanquished, already experienced by the northern kingdom—deportation into exile. The irony is that YHWH Himself, to whose divine presence in the temple the Judahites complacently appeal as protection against disaster, will be the primary cause and agent of that disaster.

## Summarizing the Temple Sermons

I hope it will be readily apparent why I have grouped these three passages together as temple sermons. Each criticizes corrupt practice in a temple, which could be summarized as a failure to practise justice (*mišpāṭ*); each criticizes spurious trust in YHWH, focussed in some way upon His presence in the temple; each sees the trust as spurious because it is complacent and has become detached from an obedience commensurate with the trust; each warns of a coming destruction of the temple and/or a deportation into exile; and each sees the destruction and/or exile as the act of YHWH (albeit through human agency).

Because the implied dynamics of these prophetic messages are in principle familiar within Jewish and Christian thought, it would be easy to resort to shorthand formulations to summarize our expositions. One possible shorthand would be some form of "Ethics trumps ritual." However, I consider such a formulation unhelpful, as it oversimplifies the complex relationships between moral practice and the activities of worship. It is one thing to say that the rituals of worship without appropriate moral practice are empty, indeed offensive; it is another to denigrate ritual as such in relation to moral practice. Yet shorthand formulations in this area almost always imply some such denigration. A much better shorthand would be the first line of the well-known chorus "Trust and obey," for such a combination indeed goes to the heart of the prophetic understanding of life with God. Nonetheless, even the best theological shorthands perhaps risk encouraging a certain kind of complacency, in that there is a danger that one may come away thinking "I knew that anyway" or "Nothing new here" without having felt afresh any existential challenge from the

---

words of Israel's elders in 1 Sam 4:3, "Let us bring the ark of the covenant of the Lord here from Shiloh, so that he may come among us and save us from the power of our enemies" are a close functional equivalent to "This is the temple of the Lord" and "We are safe" (Jer 7:4, 10); and YHWH's response, implicit in the narrative of 1 Sam 4–6 and explicit in Jeremiah's warning, is closely comparable.

biblical text. So, instead I propose briefly to offer a few preliminary reflections to try to exemplify what it might mean to take seriously these prophetic texts today.[37]

First and foremost, any use of these biblical texts in relation to our concern with the idolatry of security today necessarily involves the adoption of analogical and metaphorical modes of thought as the means whereby we may do our constructive thinking in attentive and faithful dialogical relation with the ancient text. For the fact that the Jerusalem (or Bethel) temple has long since disappeared does not nullify the prophetic challenge or make it anachronistic, since there remain other prime symbols of trust in God, the human dynamics in relation to which may be strongly similar to those in relation to the temple.

Within a Christian context the two prime symbols are probably the Bible and the dominical sacraments (Baptism and Eucharist). In many and various ways these are understood to be vehicles of the divine presence and as such become focal points of hope and expectation and also of assurance that God is with His people. Yet Christians who attend diligently to reading and studying the Bible and hearing it preached, or who regularly attend Eucharists and develop spiritual disciplines related to eucharistic worship (confession, fasting, etc.), may become lax in their moral practices that relate to the wellbeing of others. If so, if there develops a significant mismatch between their religious practices and their way of living, they may need to hear a challenge that their religious practices have become empty, even offensive, to God.

## Scripture, Security, and Christian Zionism

That which applies initially with relation to primary Christian symbols can pertain also with relation to larger concerns, such as church, race, and country. At the risk of raising an issue where heat can easily predominate over light, let me suggest that some of these problems are evident in major strands of premillennial dispensationalism and its outworking in Christian Zionism with its distinctive kind of political, financial, and military support for certain aspects of the state of Israel.[38]

37. One issue within OT studies is whether Jeremiah (and perhaps Amos and Micah) is opposing a "Zion theology" as expressed by Isaiah. However, I do not find this particularly helpful, not least because it tends to transpose the existential issues that intrinsically surround the implications of trust in God into a conflictual history of ideas, not that the latter may not have existed. However, we have no hard evidence; rather, we have only the varying plausibility of our inferences from a biblical corpus which never mentions such a conflict but can in places be read as implying it. See my *Prophecy and Discernment*, 59, n. 49, for the point that a study in the history of ideas redirects one's focus.

38. I appreciate that there are forms of Zionism, most obviously Jewish but also Christian, which do

At the risk of oversimplifying, there are at least two core characteristics of this movement. One is a focus on OT prophecy as predictive, indeed as predictive in an as yet unrealized way, awaiting realization once the timetable of the end times gets under way after the rapture. Quite apart from the way in which this ignores the intrinsically conditional and response-seeking nature of much biblical prophecy,[39] the peculiar emphasis of this approach also effectively ignores the kind of prophetic material we have been looking at, which stresses that without the practice of justice God's favour and protection is forfeited. Thus the more or less no-questions-asked support for Israeli militarism and for Israeli settlements in the West Bank in disregard for Palestinian concerns represents a failure to grasp that which is central to prophetic concerns. It is an approach that is incapable of hearing Jeremiah's warning that a land given in perpetuity may be forfeited through, among other things, unjust oppression of the weak and vulnerable.[40]

A second characteristic is the indirect concern for America's own security through the prime emphasis given to God's words to Abraham in Gen 12:3a, "I will bless those who bless you, and the one who curses you I will curse."[41] The explicit logic of some Christian Zionism is that America must bless Israel (i.e., provide financial and political support) *so that* God may bless America (i.e., give America security and victory over its enemies). There is here a deeply chauvinist streak, perhaps most famously exemplified in Hal Lindsey's scenarios of God giving America ultimate victory over its enemies in the end times.[42] There is less concern with America discerning and doing what is just—in Lincoln's enduring words "with firmness in the

---

not depend on a premillennial dispensationalist frame of reference. However, it is Zionism within this frame of reference which is its most potent form in the United States today and is my concern here.

39. This is specified axiomatically in Jer 18:7–10, and exemplified in the appeal to Mic 3:12 in Jer 26:17–19 and also in Jonah 3–4, esp. 3:10, 4:2 which draw upon the axiomatic formulation of Jer 18:8. See also the comments above on Jer 7.

40. Any attempt at depicting the situation is fraught with difficulty, for of course many Israelis feel vulnerable in relation to hostile neighbouring countries, and appalling acts of murderous violence have been committed by both Israelis and Palestinians. Nonetheless, to adapt Moses' words in Deut 8, some of the prime lessons that many Jews learned over the centuries when living in countries where they were at the mercy of an often-hostile populace and/or government have too often been neglected in Israeli attitudes and actions towards Palestinians since the reestablishment of the state of Israel.

41. For the importance of this text within Christian Zionism, see Victoria Clark, *Allies for Armageddon: The Rise of Christian Zionism* (New Haven & London: Yale University Press, 2007), *passim*, esp. 12. I have discussed this use of Scripture in my forthcoming *The Theology of the Book of Genesis* (Cambridge: Cambridge University Press: 2009), ch. 9.

42. Probably Lindsey's most famous work, whose emphases are characteristic of his larger oeuvre, is *The Late Great Planet Earth* (Grand Rapids: Zondervan, 1970).

right, as God gives us to see the right"—than with America positioning itself advantageously to receive blessing (security) now and in the end times.

This kind of Zionism involves at its heart a self-serving reading of the Bible which fails to understand how God's promises relate to God's demands. It is ironic, indeed tragic, that Christians who seek to be distinctive by their faithfulness to Scripture should have allowed themselves to be misled in this way into idolatrous practice. As in the days of Micah, those who lead bear special responsibility.[43]

## Justice, Love, and the Wrath of God

I would also like briefly to touch on a major theological issue posed by our prophetic texts: how are we to understand God? The OT portrayal of YHWH as one who brings conquering armies against His people, armies which destroy cities and carry the defeated into exile, is one that makes some believers nervous, especially in a contemporary context of heightened anxieties about the relationship between religious belief and violence.

On the one hand, at the risk of grossly oversimplifying, let me suggest that a major problem for much contemporary Christian thinking is that of "demoralizing" God.[44] We rightly proclaim and celebrate God's love and grace, yet we wrongly fail to understand the inescapably moral and demanding nature of that love and grace. In the terminology made famous by Bonhoeffer in the opening words of his *The Cost of Discipleship*[45] we are prone to "cheap grace." Or, in the terms of this paper, we have forgotten and/or neglected the nexus between knowing God and doing His will which is repeatedly formulated within both testaments and given particular emphasis by the prophets.

---

43. Victoria Clark, in the context of attending a weekend at Pastor Hagee's Cornerstone church in San Antonio, reflects: ". . . it occurred to me that American Christian Zionism's influence might be negligible were it not for the fact that so many of its noisiest exponents were implicitly trusted churchmen. Hal Lindsey, Tim LaHaye, Jerry Falwell, and Pat Robertson were all pastors" (*Allies*, 279–80).

44. I am deliberately alluding to the language and conceptuality of Gertrude Himmelfarb's important study, *The De-moralization of Society: From Victorian Virtues to Modern Values* (New York/London: Knopf/IEA Health & Welfare Unit, 1995). In the question time at the symposium John Barclay helpfully queried my point, on the grounds that the churches' obsession with sexual issues suggests too much rather than too little moralizing. For some contexts, though not all, this must be granted. Nonetheless the point of Himmelfarb's language is not that people today have lost moral principles. It is rather that virtues imply qualities of life which need to be acquired over time and are only meaningful when practically displayed, whereas values can be opinions and preferences that are changeable at will. It is in this sense that the Christian understanding of God has become shallower and less demanding.

45. London: SCM, 1959; ET by R. H. Fuller from German of 1937.

Another way of putting this in general theological terms is that we have become uneasy and/or unfamiliar with the biblical concept of the "wrath of God" (*'ap yhwh, orgē theou*).[46] Yet it is one thing to recognize how easily this language is corrupted and another to fail to understand its right use. In general biblical and theological terms "wrath" is what happens when God's good and loving purposes (*ḥesed, agapē*) encounter human complacency and intransigence (stiffness of neck, hardness of heart, impenitence, unbelief). Here a prime way in which the reality of God's moral character can be expressed is through warnings to try to engender a right response, rather than through affirmations of love and mercy, which can simply engender in the unresponsive the sense that they can get away with whatever they want.[47] Or, differently expressed, heaven and hell are related dimensions of the realities of responsiveness, or its lack, to the call of God.

On the other hand, there is the issue of what might be called "moral causality." The notion that moral corruption and decadence should bring national disaster is widely considered problematic, a problematic not eased by the fact that the most vocal proponents of such a view today are Islamists such as al-Qaeda, whom most in the United States and Europe, Christian and non-Christian alike, are not inclined to see as agents of the Almighty. To be sure, Christians (and others) need to be open to recognize critique and challenge from unexpected quarters, but even so, the indiscriminate murderousness of Islamism makes it hard to hear possibly valid Islamist critiques of Western culture. Likewise generalized Christian denunciations of moral decadence (or those with special focus on sexual practices) are simply shrugged off. More broadly, however, "moral causality" remains a difficult notion in a culture which prefers to think of national wellbeing (and/or decline) in political, economic, and sociological terms. If a Christian account of "moral causality" is to be meaningful, it will need explicitly to be inclusive of, and not alternative to, political, economic, and social categories; that is, it is primarily the injustices that characterize public life and social interactions, more than those that characterize private life, that need to be in the forefront of a Christian concern that stands in continuity with the prophets.[48] Moreover, "moral causality" will only make sense, if at all, within the context of an

---

46. There is, however, a valuable collection of material from the 2004 North Park Symposium on Judgment in *Ex Auditu* 20 (2004).

47. Another prophetic text which is illuminating of these dynamics is the story of Micaiah ben Imlah (1 Kgs 22); see my *Prophecy and Discernment*, 109–125, esp. 120.

48. This is *not* to say that "private" morality does not matter (I use scare quotes because the demarcation of "private" and "public" is itself highly contestable); the issue is one of relative emphasis.

overall understanding of God that is also continuous with that of the prophets—that God is not some kind of external intruder into otherwise autonomous human affairs but is the one in whom all life is upheld and to whom all life is accountable, such that offence against humanity is also offence against God. If such a critique is to be formulated meaningfully today, there is still much work to be done.

## Conclusion

In the above reflections I have tended somewhat to narrow our theme of "the idolatry of security" into a focus primarily upon two issues: the use of Scripture and the relationship between grace/gift and demand/expectation. The reason for my approach is that it is all too easy, within a context of Christian theologians in a Christian academic setting, to use familiar biblical language and concepts with insufficient reflection on their real significance. Those who have learned to inhabit the world of the Bible can readily bring biblical content to bear upon today's world—and I am all in favour of that! But a little reflection upon what we are doing ought to make us more alert in both watching our language and attending to our practice. As we ponder some of the many ways in which the human longing for security can become idolatrous and lead to corruption of self and injustice towards others, I hope that we will not ourselves be beguiled by the security of familiarity with the Bible and an academic context into idolatrously detaching ourselves and our love of the Bible from obedient attentiveness to God's priorities for His world.

# RESPONSE TO MOBERLY

## *Robert L. Hubbard, Jr.*

I find myself in basic agreement with the main thrust of Prof. Moberly's paper and am intrigued by his reflections on the topic. My response will also propose a slightly different reading of two texts, pose two questions for further reflection, and comment on several other voices that we might include in our deliberations.

There is much to like in this paper. Moberly defines what he means by "security" as a human need—in a negative sense (freedom from dangers) and more positively (a context in which people flourish). I might have liked also to have a definition of "idolatry," but he apparently means by it something like the "misdirection and malpractice . . . of the longing for security." He next shines his exegetical spotlight on three OT prophetic texts broadly classed as "temple sermons." Each critiques a temple—the Jerusalem one in Micah 3 and Jeremiah 7, and one at Bethel in Amos 5. The three prophets each announce the temples' destruction as symbols—"idolatrous" ones, to be sure—of misplaced trust and a misguided grasping for security. Put differently, they mirror Israel's larger problem—"the mismatch between the priorities of YHWH and those of Israel/Judah." Finally, Moberly leads the reader across a bridge of analogical and metaphorical thinking to reflect on contemporary ways in which similar mismatches occur.

I am one who grew up on dispensationalist eschatology, and so—having shifted positions decades ago—resonate with his critique of that prophecy-driven movement and its shaping of Christian Zionism. I also rue the fact that the latter ignores prophetic calls for justice, unwaveringly supports Israeli policies, and disregards Palestinian concerns—ironically, despite the large numbers of fellow Christians among the latter. Moberly highlights the further irony that Christian Zionists so devoted to faithfully obeying Scripture end up being misled into a form of idolatry. Finally, I am also a recovering fundamentalist, but I share his concern over the recent aversion among Christians to God's demanding side. In short, I find Moberly's focus on "the use of Scripture, and the relationship between grace/gift and demand/expectation" intriguing and, for the most part, persuasive.

On the other hand, I find myself reading two of his "temple sermons"—Micah 3 and Amos 5—slightly differently. Moberly rightly concedes that, at first glance, Amos 5 seems not to be a "temple sermon" but proposes that we imagine it being given at the temple in Bethel (see Amos 7:10–13). This is possible, but some indicators in Amos 5 and 7 also commend a "high place" as its possible location (see Amos 5:5–6; 7:9). Whatever the case, what strikes me as interesting is that Yahweh addresses his people at a Northern Kingdom temple or high place (i.e., an illegitimate sanctuary that enjoys royal backing), rejects worship done there in his honor, and alludes to the worship of other gods (v. 26). In this case, the "idolatry of security" apparently involves actual idolatry at an illegitimate holy place, and not simply the "misdirection and malpractice ... of the longing for security" applied to a biblically legitimate religious symbol.

As for Micah 3, the textual markers suggest to me a sermonic critique of Zion (or Jerusalem), the city of which the temple forms a key part, rather than a "temple sermon." Granted, Zion can also refer to the temple, but the parallelism in vv. 10 and 12 persuades me that the city is meant. If so, the basis of the "idolatry of security" in this case derives from the election of Jerusalem as Yahweh's hometown and its role as Israel's capital. Further, that election accords it theological legitimacy, unlike the site in Amos 5 (see Isa 10:24; Pss 87:2–3; 132:13). It is that legitimacy that attracts Israel's "malpractice" (Moberly's term) in seeking security there. The malpractitioners, by the way, include both the civic and religious leaders of the capital city, probably as representatives of the general populace of Judah. If I am right, Micah 3 and Amos 5 further flesh out the situation to which the eighth-century prophets respond: the "idolatry of security" typifies both northern and southern sanctuaries—what Joshua calls, "all Israel" (Josh 8:33); in the north it even involved a form of polytheism. It also faults both civic and religious leadership for the lapse into idolatry.

This leads me to the first of my two questions. These three texts reflect a pattern that I have observed elsewhere in the prophets. Driven by the need for security, God's people seem usually to seek sanctuary in what I call the "cultic option"—the rituals of sanctuaries and sacrifices—rather than the alternative, what Moberly calls "the priorities of YHWH" (i.e., ethical demands like justice). My question is: Why is this so? What makes the latter option preferable to the former? The obvious, related question, of course, would also ask whether in obvious or subtle ways we show a similar preference—and what we can do about that.

My second question crosses the bridge from the prophetic texts to the contemporary cultural motifs of "God and country" and patriotism. I ask this as a retired

Navy Reserve chaplain, someone who for three decades navigated the tricky terrain of being "in" that military world but not "of" it. We are all well aware of deals struck in history between church and state, compacts we acknowledge in retrospect as disastrous for the advance of God's kingdom. Given the models of Israel and Judah before us, and given what I see as a post-Vietnam resurgence of American nationalism, is a non-idolatrous relationship to our government possible at all? If so, what might that look like? In a sense Israel and Judah had it easier than we do. God had thrown temple and capital city together as a unity, a unity full of tensions and grabs for power among the parties, to be sure, whereas we may negotiate the relationship more freely. How do we engage, if not influence the body politic, without succumbing to its idolatrous lure of power and influence?

Finally, a comment concerning other voices we might invite into the present discussion. When I first read the paper's focus on prophetic "temple sermons," I had two thoughts. The first was: "Okay, that's what I would expect; the prophetic corpus is the obvious resource on idolatry." My second was: "Once again, as so often happens, the wisdom tradition is not invited into the conversation." So, just to keep us canonically "honest," I suggest that we come at the topic of "idolatry as security" from the direction of biblical wisdom. Just for discussion, we might imagine a meeting somewhere in Jerusalem around 500 BC attended by the compilers of Proverbs, Job, and Ecclesiastes. They have just read the three "temple sermons" and begin to discuss them from the viewpoints of the three wisdom books. What would they say about the concerns of the prophets about our topic?

Professor Moberly has served us well in his paper. We have texts to work with and his reflections on their contemporary significance. He has raised fundamental questions about how we read the Bible, our vision of God, and of complacency around us. In his conclusion he has also denied us a safe escape back to the security of our ivory towers. Now it is our turn to wrestle with these and other important matters.

# IMAGINING THE UNTHINKABLE
Exposing the Idolatry of National Security in Amos

## *M. Daniel Carroll R.*

### Setting a Direction

In OT studies research on idolatry often concentrates on the relationship between Yahweh and other deities. Discussions deal with the interconnected issues of the extent of belief in and worship of other deities among the people of God, how these other gods are portrayed in different texts, possible reconstructions of the development of monotheism in ancient Israel, whether Israel's faith was aniconic, and the uniqueness of its faith (and its expression in the Hebrew Bible) vis-à-vis the surrounding cultures.[1] Some utilize insights gleaned from this material for the life and mission of the church today. These modern applications tend to point to such dangers as the powerful lures of materialism, sexuality, and the cult of self that can take the central place in our lives that only God deserves.[2]

This approach to idolatry certainly reflects much of what the OT has to say on the topic. It also is quite relevant, and the lessons that are drawn can be enlightening and challenging. Nevertheless, I would like to go in a different direction. My purpose in this paper is to explore the "idolatry of the true God"—that is, the deity created by civil religion whom biblical texts consider to be an unacceptable formulation of Yahweh. The problem in this case is not credence in other gods but rather in another Yahweh. A false Yahweh is the most insidious idol of all, because its followers judge

---

[1]. For a survey of the archaeological data see Richard S. Hess, *Israelite Religions: An Archaeological and Biblical Survey* (Grand Rapids: Baker, 2007). Note the helpful discussions in John Barton, "'The Work of Human Hands' (Psalm 115:4): Idolatry in the Old Testament," *Ex Auditu* 15 (1999): 63–72; Richard Bauckham, "Biblical Theology and the Problems of Monotheism," in *Out of Egypt: Biblical Theology and Biblical Interpretation* (ed. C. Bartholomew et al.; Scripture and Hermeneutics Series 5; Grand Rapids: Zondervan, 2004), 187–232.

[2]. Ian Provan, "To Highlight All Our Idols: Worshipping God in Nietzche's World," *Ex Auditu* 15 (1999): 19–38; Christopher J. H. Wright, *The Mission of God: Unlocking the Bible's Grand Narrative* (Downers Grove, Ill.: InterVarsity, 2006), 136–88; cf. Douglas K. Stuart, *Exodus* (NAC 2; Nashville: Broadman & Holman, 2006), 450–54.

themselves and the nation to be doing the will of the true God and so enjoying his favor. After consideration of several introductory matters, the book of Amos will serve as the focus of our reflections.

The blending of patriotism and religion, then and now, lodges itself deep within the soul of a people. The fact that a heterodox faith weaves its way into the people's psyche and becomes inseparable from national identity makes it difficult to recognize and dangerous to denounce. To question it is to contradict the commonly accepted faith; it is to deny the country's favored status before God and to betray the body politic to its enemies. The sinister yet subtle allure of such a religion is captured magnificently in C. S. Lewis's memorable *The Screwtape Letters*. Writing during the throes of the Second World War and with Britain under grave threat, Lewis appreciated the dangers of a religion driven and defined by political convictions, whether of the hawk or dove. In a letter to his neophyte nephew Wormwood about how best to secure the downfall of the human entrusted to his "care," the experienced demon counsels:

> Let him begin by treating the Patriotism or the Pacifism as a part of his religion. Then let him, under the influence of partisan spirit, come to regard it as the most important part. Then quietly and gradually nurse him on to the stage at which the religion becomes merely part of the "cause," in which Christianity is valued chiefly because of the excellent arguments it can produce in favour of the British war-effort or Pacifism. . . . Once you have made the World an end, and faith a means, you have almost won your man, and it makes very little difference what kind of worldly end he is pursuing. Provided that meetings, pamphlets, policies, movements, causes, and crusades, matter more to him than prayers and sacraments and charity, he is ours—and the more "religious" (on those terms) the more securely ours. I could show you a pretty cageful down here.[3]

## Versions of Faith in Conflict

The association of politics, society, and religion in the United States is an ongoing topic of research and debate. Scholars trace the tensions back to the colonial era and to the founding of the republic.[4] Today not a few disapprove of the connec-

---

3. C. S. Lewis, *The Screwtape Letters, with Screwtape Proposes a Toast* (New York: HarperSanFrancisco, 2000), 34–35. This passage was brought to my attention in David Kuo's *Tempting Faith* (below, n. 7).

4. E.g., Noah Feldman, *Divided by God: America's Church-State Problem and What We Should Do about It* (New York: Farrar, Straus and Giroux, 2005).

tions between this civil and cultural religion—especially that labeled the Religious Right—and United States internal politics and foreign policy.

The invasion of Iraq and its impact on citizens' rights at home and on the nation's image abroad are the primary motivations of many new analyses. Among the disapproving assessments that I have read are works with provocative titles like *Captain America and the Crusade against Evil*[5] and *America's Battle for God*.[6] There have been critiques from individuals of strong Christian convictions, who have worked within the Bush administration, such as David Kuo's *Tempting Faith*.[7] Jim Wallis is a prominent contrarian, who has called Christians to move beyond traditional simplistic partisan politics with their respective truncated views of God.[8] Others have incorporated the civil religion impulses of Christianity in the United States as part of wider portrayals of God and Jesus in this country.[9] Stephen Prothero wryly comments: "At least in the United States, Jesus has stood not on some unchanging rock of ages, but on the shifting sands of economic circumstances, political calculations, and cultural trends."[10] Another negative perspective on these matters is one that claims that the Christian faith itself as well as its Scriptures—the OT in particular—are inherently violent and legitimize war.[11]

The mixing of context and religion, of course, is not limited to the United States. The evidence elsewhere is both historical and contemporary. The tendency, for example, has been manifest in Latin America since the coming of the Spanish over five centuries ago. I cite that continent because of my own background (I am

---

5. Robert Jewett and John Shelton Lawrence, *Captain America and the Crusade against Evil: The Dilemma of Zealous Nationalism* (Grand Rapids: Eerdmans, 2003).

6. Geiko Müller-Fahrenholz, *America's Battle for God: A European Christian Looks at Civil Religion* (Grand Rapids: Eerdmans, 2007).

7. David Kuo, *Tempting Faith: An Inside Story of Political Seduction* (New York: Free, 2007). Earlier examples of disillusionment by two who had been involved in the rise of the Religious Right are Cal Thomas and Ed Dobson. See their *Blinded by Might: Can the Religious Right Save America?* (Grand Rapids: Zondervan, 1999).

8. *God's Politics: Why the Right Gets It Wrong and the Left Doesn't Get It* (New York: HarperOne, 2006); *The Great Awakening: Religious Faith in a Post-Religious Right America* (New York: HarperOne, 2008).

9. Stephen Prothero, *American Jesus: How the Son of God Became a National Icon* (New York: Farrar, Straus & Giroux, 2003); Stephen J. Nichols, *Jesus Made in America: A Cultural History from the Puritans to the Passion of Christ* (Downers Grove, Ill.: InterVarsity, 2008).

10. Prothero, *American Jesus*, 8.

11. J. G. McConville responds to some of these claims in *God and Earthly Power: An Old Testament Political Theology, Genesis—Kings* (LHB/OTS 454; London: T. & T. Clark, 2006).

half-Guatemalan) and work in Guatemala City for fifteen years before coming to Denver Seminary. (I continue to teach at a seminary there every summer).

The Christianity brought by the Spanish in the fifteenth century was militant. It was fresh from the victorious expulsion of the Moors from the Iberian Peninsula after a long struggle stretching over hundreds of years. It also was dogmatic. The uniting of Spain was followed by the institution of the Roman Catholic Inquisition. It was a Christianity that wedded the cross and the crown with the help of the sword.

At one level the conquest of the New World was a religious one. The subjugation of the great Amerindian civilizations was a war between the god of the Europeans and the gods of the indigenous. All had their own expressions of civil religion, and so, not surprisingly, the conflict generated theological discussions on both sides. On the one hand, for example, the Aztecs wrestled with the theological crisis brought by the defeat of their deities, the spoliation of their cities and towns, and the death and exploitation of so many.[12] On the other, the conquest spawned distinct appreciations of the Christian faith and God. There were ongoing religious and political disputes (inseparable at the time) regarding the definition of what constituted suitable evangelization of these lands and the corresponding socio-economic and governmental arrangements best suited to accomplish that end (e.g., the *encomienda*).[13] The great defender of the indigenous, the Dominican friar Bartolomé de las Casas, in his written works and proposals of alternative laws and projects tried to counter the cruelty of what his country had wrought and his faith had sanctioned.[14] His efforts are applauded to this day. They stand in stark contrast to those of others, such as the jurist Juan Ginés de Sepúlveda in his *Un tratado sobre las justas causas de la Guerra*, which is a biblical, theological, and historical apologetic for the conquest.[15]

---

12. See Miguel Léon-Portilla (ed.), *Visión de los vencidos: Relaciones indígenas de la Conquista* (Biblioteca del Estudiante Universitario 81; México, D. F.: Universidad Nacional Autónoma de México, 1992); cf. Tzvetan Todorov, *The Conquest of America: The Question of the Other* (trans. R. Howard; New York: Harper & Row, 1984).

13. Luis N. Rivera, *A Violent Evangelism: The Political and Religious Conquest of the Americas* (Louisville: Westminster John Knox, 1992).

14. G. Sanderlin (ed.), *Witness: The Writings of Bartolomé de las Casas* (Maryknoll, N.Y.: Orbis, 1992); Bartolomé de las Casas, *The Only Way* (ed. H. R. Parish; trans. F. P. Sullivan; Sources of American Spirituality; New York: Paulist, 1992); cf. Gustavo Gutiérrez, *En busca de los pobres de Jesucristo: El pensamiento de Bartolomé de las Casas* (Lima, Peru: Instituto Bartolomé de las Casas; Centro de Estudios y Publicaciones, 1992).

15. Juan Ginés de Sepúlveda, *Un tratado sobre las justas causas de la guerra contra los indios* (México, D. F.: Fondo de Cultura Económica, 1986).

This intermingling of religion, society, and politics is with us even now. It appears across the ideological spectrum. For example, for some *la Revolución* of Sandinista Nicaragua (1979–90) was a milestone of Christian commitment to radical social change, perhaps even a manifestation of the kingdom of God on earth.[16] The electoral defeat of Daniel Ortega in February 1990 to Violeta de Chamorro stunned the party faithful. It created too a theological dilemma for the regime's religious supporters at home and its sympathizers outside the country. If God had been with the Revolution—its genesis, its initial flourishing, and its defense against foreign aggression (the United States sponsored Contra forces)—how could they have lost at the polls? This last summer in Guatemala I picked up the third volume of Ernesto Cardenal's memoirs (*La revolución perdida*). In it this priest and former Minister of Culture, laments this reverse of fortunes, but he continues to maintain his theological-political convictions. The last lines of the book read: "Toda revolución nos acerca a ese Reino, aun una revolución perdida. Habrá más revoluciones. Pidamos a Dios que se haga su revolucion en la tierra como en el cielo" ("Every revolution, even one that has lost, brings us closer to the Kingdom. There will be more revolutions. Let us pray to God that his revolution be done on earth as in heaven").[17] This defeat, coupled with the setbacks to the socialist government in Cuba, the dismantling of the former Soviet Union, and the end of the armed conflicts in El Salvador and Guatemala led to much introspection about the future viability and direction of Liberation Theology.[18] There have been as well, of course, forays into politics by evangelicals of more conservative persuasions. Again, on occasion, ideological convictions have

---

16. The bibliography for this is massive, and much in Spanish was never translated into English. An interesting "insider" view is that of Ernesto Cardenal in his *Memorias*, vol. 3: *La revolución perdida* (Madrid: Trotta, 2004). Note esp. the chapter "Gracias a Dios y la Revolución," 301–30; cf. *Flights of Victory/Vuelos de Victoria* (trans. M. Zimmerman; Willimantic: Curbstone, 1988). In the United States Cardenal perhaps is best known for *The Gospel in Solentiname* (trans. D. Walsh; Maryknoll, N.Y.: Orbis, 1977–1982).

17. Cardenal, *La revolución perdida*, p. 473; cf. Uriel Molina, "Dios, el proceso revolucionario y las elecciones del 25 de febrero de 1990," *Revista de Interpretación Bíblica Latinoamericana* 7 (1990): 113–20.

18. Again, the bibliography here is immense, esp. in Spanish. E.g., Juan José Tamayo, *Presente y futuro de la teología de la liberación* (Teología Siglo XXI; Madrid: San Pablo, 1994); Hugo Assmann, "Teología de la liberación: Mirando hacia el frente," *Revista latinoamericana de teología* [*RLT*] 34 (1995): 93–111; Pablo Richard, "Futuro de la teología de la liberacion (una visión desde América Latina)," *Carthaginensia* 15 (1999): 325–45; Pedro Trigo, "¿Ha muerto la teología de la liberación? La realidad actual y sus causas (I)," *RLT* 64 (2005): 45–74; idem, "¿Ha muerto la teología de la liberación? La realidad actual y sus causas (II)," *RLT* 66 (2005): 287–313.

overridden fidelity to gospel values. The most unfortunate case in Guatemala was the presidency of Efraín Ríos Montt (1982–1983).[19]

Each of the instances in North and Latin America I have cited—and there are many more one could point to all around the world—is an example of the intersection of Christian faith and politics. Each at its core is a battle over defining the person of God himself, what he expects of his people, and the shape of society that such beliefs generate and sustain. The theological stakes are high. The issues are more than simply intellectual, and they cannot be limited to the interiority of the soul.

## Defining the Problem

The first and second of the Ten Commandments (Exod 20:3–6; Deut 5:7–10)[20] prohibit, respectively, the worship of any other gods but Yahweh and the manufacture of images of any kind. The proscription against making idols would have included representations of Yahweh.[21]

It is not uncommon for commentators to point to Deut 4:10–19 as indicative of the underlying reason for this ban on images. At Sinai Yahweh had not been seen, only heard. An image was not adequate to encompass the transcendence and authority of Yahweh and could easily become misunderstood as embodying the very presence of God. This interpretation is true as far as it goes, but I believe there is more here that needs to be emphasized. These verses in Deuteronomy are bracketed by declarations that Israel's laws are exceptional, worthy to be admired by other nations and a source of special blessing (4:1–9, 32–40). What is the import of these "laws"? How might they be related to the issue of idolatry? A look again at the giving of the Ten Commandments at Sinai can be instructive.

---

19. Efraín Ríos Montt has been a very controversial figure in Guatemalan politics. He claims to be a born-again Christian, but many believe that the time of his presidency was one of the most brutal periods of the war between the government and the Marxist guerillas. Note the surveys and extensive bibliographies of evangelicals and politics in Latin America in Paul Freston, *Evangelicals and Politics in Asia, Africa, and Latin America* (Cambridge: Cambridge University Press, 2001), 191–280; idem (ed.), *Evangelical Christianity and Democracy in Latin America* (Evangelical Christianity and Democracy in the Global South; Oxford: Oxford University Press, 2008). For Ríos Montt, see Freston, *Evangelicals and Politics in Asia, Africa, and Latin America*, 266–73.

20. As is well known, the enumeration of the Commandments differs between the Hebrew Bible and Reformed tradition and that of the Roman Catholic and Lutheran traditions. I am following the former.

21. For a thorough discussion of the critical and theological issues, see esp. Brevard S. Childs, *The Book of Exodus: A Critical, Theological Commentary* (OTL; Philadelphia: Westminster, 1974), 404–9.); cf. Walter Harrelson, *The Ten Commandments and Human Rights* (Overtures to Biblical Theology; Philadelphia: Fortress, 1985), 61–72.

The narratival context in Exodus 20 is the exodus, and the prologue in v. 2 makes it clear that the God of that liberating event is the one who is revealing these laws to Israel. The exodus was both political and religious. The emancipation from Egyptian oppression was to be the first step toward moving to a new land and establishing a way of life different from what had been experienced in Egypt.[22] Under Yahweh, Israel was to construct what the sociology of knowledge and cultural anthropology would call an alternative social construction of reality. Allegiance to Yahweh was to be fundamental to and inseparable from the web of social, economic, political, and familial relationships, structures, and activities that would be established in that land. The religious system, with its personnel, holy sites, and rituals, would legitimate and sanctify this different reality.[23] It is not surprising then that the Ten Commandments combine "religious" items with integrity in the legal process, graciousness toward laborers, the importance of familial and interfamily relationships, the sanctity of life, and the inviolability of property (Exod 20:7–17; Deut 5:1–21). This intermingling of the multiple spheres of life is characteristic of the law codes in Exodus, Leviticus, and Deuteronomy. Another deity or a divergent understanding of Yahweh would yield a different society. The ban on idols then meant more than simply the prohibition of fashioning an image of the God who had spoken; *what had been said* also was key.

Like other peoples in ancient times, Israel's "world" was defined—both by the official state religion and at the level of the general population in different popular beliefs—by the connections between its deity, the national territory, and the capital city with its primary temple and cult to the chief deity. Because Jerusalem/Zion were believed to be the chosen abode of Yahweh and the Davidic line to be the covenanted rulers of God's people who ruled from that place, there arose the settled conviction in its sanctity and impregnability.[24] When Jeroboam lead the succession from

---

22. I am fully aware that there are a host of moral issues that many would raise at this point about the exodus, the laws themselves, and the entrance into the land. These lie beyond the purview of this essay.

23. Concerning these disciplines in relationship to the study of Amos, see my *Contexts for Amos: Prophetic Poetics in Latin American Perspective* (JSOTSup 132; Sheffield: Sheffield Academic Press, 1992), 49–76; "Reexamining Popular Religion: Issues of Definition and Sources—Insights from Interpretive Anthropology," in *Rethinking Contexts, Rereading Texts: Contributions from the Social Sciences to Biblical Interpretation* (ed. M. D. Carroll R.; JSOTSup 299; Sheffield: Sheffield Academic, 2000), 146–67; "Can the Prophets Shed Light on Our Worship Wars?—How Amos Evaluates Religious Ritual," *Stone-Campbell Journal* 8.2 (2005): 215–27; cf. Gerald A. Klingbeil, *Bridging the Gap: Ritual and Ritual Texts in the Bible* (Bulletin for Biblical Research Sup 1; Winona Lake: Eisenbrauns, 2007).

24. G. W. Ahlström, *Royal Administration and National Religion in Ancient Palestine* (SHANE 1;

Rehoboam, he recognized the need to establish an alternative substitute religion, since he was appealing to the same god—Yahweh—that Judah would use to substantiate its government and social system (1 Kgs 12:25–33).

Faith in the throne and temple can fall prey to a self-perpetuating system favorable to those in power, which can be both self-deceiving and abusive in its policies. Walter Brueggemann has written extensively on this misplaced ideology[25] of kingship and religion in the biblical materials, even as he has provided helpful insights into the power of rhetoric to fund and energize another kind of imagination and praxis.[26] Though sometimes his categories and their distinctions may appear to be a bit too neat, he has captured better than most the destructive character of *Realpolitik* and the role of religion in the creation and maintenance of a sociopolitical and economic creed and system.

Among theological movements within the last several decades, perhaps Latin American Liberation Theology has best appreciated the mutual investments between religion and the status quo. This awareness surely is due to the harsh socioeconomic realities of the continent and the brutality of the various dictatorships that governed much of the continent for many decades, oftentimes with the blessing of religious authorities. In his description of the "Doctrine of National Security" of these governments, José Míguez Bonino comments, "The rhetoric used by the military regimes abounds in religious references. It defines their aim as the defense of Christian civilization and the struggle against atheism and materialism. It extols religious

---

Leiden: Brill, 1982); J. J. M. Roberts, "Zion in the Theology of the Davidic-Solomonic Empire," in *Studies in the Period of David and Solomon and Other Essays* (ed. T. Ishida; Winona Lake: Eisenbrauns, 1982), 93–108; B. C. Ollenberger, *Zion—The City of the Great King: A Theological Symbol of the Jerusalem Cult* (JSOTSup 41; Sheffield: Sheffield Academic, 1987); Dale Launderville, *Piety and Politics: The Dynamics of Royal Authority in Homeric Greece, Biblical Israel, and Old Babylonian Mesopotamia* (Grand Rapids: Eerdmans, 2003). For an extensive discussion from the perspective of an empire, see Steven W. Holloway, *Assur Is King! Assur Is King!: Religion in the Exercise of Power in the New-Assyrian Empire* (CHANE 10; Leiden: Brill, 2002).

25. The term "ideology" is understood in various ways. For a survey of definitions and implications for biblical studies, see Jonathan E. Dyck, "A Map of Ideology for Biblical Critics," in *Rethinking Contexts, Rereading Texts*, 108–28. He categorizes approaches to ideology according to one of three principal contexts in which it is analyzed: social science, social criticism, and interpretive sociology. I am using the term a bit loosely, more in a descriptive sense of a worldview and its social world. Each of the categories that Dyck develops eventually needs to come into play at some level for a full reading of the biblical text, the reality behind it, and the use of that biblical text for the modern context.

26. Walter Brueggemann, *Israel's Praise: Doxology Against Idolatry and Ideology* (Philadelphia: Fortress, 1988); *Theology of the Old Testament: Testimony, Dispute, Advocacy* (Minneapolis: Fortress, 1997), 600–21; *The Prophetic Imagination* (2d ed.; Minneapolis: Fortress, 2001).

values, particularly those of family and the religious tradition."[27] These theologians saw clearly that the injustice and the violence of our societies was inseparable from and defended by a perverse conception of God. The idolatry, in other words, was ideological, and—most importantly—concerned not another deity but the very One of the Christian faith.

Several theologians made distinct contributions to this perspective on idolatry. José Porfirio Miranda argued that the prophets believed that the true God can only be found in the practice of inter-human justice, in the ethical demand, not in the cult;[28] Gustavo Gutiérrez offered a detailed historical study of the work of Bartolomé de las Casas that looked at the idol of the Spanish conquistadores for lessons for Latin America today regarding the utilization of religion for nefarious ends;[29] Enrique Dussel appealed to (and also critiqued) Marx's idea of the fetish to explain the falseness of the god of the Christian religion that allows injustice and violence against the weak;[30] and Pablo Richard contrasted the god of death, the dominant idol of the reigning capitalist system that had brought so much misery, to the God of life, that God of the poor who is confessed and celebrated in the struggle for a new society.[31] Richard voices the core point: "La tarea teológica fundamental en América Latina no es tanto probar la existencia de Dios, sino discernir al Dios verdadero de los dioses falsos. El problema no es saber *si* Dios existe, sino demostrar en *cuál* Dios creo" ("The fundamental theological problem in Latin America is not so much to prove the existence of God, but rather to discern the true God from the false gods. The problem is not to know *if* God exists, but to demonstrate in what *kind* of God I believe.")[32]

---

27. José Míguez Bonino, *Toward a Christian Political Ethics* (Philadelphia: Fortress, 1983), 71 [65–78]; cf. José Comblin, *The Church and the National Security State* (Maryknoll, N.Y.: Orbis, 1979); Jeffrey Klaiber, *The Church, Dictatorships, and Democracy in Latin America* (Maryknoll, N.Y.: Orbis, 1998).

28. José Porfirio Miranda, *Marx and the Bible: A Critique of the Philosophy of Oppression* (trans. J. Eagleson; Maryknoll, N.Y.: Orbis, 1974), 35–76 [Spanish 1971].

29. Gutiérrez, Gutiérrez, *En busca de los pobres de Jesucristo*.

30. Enrique Dussel, *Las metáforas teológicas de Marx* (Estella, Spain: Verbo Divino, 1993).

31. Pablo Richard, "Nuestra lucha es contra los ídolos—teología bíblica," in *La lucha de los dioses: Los ídolos de la opresión y la búsqueda del Dios Liberador* (ed. research group; San José, Cost Rica: Departamento Ecuménico de Investigaciones; Managua, Nicaragua: Centro Antonio Valdivieso, 1980), 9–32; idem, "Teología en la teología de la liberación," in *Mysterium Liberationis: Conceptos fundamentals de la teología de la liberación* (ed. I. Ellacuría and J. Sobrino; El Salvador, San Salvador: UCA), 201–22.

32. Richard, "Teología en la teología de la liberación," 207.

Whatever one may think of the political options of Latin American Liberation Theology or of some of the positions taken by its theologians, or whether their critique of the wedding of religion and the Right appears ironic in light of its role in Sandinista Nicaragua, they, along with scholars like Brueggemann, have identified the immense problem of an idolatry of Yahweh that is connected to the ruling authorities and structures and which condones oppression within national borders and justifies involvement in war. The prophetic literature is strident in its denunciation of a counterfeit Yahweh. Some of the most biting words are found in the book of Amos.

## A Reading of Amos

I will base the following reading of this prophetic book on its final form. Some defend the unity of the book for biographical reasons (arguing that different sections arose at different times in the prophet's ministry), others on the grounds that the finished work can be explained by its historical context, and still others simply take it as a literary work without seeking an historical explanation for that stance.[33] I forego here a defense of an eighth-century setting for the book (although I do think one can be made), and I assume the literariness of the received text. This is the text that informs and shapes the people of God today.[34]

Amos is often singled out as the prophetic book of social justice *par excellence*, and a number of studies have tried to identify the socioeconomic system that triggered its invective.[35] The reproof of religious rituals at the sanctuaries is typically explained in conjunction with the denunciation of oppression of the poor (most famously at 5:21–24). This is helpful and obviously does reflect in some measure what the text presents. Nevertheless, another dimension of the prophetic diatribe that

---

33. Note a survey in M. Daniel Carroll R., *Amos—The Prophet & His Oracles: Research on the Book of Amos* (Louisville: Westminster John Knox, 2002), 24–26, 43–47. A new work that defends a final form but from the Persian period is James R. Linville's *Amos and the Cosmic Imagination* (Society of Old Testament Study Series; Aldershot: Ashgate, 2008); cf. Jennifer M. Dines, "Amos," in *Oxford Bible Dictionary* (ed. J. Barton and J. Muddiman; Oxford: Oxford University Press, 2001), 581–90.

34. For a discussion of the final form as a moral and pastoral choice, see my *Contexts for Amos*, 140–75. For a variety of reasons, others have been critical of the book's ethics. For summaries, see my *Amos—The Prophet & His Oracles*, 61–66; cf. Richard James Coggins, *Joel and Amos* (New Century Bible; Sheffield: Sheffield Academic, 2000), 74; Walter J. Houston, *Contending for Justice: Ideologies and Theologies of Social Justice in the Old Testament* (LHB/OTS 428; London: T. & T. Clark, 2006), 52–98.

35. For summaries, see my *Amos—The Prophet & His Oracles*, 23–24, 42–43; Houston, *Contending for Justice*, 18–51.

should be considered is the censure of (to steal a phrase from Liberation Theology) Israel's "Doctrine of National Security." What is unacceptable is not that the nation state has become an idol,[36] but rather that the Yahweh that it worships supports this sinful state. *He* is the idol, an ideological creation, who sustains and sanctions the regime.[37]

It is a bit arbitrary to separate the political-military critique from the socioeconomic. But, this will serve to highlight this missing dimension in the study of the ethics of the book. I will return to the socioeconomic briefly later on. I have explored the issue of military pretense in Amos elsewhere,[38] but this essay hopes to carry some of those arguments a bit further. The critique of the idolatry of national security is divided into two parts: the exposé of the false foundations of Israel's military pride and the disallowing of any future for the present regime.

### Unmasking Military Pretense and Its Idolatry

One of the aspects of the description of the past, present, and future of the world of the text of Amos that stands out is the pervasive reality of war. This is evident from the opening chapters. The Oracles against the Nations (1:3–2:3) announce the destruction of important cities of the surrounding peoples because of violence committed in war. They had ravaged the land of others (1:3b), trafficked in the survivors (1:6, 9), and violated the integrity of the victims and the dead (1:13; 2:1). Therefore, their fortresses will be razed by fire (1:4, 5a, 7, 8b, 10, 12, 14; 2:2), and their leaders killed (1:5, 8a, 15; 2:3).

Israel is not exempt from this terrible fate. Although the transgressions that are listed in 2:6–8, 12 are not those perpetrated in combat, the judgment is the same: utter military defeat (2:14–16; note the list of seven kinds of soldiers, implying perfect defeat). While from the perspective of the oracle this defeat still lies in the future,

---

36. See, e.g., Provan, "To Highlight All Our Idols," 30–31.

37. Other deities surface at 5:26 and possibly at 2:8, 7:9, and 8:14. Whatever the identity of the references in these verses, they are not the primary focus of the text.

38. *Contexts for Amos, passim*; "Reflecting on War and Utopia in the Book of Amos: The Relevance of a Literary Reading of the Prophetic Text from Central America," in *The Bible in Human Society: Essays in Honour of John W. Rogerson*, (ed. D. J. A. Clines, P. R. Davies, and M. D. Carroll R.; JSOTSup 200; Sheffield: Sheffield Academic, 1995), 105–21; "The Prophetic Text and the Literature of Dissent in Latin America: Amos, García Márquez, and Cabrera Infante Dismantle Militarism," *BibInt* 4 (1996): 76–100; "Living Between the Lines: A Reading of Amos 9:11-15 in Postwar Guatemala," *R & T* 6 (1999): 50–64; "'For so you love to do': Probing Popular Religion in the Book of Amos," in *Rethinking Contexts, Rereading Texts*, 168–89.

the past had been characterized by the same. The stench of death in battle is cited later as one of the litany of disasters that should have brought the nation back to God (4:10). If the atrocities of the nations were committed against Israel—and that is a possibility (esp. 1:3, 9, 11, 13)—the very fact that these occurred and that Israel had not been able to defend itself reveals any posturing of strength as a lie and any confidence in its military power as self-delusion.

The futility of trusting in military strength is communicated in several passages beyond the Oracles against the Nations. It is announced that the fortresses of Samaria will be taken by an (anonymous) enemy (3:11) and that the attack will leave holes in what some would have thought were impenetrable walls (4:3). Amos 6:13 mocks the celebrated victories of Israel's armies in a word play: the prize that had been taken was the town of *Lōʾ Dābār*—"nothing" really. What awaited the country was occupation from border to border (6:14). Other passages are even more telling.

Amos 5:1–17, as is well known, is in the form of a chiasm. The lament that begins the chapter (5:1–3) speaks of horrific losses (either of ninety or ninety-nine percent, depending on how the relationship between the two lines in 5:3 is defined). Its matching pericope in the chiasm speaks of wailing and mourning everywhere (5:16–17). Death fills the air. The difficult phrases of 5:9 also point to the destruction of Israel's fortresses. What is especially important for the topic at hand is that the passage reveals, as does the rest of the book, that Yahweh is the sovereign God who brings this judgment of military defeat. He is *Yahweh ʾĕlōhê-ṣĕbāʾôt*, the God of the armies (this name is mentioned three times in 5:14–16), the all-powerful One who will mobilize the enemy, who will cause the casualties and bring so much grief. He is the focal point of the chiasm, too. The center of the poetic structure is the last line of 5:8, which reads, "Yahweh is his name." "Perhaps" he will have mercy on those who remain after the demise (5:16).

This Yahweh stands in sharp contrast to the Yahweh of the misunderstood "Day of Yahweh" (5:18–20). The people yearned for that day, which they assumed would be a day of light—that is, of triumph, not of death and darkness. Interestingly, the denunciation of the cult follows these lines (5:21–23). It would have been in the ceremonies at the sanctuaries that the people would have offered sacrifices and sung their songs to the national god, whom they thought would direct them to victory. Instead, what awaits Israel is exile from the land; defeat would lead to deportation. Yahweh, whose name is *ʾĕlōhê-ṣĕbāʾôt*, had so decreed (5:27).

Chapter five provides a window into the theology of the national ideology. Its god is one of triumph, even though recent history and Israel's future destiny actually point in the opposite direction. The belief in this sort of Yahweh helps explain, too, the incoherence of the cult described (and denounced) in 4:4–13. The prophet labels going to the national shrines as so much sin (4:4–5). This at first seems odd, but a closer look at what is said explains this surprising evaluation. The vocabulary of worship in these two verses suggests a religion of celebration and thanksgiving. Yet, the reality "on the ground"—hunger, drought, agricultural disaster, and death in war (4:6–10)—should have led the people to repentance. There was a disconnect between what life was really like and what was commemorated in the rituals. The people that crowded the sanctuaries thought that they were meeting their benevolent and powerful god and that they were pleasing him with their sacrifices and tithes. The true Yahweh will have none of it. He tells them to get ready for a terrifying encounter with the omnipotent One (4:12–13). That "hymn" passage is then followed by the opening lines of chapter five, the lament to fallen Israel.[39]

Here I return momentarily to the issue of socioeconomic injustice. Note how the shrines are full. This Doctrine of National Security is no respecter of persons. Powerful and poor alike, the privileged and the exploited, rally together around the great god of the nation. The patriotic call to the heart of the Israelites would have all cheering and honoring their divine champion. Herein lies another tragedy—and transgression: those who suffer at the hands of the system are some of the very ones that perpetuate it and defend it, even to their death.

The undermining of the military pretensions of Israel continues in the first three visions of chapter seven. The pertinent phrase in the first two appears in the prophet's plea for mercy: "He [i.e., Israel] is so small" (7:2, 5). This description could include reference to the nation's military weakness before its adversaries (past and future). Such an interpretive option is a possibility in light of the immediately preceding context (6:13–14) and because of what follows in the third vision (7:7–8). The key term there is ʾănāk. It is usually translated "plumb line." Recent studies, however, make clear that a more correct rendering is "tin."[40] This translation conveys the self-deceiving ideology of Israel's defenses. From a distance the walls of their

---

39. Three passages that declare the power of the Creator have been designated "hymnic" or "doxologies" in Amos research (4:13; 5:8–9; 9:5–6). Scholars disagree about whether these three passages were originally part of a longer poem or if each was created for its particular location in the book; there is also debate regarding their authorship and dating. For convenient discussions see the commentaries (e.g., Shalom M. Paul, *Amos: A Commentary on the Book of Amos* [Hermeneia; Minneapolis: Fortress, 1991], 152–53).

40. Carroll R., "'For so you love to do,'" 185–86, and the references there. Also see Alan Cooper, "The Meaning of Amos's Third Vision (Amos 7:7–9)," in *Tehillah le-Moshe: Biblical and Judaic Studies in Honor of Moshe Greenberg* (ed. M. Cogan, B. L. Eichler, and J. H. Tigay; Winona Lake: Eisenbrauns, 1997), 13–21; Linville, *Amos and the Cosmic Imagination*, 138–40.

fortresses might appear to be made of iron, a strong metal; surely, they could resist attack. In reality, however, they are but tin. Perhaps the meaning of the vision is that Yahweh has reached down and ripped out a piece of this fragile wall and thrown it in the midst of his people, as if to say, "This is nothing!" What is coming is the unstoppable destruction of the sanctuaries of the idol Yahweh and the eradication of the monarchy that has staked its existence on it (7:9).

This reading of the initial visions helps explain the confrontation between the prophet and the high priest at the principal national sanctuary (7:10–17; presumably Bethel, although this is nowhere stated). Amaziah correctly sees that Amos's words connote a conspiracy against the crown (7:10). They proclaim its military demise and thus hit at the very heart of the ideology of national power and security (7:13). Part of the prophet's retort to the priest is a repetition of death in war and exile, now concentrated and personalized in Amaziah's family (7:17).

After this judgment linked to defeat in war comes 8:1–3, with its wailing, interspersed with the silence of shock, inexpressible grief and defiance, and the presence of multiple dead bodies (cf. 6:9–10). This will occur in the *hêkāl* (v. 3). This word can mean "temple" or "palace" (or both as a word play?), and different commentators and versions opt for one or the other translation. Either choice yields an appropriate interpretation. The ruin of the "temple" would certainly happen as part of the coming invasion, as the profaning of the holy ground of the conquered and the tearing down and sacking of sanctuaries was part of the conduct of warfare at that time. This passage would reiterate in more graphic fashion the predictions of earlier oracles, which announce the elimination of the sanctuaries of the false Yahweh (3:12; 5:5; 7:9). On the other hand, if the meaning is "palace," the significance is that the fate of the king's home and throne room would be no different than those of the deity. Wedded together in the national ideology, they would fail together at the system's downfall. In addition, palaces and temples usually were constructed side-by-side, or at least in close proximity, on the acropolis of the capital or principal cities in the ancient world. So, if one were to perish, the other would too. The ambiguity, whether intentional or not, is fitting.

As in the case of the previous four visions (7:1–8, 8:1–3), there is a gap before the next vision at 9:1–4. It is preceded by a lengthy passage (8:4–14). This last vision is a description of the collapse of the temple. The most natural reading would be to assume that this structure is the same one as that of Amos's altercation with Amaziah (7:10–17) and of the mourning of the fourth vision (8:1–3).[41] What Yahweh had said

---

41. Linville argues that this is the heavenly temple (*Amos and the Cosmic Imagination*, 159–68).

before concerning his ordained demolition of Bethel ("I will destroy the altars of Bethel," 3:14; "Bethel will be nothing," 5:5) climaxes at 9:1. Here he stands on the altar of his counterpart, the Yahweh of Jeroboam's regime, and demands that its sanctuary come crashing down, again probably in relationship to the approaching invasion (although some commentators relate this to the earthquake mentioned in 1:1). After this vision comes the last of the "hymns" to Yahweh ṣĕbāʾôt. He is matchlessly powerful and rules the earth from heaven, shaking the earth and disturbing the grandest river Israel had seen, the Nile; Yahweh is his name (9:5–6; cf. 8:8–9).

Finally, if I may indulge in a bit of intertexuality: The exodus, which is the theological foundation to which Jeroboam appeals in 1 Kings 12 for his new regime, is turned on its head. Israel will be judged precisely because they did not respond properly to that event (2:10; 3:1). The true Yahweh negates the idol Yahweh of the manipulated exodus. In addition, the true God declares that that liberation was part of his larger work among the nations (9:7). That is, election demands responsibility and a clearer vision of Yahweh and his ways. Neither Jeroboam I nor Jeroboam II could use the exodus for their political ends.

In sum, what one witnesses in the book of Amos is that the ridicule of Israel's military and of the national confidence in its fortresses is accompanied throughout by the exaltation of the true God and this in sharp distinction from the misconceived Yahwism of the nation. The Yahweh of the country's ideology will be exposed as helpless and left without sanctuaries. There is still one more element to mention of this subversion of the idolatry of national security.

## *An Alternative Future*

By the second verse of the book the reader knows that the government and the religion of the Northern Kingdom are illegitimate. Yahweh roars from Zion and Jerusalem—that is, from Solomon's Temple and the capital city of Judah (1:2). He does not support the pretenses of Israel and will not allow another god of his name to take his place.

In addition, Amos is presented as a Judean prophet. It makes sense that the priest Amaziah commands him to leave (7:10–13). What right does this foreigner have to criticize the government and society of the North! What is more, the most prominent name for God in Amos, *Yahweh ʾĕlōhê-ṣĕbāʾôt*, itself is associated with Zion and the Solomonic Temple.[42] The book also ends by proclaiming that the future

---

42. See, e.g., Tryggve N. D. Mettinger, "YHWH SABAOTH—The Heavenly King on the Cherubim

does not lie with the line of Jeroboam nor with the regime whose capital is Samaria. No, the future is connected to the "booth" of David, which I take as the Southern monarchy (9:11–15). Subversive conspiracy, indeed! Several comments are in order in relationship to these words.

First, the book does not suggest that Amos's words arise from a blind nationalism and allegiance to the Davidic line. It includes an oracle against Judah among the Oracles against the Nations that says that the South has committed serious transgressions against God and will be judged (2:4–5). Chapter six also suggests that the destructive complacency of Israel's leaders exists as well in Judah (6:1). The Southern Kingdom, in other words, is not some paradise without sin. Its time will also come.

Second, the description of that future is one of plenty. This abundance is a contrast to the want and suffering of the general population (4:6–9; 6:6). There are those who glory in their plenty, which had been gained at the expense of others (4:1; 5:11; 6:4–6). Yet, "in that day" there will be more than enough for all, and that different kind of social world will come under a different government.

Third, the future of 9:11–15 speaks of rebuilding ruins, of reconstruction after the war that will come as divine judgment. In other words, peace and prosperity lie on the other side of incredible suffering. The doctrine of national security is the way of disaster and death. Not only had it misrepresented the military failures of the regime, it would also be the set of attitudes and policies that would result in the nation going into one last, fatal, armed conflict. Its fruits—past, present, and future—are its condemnation. The picture that closes the book does not mention armies or fortifications.[43] Neither is there a temple. In the ancient world one would expect that the cities to be rebuilt would include walls for protection and a place for worship, but neither are mentioned in the passage. Whether the omission is what is actually envisioned or simply a rhetorical ploy, the point is that the world beyond that sociopolitical system will be different. There are no bases for another doctrine of national security, but there is hope for relationship with "Yahweh your god." This is the only place in Amos that this combination appears. Israel will finally live with its true Yahweh.

---

Throne," in *Studies in the Period of David and Solomon and Other Essays* (ed. T. Ishida; Winona Lake: Eisenbrauns, 1982), 109–38; idem, "Yahweh Zebaoth," *DDD*, 920–24; H.-J. Zobel, "$s^eb\bar{a}{}^{\ni}ôt$," *TDOT* 12: 215–32.

43. In this context 9:12 deserves a fuller exposition, but this lies beyond the purview of this paper. Questions that need to be answered are what kind of possession is the text hinting at and how is that achieved.

## Conclusion

The book of Amos imagines the unthinkable: The defeat of the mighty armies and the strong fortresses of Israel, the destruction of its sanctuaries, and the exile of its leaders and general population. This would be a military and political event, but also a theological resolution of the conflict between the true Yahweh and the idol of national security. The doctrine of national security would prove in the end to be an ideology for defeat.

There is a lesson for the ages here, I believe. Any such set of convictions and the rituals that sustain it cannot last. God will not be mocked. I have lived in four countries and visited many more. This doctrine and its accompanying idolatry is a common malaise, and it manifests itself with the right and the left. Unmasking the pretense is a never-ending challenge.

The prophet in this text also allows the reader to appreciate that such a parody of God in such celebratory rituals, which mask the cruelties and self-delusions and demands great cost in human lives, deserves an angry retort, a pointed denunciation. The anger is but one part of the prophet's message. At the same time, it must involve a call to choose life with the true Yahweh (5:4-6, 14-15). These determined choices may not change the regime's agenda nor move the masses of people to forsake the temples of the national deity, and the violent end that such a militaristic world brings may still come. It most assuredly will bring opposition—perhaps from both the secular and religious authorities. But, it is the right thing to do. It is to stand with the prophet to offer an alternative version of reality with a different God and a hope for a future beyond the ruinous posturing of power.

## Appendix

I appreciate very much Prof. Haak's gracious response to this paper. The observations that he makes are important ones. I would like to offer a few brief remarks to some of those points.

I do not address directly the economics of the reign of Jeroboam II. The reason I do not is that this is commonly done in relationship to the ethics of the book of Amos.[44] The problem of the ideology of the regime and its relationship with military issues is hardly ever dealt with; hence, the focus of this article. It also should be mentioned that there are several theories as to how the prosperity of Jeroboam's

---

44. For a survey of this kind of data, see my *Amos—The Prophet & His Oracles*, 22–24, 41–43, 49–50.

rule should be understood: Was there economic and military success throughout his reign, or was it concentrated at the beginning or toward the end? I favor the view that prosperity and peace were characteristic of the early years of his time on the throne. If the Oracles against the Nations in 1:3–2:3 (cf. 4:10) refer to events in the general time period of the prophet's ministry—and I believe they do, then things seem to be unraveling. After Jeroboam's death, Israel went through a series of coups and would cease to exist just a couple of decades later (722 BCE).

The canonical form of the OT (and, thus, the book of Amos) does privilege Judah and its Davidic line and a certain perception of Yahweh. One may question this as an arbitrary choice that was not fair to the Northern Kingdom of Israel and also claim that some material from the North has been incorporated into the OT as we have it today. At one level these are correct historical observations. Two comments are apropos by way of response. First, final form, or literary, approaches are acceptable as one of the options for textual study. Prof. Haak takes a decidedly historical reconstruction view in his treatment, whereas my study looks at the received text. This clarification, however, still leaves unanswered the issue of the prioritizing of that canonical form, which leads to the second point. As a Christian reader who comes to this canon as Scripture, I accept the OT as received as normative. This is a faith choice grounded in the historical witness of the Christian church (and Jews, too, in regards to the OT) for millennia (cf. n. 34).

The argument offered here attempts to inform this final form reading with historical data that is both particular (data from the time of the prophet in the eighth century) and more universal. The latter would be of the *longue durée* sort—that is, setting the discussion against the broader socioreligious and political realities and belief systems of the ancient world (e.g., the relationship between the regime and the national god and his temple).

Finally, it is true that the Davidic monarchy ultimately was found wanting. (The monarchy of Judah over a century later would be defeated by Babylon.) This observation needs to be tempered by the recognition that Amos was no blind nationalist. The canonical text (in contradistinction to some critical approaches that consider the Judah material as later additions) is not naïve about the Southern Kingdom. It too is sinful and deserving of judgment (2:4–5; 6:1). The future hope that is announced points to a monarchy based in Jerusalem which will have a Davidic king (9:11; cf. 1:2), but there is no illusion that what exists at that time meets the standards that Yahweh demanded.

# RESPONSE TO CARROLL

## Robert D. Haak

What is the object of complaint in the prophecy attributed to Amos, and what word might that text speak to us today? That is the central question raised in Prof. Carroll's essay. He sets the texts within an ancient context. His basic premise is that the text of Amos reflects two "YHWHs"—two understandings of god that we in the Christian tradition claim to share. The first of these is the "true YHWH"—the god of Amos and the god of Judah. This is contrasted with the "idol YHWH"—the god of national security associated with the nation of Israel.

There is no question that this basic premise is correct. We often think of the polytheism of the ancient world in terms of other divinities beside YHWH—Baal or Asherah or Marduk or others. What has been less clear in the history of scholarship is that there are also multiple YHWHs—different (and in some cases competing) understandings of god—different understandings that try to lay claim to the "name of god," YHWH.[1]

Prof. Carroll acknowledges that there are two competing "YHWHs," at least since the time of Jeroboam. Jeroboam, the founder of the kingdom of Israel, understood that the YHWH worshipped in Jerusalem could not function as the divinity in the north. In fact, it seems clear that Jeroboam felt that the YHWH worshipped in Jerusalem was a corruption of true YHWH worship. What he attempted to create, of course, was true worship of YHWH in his kingdom. Clearly, this understanding of YHWH was not that of the author of the books of Kings—and not that of the author of Amos either.[2]

In spite of this, I would not characterize Amos' view as the "true" understanding of YHWH as opposed to the idolatrous worship. It seems clear to me that those who took religion seriously in both the north and the south would surely have seen

---

1. Mark S. Smith, *The Early History of God: Yahweh and the Other Deities in Ancient Israel* (San Francisco: Harper & Row, 1990).

2. Anne Marie Kitz, "The Cult of Jeroboam and the Religious Heritage of the North" (Thesis, Harvard University, 1986); William J. Doorly, *The Religion of Israel: A Short History* (New York: Paulist, 1997), 81–120.

the opposing view as "idolatrous." Each surely felt they were worshipping the "true" YHWH in the proper way and probably had little patience and understanding of those on the other side of the border. Prof. Carroll is surely right when he says, "Each at its core is a battle over defining the person of God himself, what he expects of his people, and the shape of society that such beliefs generate and sustain." I would rather just characterize the two views as "Israelite YHWH" and "Judahite YHWH."

One might well ask whether these are different gods or just different views of the same deity. That probably depends more on one's point of view than anything that can be considered objective reality. I grew up in a Lutheran parsonage. I remember understanding that the folks down the street in the Catholic church were idolaters—after all, they worshipped all those statues, right? I am quite certain that the priest down the street was just as sure that we "Protestants" down the street were on a seriously wrong path. Today I (and my Catholic friends) might have a different view of the others' tradition.

The understanding of the relationship between the YHWH of Israel and the YHWH of Judah becomes even more complex because ideas of the North (seen clearly, for example, in the writings of Hosea) move to the south at the time of Assyrian conquest. They come to inform the understanding of God in Judah and, in fact, become a part of the heritage that we ourselves claim.

I would suggest that the reading of Amos suggested by Prof. Carroll needs to be placed in a larger context in at least two ways. The first of these is the context provided by the evidence of archaeology.[3] Prof. Carroll highlights the societal problems indicated by the text. I will not argue that Israel under Jeroboam II never had any problems, but historical evidence would seem to indicate that on a realistic level the reign of Jeroboam II was successful, at least if we define the term in ways that we would consider normal. He had a very long reign. The economic situation of the region seems to have generated wealth and a measure of political and military power that kept the nation from war for an extraordinarily long time. The text of Amos, in fact, confirms this judgment. It was assumed by the audience of the text that a "Day of YHWH" was a day of light and prosperity. Later Deuteronomic authors felt they had to justify Jeroboam's success—even as they disagreed with him.

This is not to say that Prof. Carroll's description of economic exploitation in Israel is wrong. The disruption of traditional economy in Israel in this period has long been recognized. The new basis of the society in the production of exportable

---

3. Israel Finkelstein and Neil Asher Silberman, *The Bible Unearthed: Archaeology's New Vision of Ancient Israel and the Origin of the Its Sacred Texts* (New York: Frees, 2001), 149–225.

surpluses and the extraction of wealth from the land and its people is different than the "old days" and different (usually) from the system in Judah. But, there is no question that the North was "better"/"more successful" by most modern standards. It might be noted that this raises the *real* critique *for us*—how do we evaluate "success"? A rising (or today falling!) stock market? What is the symbol of our "idol of national security"?

What is the real issue for Amos though? Often this is put in essentially economic terms. The basic problem is seen as the weak oppressed poor. Surely there is evidence of that (for example, in the critique of judicial system in 5:10–11). But I believe the key to a broader understanding are verses such as the critique of worship in 5:4–5. What can be wrong with that? There does not seem to be a direct critique of the types of activities mentioned or even of the motivation of the worshippers. There may be different ways of answering this question. Some might contend it is because of the moral failure of these same people who are oppressing the poor of the land. I would contend that it is not the oppression of the poor itself that is the problem for Amos. That is only symptom of a larger issue. *All of society failed because they have the wrong king.* Because they have the wrong king, they have the wrong YHWH and the wrong religion and the wrong judicial system and economic system, etc. Because of this, they will fall.

This essential issue is recognized by the "story" of the book itself. In 7:10–17, Amaziah sees the point of the attack. Amos' goal is not to change the economic or any other single system. It is an attack on the king.

For Amos the outcome is already certain. The timing of these things is not crucial. Prof. Carroll has argued that the events on the ground have already made the judgment evident (the natural disasters of 4:6–10). But, it may well be argued that the conditions described in these verses reflect "normal" variation in weather and harvest. Most of the tone is certainly focused on *coming* disasters, not on present conditions. It also cannot be ignored that some of these specifics might have been added by later editors.

Prof. Carroll is correct. From Amos' view, all that is set up in Israel is idolatry. It must be because the whole society is based on the system set up by an illegitimate king—the non-Davidic king of Israel. Because of this Amos concludes that the seemingly stronger cousin to the North is actually weaker. Their military and economic success, which people of the North surely took as a sign of YHWH's favor, will not last. Here Prof. Carroll's critique is on the mark. The theology that said that economic blessings and military success are "proof" of right actions and belief was widespread in the ancient world, even in the biblical record, and is alive and well today. "We surely have god on our side . . . look how blessed we are as a nation."

There is a second context that has to be considered as we make use of the text attributed to Amos—the longer historical conversation of which this is but a part. Amos is relatively early in a conversation considering what it takes to be "successful," "faithful" *as a society* (today's idol of individualism is not yet evident!). The answer from Amos is "you need the right king." If you have the wrong king, your whole society and all its institutions will be wrong—economy, courts, even worship. Whether Amos really expected the Israelites to overthrow their king who had led them to long prosperity and return to the more rudimentary society of Judah may be debated. The fact is that they did not. The results that Amos envisioned came to pass in the turmoil of the end of the Israelite monarchy and the destruction by the Assyrians at the end of the century.

That is not the end of the conversation, neither theirs nor ours. Prof. Carroll is not suggesting that we need a return to a Davidic king to solve the problems of our time, *but the problem of the misidentification of what it takes to have true security may be the same.* Israel assumed that the sort of king they had and the economic and military success that resulted assured their security. Amos says they are mistaken—in ways that will lead to their death and the death of their society that is based on this false foundation. With that we might agree.

However, the "solution"—a return to the monarchy of the Davidides in Jerusalem—was also tried and found wanting. The Judahites were confident if they could just get the "right" king in place—the one who followed *their* policies—then all would be well. That is surely the assumption of Amos and those who followed. Get the right king who oversees the worship of the right YHWH. Then we will be truly successful.

Like many programs, the reality was more complex than expected. We see later in the biblical text the struggle to understand what happens when the rise of the "right sort" of king—Josiah—does not result in the expected blessings. One might well compare the response pointed out by Prof. Carroll to the election of Daniel Ortega. In our story the failure of Josiah leads at least to two responses. On one hand we find a group that says that no king (i.e., no particular political system) will assure security. Others hold out hope that some day the *really* true king will appear, the long awaited messiah.

We see these two responses play themselves out throughout the biblical witness. Ezekiel has a prince rather than a king (34:23). In some places he says "only YHWH will be your king" (20:33). Others, eventually including the followers of Jesus, believe that a true messiah will (or has) appeared. Even this becomes problematic when the result is not what is expected—crucifixion and the continuation of Roman rule. The conversation about the true nature of God continues today.

I agree with Prof. Carroll that the question and critique raised by Amos continues today. We too see those who equate a certain economic system with the will of God—sure that if their understanding is adopted that "salvation" will result. In this political day we see supporters of candidates assuring us that *their* candidate will be the "true" leader who will lead us to prosperity. Amos is a voice of caution that the usual understanding of prosperity may mask underlying problems, that current prosperity may be the prelude to a day of reckoning.

The lesson that may be learned from the broader context is that *no political or economic* system will provide the security and "success" for which we long. What is the message of biblical scholars today? I would suggest that calling into question all schemes of national security based on any particular person or system should be exposed for what they are—attempts to gain security through our own efforts, efforts that the biblical authors come to believe will fail.

This does not mean that we do not participate in the political system. It just means that we recognize the limitations of all messiahs (and all our idols of God)—then and now. The truth is that neither the vision of YHWH of Israel nor that of the YHWH of Judah is able to contain the God behind these visions. The truth is that *our* visions of God are also limited and proximate. In the context that Prof. Carroll sets for the conversation—neither the god of the rich, powerful, successful North nor the god of the poor of the liberation theologian can capture all.

I do not think that the result is that we do not create and promote visions of YHWH, but that as we do, we recognize that the experience of the community of faith over all these years tells us that all of these visions are idols. Never can we capture God in our vision. In the end the best we can hope for is that the God of the Scripture captures us.

# SECURITY AND SELF-SUFFICIENCY
A Comparison of Paul and Epictetus

## *John M. G. Barclay*

It is one of the ironies of modern life that, for all their efforts to make us secure, governments are powerless to make us *feel* secure. All kinds of legislation and practical measures can be put in place to tighten security, and all kinds of information (or propaganda) can be disseminated to tell us how safe we are. But, no one can legislate or inform us in such as way as to make us feel safe. At the psychological level insecurity and vulnerability remain stubbornly resistant to government intervention. Can this psychological insecurity, with all its debilitating consequences both individual and social, be treated? If so, how? Or, is it an ineradicable feature of the human condition, for which we may seek mitigation or compensation but no satisfactory cure? I wish to place here side by side two contrasting answers to such questions, as formulated by the Stoic philosopher Epictetus (c. 55–c. 135 CE) and his near contemporary Paul. Although Paul does not address these questions as directly as Epictetus, the comparison helps to show why he is not a Stoic in this respect and why the Stoic ideal of imperturbability, although hugely attractive, has never quite been reconcilable with the Christian ethos.

## Epictetus and Stoic Security

Epictetus's vivid discourses, preserved by his student Arrian, are designed to jolt, tease, cajole, and harangue his students out of the ordinary assumptions and evaluations of life and to show the path to freedom, security, happiness, and integrity in a life lived according to nature, in tune with God, and at peace with the universe. Although psychological security—tranquillity of mind—is not the sole or even, perhaps, the chief goal of his philosophy, it is a theme to which he returns time and again, since he is convinced that God has ordered this world to enable us to thrive in the achievement of happiness and that the disturbances, constraints, frustrations, and disappointments we suffer arise from self-inflicted errors of judgment, not a failure in providence.¹ Epictetus thinks that it is possible to live a life free from the sorts of passions that so often shipwreck lives and ruin society: free from the grief or distress that cause emotional collapse (and can lead to impiety, in casting blame on the Gods; *Diatr.* 1.22); free from fear and anxiety regarding the future; free from the anger, envy, lust, and ambition that cause us to harm others; in short, free from every passion that represents the frustration that what we want to happen *has not* happened or *may not* happen. It is possible, he believes, indeed part of our highest human calling, to be rid of all such passions and to live in serenity and security, maintaining an undisturbed psychological stability whatever the external conditions of our life.² He is well aware that this famous Stoic virtue of passionlessness (*apatheia*) may appear, at first glance, not the highest human achievement, but actually inhumane. Among our strong social duties to others it may well be right to groan when they groan, but we should take care, he insists, not to groan "inwardly" (*esōthen*, 1.18.19; *Ench.* 16). Some element of mutual sympathy, he recognizes, is essential to human sociability: in the face of others' sorrows one should not be unmoved (*apathēs*) "like a statue" (3.2.4). Still, it is crucial not to internalize this grief too deeply and thus to lose one's inner freedom and tranquillity. Unless emotions are kept at this necessary critical distance, they will damage our lives and ruin our relationships with others, with the cosmos, and with God.³

The essence of Epictetus's prescription is his claim that bad emotions arise from bad judgments, that we wrongly evaluate things as "evil" which are not really so. Epictetus's cardinal rule is "to make correct use of impressions," and the essential distinction he draws is between what God has left "up to us" (*eph' hēmin*) and what is outside our control and, therefore, ultimately of no concern to us. What is "up

---

1. See A. A. Long, *Epictetus. A Stoic and Socratic Guide to Life* (Oxford: Clarendon, 2002), 193-94: "Tranquillity enters his argument not as its beginning but as the response to such questions as: How can I live in accordance with nature? How can I follow and obey God? . . . How can I put the resources God has given me to proper use? He gets to tranquillity as the content of happiness not by privileging this mental state *per se*, but because he takes it to be the most subjectively satisfying condition available to us and also the condition that will best enable us to perform our social functions in a world governed by a benevolent deity."

2. For *asphaleia* among the other attributes of this life (such as *euroia, ataraxia,* and *eustatheia*), see, e.g., 2.2.2; 4.5.25ff.; 4.1.91-98; 4.10.3.

3. On Epictetus and emotions, see Long, *Epictetus*, 244-50. For the ancient philosophical tradition on this topic, and the distinctive Stoic stance on "emotions" (*pathē*), see M. C. Nussbaum, *The Therapy of Desire: Theory and Practice in Hellenistic Ethics* (Princeton: Princeton University Press, 1994); R. Sorabji, *Emotion and Peace of Mind: From Stoic Agitation to Christian Temptation* (Oxford: Oxford University Press, 2000).

to us" is our assessment of life and our reaction to it and crucially what Epictetus calls our *proairesis*, our "volition,"[4] our ability to choose, to formulate objectives, and to try to put them into practice. It is not within my control whether my body gets sick, if I break my leg, or if someone threatens to kill me; what is "up to me" is how I react to this sickness, this accident, or this threat, whether I let them "get to me" (as we would say) and thus enslave or inhibit me. It is not within my control what happens to my possessions, or my career, or my family. Disaster may consume them all in ways I cannot prevent, but if I let this affect me at the deepest level I have made myself a slave to external conditions. It is not up to me how others treat me (whether well or ill), nor whether my well-made plans come to fruition, nor when or how I will die. What *is* up to me—and here I have been given complete and untrammelled freedom—is how I evaluate all these things and how I conduct myself in relation to them. This is the one area in which no one can constrain or force me to do anything and in which I can be guaranteed success. If I wish for the success of externals—for promotion, for the good health of my family, or for a long life for myself—I will be enslaved to conditions beyond my control and therefore inevitably subject to grief, disappointment, anger, anxiety, and all the other passions that will toss me about. But if I wish only to live rightly within the sphere I can control, the sphere of my volition, if I *intend* the right (whether or not it succeeds), and if I am content to welcome whatever happens in external circumstances as part of the necessary and benevolent ordering of the universe, I will retain a tranquillity that nothing at all can touch.

Epictetus's philosophy depends on a conviction that the cosmos is well administered by a benevolent power (generally called God or the Gods), which ensures that all things, ultimately, and on a global scale, work for the good. It may be necessary for me to undergo what superficially appear to me to be "bad" experiences, but these are necessary for the good ordering of the whole, just as a foot must sometimes get muddy stepping into a puddle for the sake of the body's progress down the street (2.5.24). Epictetus draws here on the long tradition of Stoic reflection on Fate and Providence (he cites Cleanthes' famous hymn on this topic a number of times, 2.23.42; *Ench.* 53), but he uses strikingly personalist language about God and encourages a strong sense of personal, even emotional, engagement with the divine. What we cannot control we must accept as reasonable and necessary; what we can control, and what God has given as an inalienable gift, is all we need for a perfectly happy and perfectly fulfilled life.

---

4. For the translation, and the concept, see Long, *Epictetus*, 210–20.

Epictetus knows that it is extremely difficult to break out of the habit that accords the labels "good" or "bad" to what is really indifferent to us and to learn to give true value only to our own exercise of volition. When a family member dies, we instantly count this a disaster, but this is not, he insists, a "natural" reaction, only one instilled by social environment and poor judgment; death is entirely natural and necessary in order to make room for the next generation.[5] It takes persistent practice, self-criticism, and huge mental readjustment to evaluate life aright, but progress is possible. (Epictetus only rarely evokes the notion of the ideal sage). There may be events that uncontrollably damage our reasoning and thus our volition—such as sleep, drunkenness, and depression (melancholy), but in normal waking life Epictetus is confident that we have the capacity to control our evaluations of life and thus to pass serenely through any and all circumstances, up to and including death. It is not easy to maintain that what is not the outcome of my own volition is truly nothing to me (1.29.24), but the freedom won through this discipline is immense. This means that no one and nothing can truly harm me, not even the ill-will of a close family member (3.10.19–20) or the cruellest treatment by a tyrant: they may harm my property, my reputation, or my body, but they cannot harm *me*; I can never be made unfortunate because of someone else (1.9.34; 1.28).

Does this mean that the Epictetan ideal is fundamentally egoistic, self-centered, and socially aloof? So it is often said by those impressed by the premium he places on the immunity of the self from exterior conditions.[6] He does indeed insist on the "autonomy" of the volition (*autexousios*, 2.2.2) and the proper priority of acting for one's own sake. Still, he equally insists that, in accordance with our nature, our own interests are served only in our sociability with others (1.19.11–15), that our dignity, integrity, and rationality are embedded in our duty to others.[7] We are by nature social beings (*pros koinōnian*, Frag. 1), properly characterized as "gentle, generous, patient, and affectionate" (*hēmeron, koinōnikon, anektikon, philallēlon*, 4.5.17; cf. 4.4.17); it is appropriate to pray for others (4.1.22) and to share their burdens (4.13.16). Like other Stoics, Epictetus distinguishes himself sharply from the escapist doctrines of Epicureanism (2.20; 3.7), insisting that we should fulfil the duties of whatever "sta-

---

5. Cf. the famous anecdote cited by Epictetus (3.24.105) of the philosopher who was told, mid-lecture, that his son had died and who replied calmly: "I never thought he was immortal."

6. See P. Esler, "Paul and Stoicism: Romans 12 as a Test Case," *NTS* 50 (2004): 106–24, with the robust response by T. Engberg-Pedersen, "The Relationship with Others: Similarities and Differences between Paul and Stoicism," *ZNW* 96 (2005): 35–60.

7. See, especially, Long, *Epictetus*, 115–16, 196–98, 232–44.

tions" we find ourselves called to occupy in the household, the state, or the wider cosmos (2.22). He strongly criticizes a father who, distraught at his daughter's illness, ran away from home rather than help those looking after her, insisting that what is natural and reasonable in this case is to show love to the suffering girl (1.11). Service for others and the fulfilment of social duties (*ta kathēkonta*) are integral to Epictetus's ideal. It might be necessary to risk one's life or even to die for a friend (2.7.3). At the same time, since we cannot control external circumstances and therefore cannot guarantee the success of our efforts, the only thing of importance here is our *intention* to serve others, not the actual result. Further, we cannot serve others' interests at all costs (*ex hapantos*). If what they require of us conflicts with our own integrity,[8] we simply have to let others look after their own business; in relation to us, it is another's (*allotrion*, 3.24.22–24). Otherwise we would be questioning, even countering, the divine and, therefore, benevolent administration of the universe.

Thus for all the emphasis that Epictetus puts on fulfilling our duties to others, he is equally insistent that each person's first responsibility is to preserve intact and unhindered the volition which is the one thing under his or her control. Because other people, their actions, and the benefits they might bring are *not* under our control we must never depend on them for our happiness or self-fulfilment as human beings. To do otherwise would be to make ourselves "slaves" to others and to circumstances. As A. A. Long, the best recent interpreter of Epictetus, writes:

> The correct performance of one's social roles . . . is both outwardly and inwardly oriented. It is outward in what it requires by way of sensitivity to the dignity and claims of other persons, but what it is about other persons that should concern us is not how they treat us, or who they are and how they fare independently of us, but only how we dispose ourselves in relation to them. The relevant relationship is entirely one-sided: us in relation to them, not them in relation to us. That is because, as Epictetus views the basis of proper relationships, they should be entirely translated, like everything we deal with, into the domain of our volition and integrity.[9]

Hence Epictetus insists that one should be affectionate (*philostorgos*), but not in a way that is abject or broken in spirit or that makes one dependent on another (*ex allou kremasthai*, 3.24.58). Like Socrates, we should love our children, but remember that our first duty is to love the Gods; as for him, that might require nobly accepting death and leaving our children fatherless (3.24.60–61).

---

8. On the theme of integrity in Epictetus, see Long, *Epictetus*, 222–30.

9. Long, *Epictetus*, 237.

In a typical aphoristic exchange Epictetus writes: "This is the law which God has ordained, and He says: 'If you wish any good thing, get it from yourself.' You say, 'No, but from someone else.' Do not so, get it from yourself." (1.29.4; cf. *Ench.* 48). In this sense the Stoic, while bound in a network of duties *to* others, is never bound by anything he needs *from* them. In the last resort no one can help or hurt another: we may change others' external circumstances, but their self is entirely up to them, and ours is up to us. Thus the greatest challenge issued by Socrates (Epictetus's hero) is to inculcate precisely this self-sufficiency: "If a person can hurt me, what I am engaged in amounts to nothing; if I wait for someone else to help me, I am nothing (*ouden eimi*)" (4.8.25). My responsibility is to attach myself to God, and to what God has given me, that is, my own capacity for the unhindered exercise of volition, in which I fulfil my rational and natural calling as a human being. If others, when travelling through this dangerous world, attach themselves for safety to those stronger than themselves as protectors or patrons, the Stoic will attach himself or herself to God, whose will is invincible and must be gladly accepted whatever befalls. Because the reason by which I am to live is also (a fragment of) the God who orders the world aright, *self*-sufficiency and dependence on *God* are wholly one and the same thing.[10] But they are also totally different from dependency on *others*: that would be to make oneself slavish and ultimately insecure.

## Paul and Christian Vulnerability

When we turn to Paul from Epictetus, we find a figure who often expresses confidence, hope, and joy but appears far less concerned with stability and serenity as essential virtues, often mixing his language with expressions of anxiety, sorrow, and fear. This might be because Paul's thought on this matter is less rigorous that Epictetus, that he is, as it were, only on the first steps on the Stoic road with a long way still to progress (cf. Phil 3:12–14). Or, it might be that he is on a fundamentally different road, with a different concept of human flourishing and human social relations.[11] In what follows I will first outline the ambiguous signals Paul emits regarding Christian confidence

---

10. See T. Engberg-Pedersen, 'Self-Sufficiency and Power: Divine and Human Agency in Epictetus and Paul' in J. M. G. Barclay and S. J. Gathercole (eds.), *Divine and Human Agency in Paul and his Cultural Environment* (London: T & T Clark, 2006), 117–39.

11. I do not mean to make or imply here any large claims about Paul's relationship to Hellenistic culture in general (which is in any case not incompatible with his Jewish heritage). On the topic of this essay, the Stoics were in any case atypical "Greeks," arguing against what they knew to be the normal practice among ordinary members of their culture.

and insecurity and then propose that his notion of mutual dependence suggests a significantly different vision of humanity than that proposed by Epictetus.

Even a casual reader of Galatians will notice that Paul seems torn between *confidence and doubt* in his dealings with his converts. On the one hand, he is "confident in relation to you, in the Lord, that you will think nothing other" than what he wants them to think (5:10); on the other, he is at a loss regarding them (*aporoumai en humin*, 4:20) and is seriously afraid lest he has labored over them in vain (4:11). The doubt here is not over the ultimate victory of God's purposes (cf. 5:5), but over the Galatians' relationship to that victory and the success or failure of his own efforts towards them (cf. Gal 2:2). The Epictetan distinction between intention and result does not seem to apply here. Paul cannot rest content that he has at least *tried* to do the right thing for them, reckoning that it is up to them now how they respond. It matters to him greatly whether or not they have believed in vain (3:4), sufficient for him to be angry, judgmental, and deeply upset. Elsewhere, we find the same curious combination of confidence and anxiety. He is wholly confident (*pepoitha*) that the one who began a good work in the Philippians will bring it to completion (Phil 1:6) and that whatever happens to him will turn out to their advantage (1:25). He rests secure in the sufficiency afforded by God (2 Cor 3:4–6) and does not lose heart whatever the outward circumstances (2 Cor 4:1–18). He knows that God is faithful and will confirm the work God has started (1 Cor 1:8–9), that the Lord can make his servants to stand (Rom 14:4), and that the calling and election of God are secure (1 Thess 1:4; 5:24). On the other hand, he is acutely anxious regarding the Thessalonians whether they will stand fast in their faith and whether his work has been in vain (*eis kenon*, 1 Thess 3:5; cf. Phil 1:16; 2 Cor 6:1). What surprises us is that this matters so much to him. He cannot bear being away from Thessalonica and not hearing news from them (1 Thess 3:1, 5)—"Now we live if you stand firm in the Lord" (3:8). On this news depends his joy (3:9) since they constitute his glory and his joy (2:20). One might have expected Paul to rest his confidence in God and in the fact that he had played his part as an apostle in the best possible way, as certified by God (1 Thess 2:1–12). He had surely done all that could possibly be considered "up to him," and it was the Thessalonians' responsibility whether they continued in the faith or went astray. Instead, what happens to them and what they do seems to matter very deeply to Paul, and he allows himself expressions of disturbance, anxiety, and fear that, however rhetorical, would be wholly inappropriate for a serious Stoic.[12]

---

12. Joel Willetts, in his helpful response, points to Rom 12:18 as a counter-example. I agree that Paul's "if possible, as far as it depends on you (*to ex humōn*)" constitutes a surface parallel to the Stoic

We meet the same phenomenon in relation to expressions of *joy and sorrow*. Philippians is, of course, the letter with the most expressions of joy (1:6, 25; 3:1; 4:1, etc.), exuding serenity in the midst of great trial. But within this very letter Paul expresses also his vulnerability. He sends Timothy to bring back news from Philippi "that I might be cheered (*eupsychō*) when I learn about you" (2:19); his *psychē* is not assuredly content but requires good news from the Philippians to make it so. Similarly, he confesses (despite 1 Thess 4:13) that had Epaphroditus died he would have had "sorrow upon sorrow" (*lypē epi lypēn*); he was spared this disaster by God's mercy but is still anxious to send Epaphroditus home "that I might be less grieved" (*alypoteros*, Phil 2:27–28).[13] Elsewhere he writes through tears (Phil 3:18) and is not ashamed to tell the Corinthians that they should mourn (1 Cor 5:2; 2 Cor 12:21). His letter has caused *lypē* to them, and although he does not want anyone to be consumed by grief (2 Cor 2:7), he is not averse to grief of every kind since it can have salutary effects (2 Cor 7:8–11). Although this grief contains more than "passion" in the Stoic sense, it certainly involves emotional upset, and the sentiment contrasts sharply with Epictetus's denial that others can fundamentally cause us harm. Paul urges his converts to rejoice with those who rejoice and weep with those who weep (Rom 12:15), and there is no reason to think that he would endorse Epictetus's caveat that one's weeping should never be truly internal (*esōthen*). When he expresses his own sorrow and unremitting pain for his fellow Jews, he says this grief is "in my heart" (Rom 9:2; cf. 10:1), and only a cynic could read this as empty rhetoric. On the only occasion on which he distinguishes between "inner" and "outer" in this connection, the passions are expressly inner (external battles, internal fears, 2 Cor 7:5). However we read the paradox that we live "as sorrowful, yet always rejoicing" (2 Cor 6:10), we cannot take the grief as merely an external show.[14]

---

notion of what is "up to us," but we should note that Paul's concern is with acts that may or may not prove peacemaking (the alternative is an act of retribution), and he is not discussing here the inner attitude towards or judgment of events which are the concern of the Stoics. We should also note that the relationships here discussed are with (or include those with) people outside the church, for whose actions Paul does not feel responsible. As was pointed out in discussion at the colloquium, he may feel differently in terms of mutual care and mutual dependence with regard to outsiders (and with regard to opponents and "false brothers") than he does with regard to members of his churches.

13. For Paul's attitude to grief in 1 Thess 4:13, however, see my essay, "'That you may not grieve like the rest who have no hope' (1 Thess 4.13): Death and Early Christian Identity," in *Not in the Word Alone: The First Epistle to the Thessalonians* (ed. M. D. Hooker; St. Paul's Abbey, Rome: Benedictina, 2003), 131–53.

14. When Paul talks about the crucifixion of the *pathē* (Gal 5:24), he is speaking of desires and passions which only partially overlap with what Stoics meant by the term and do not include grief or fear.

Finally, we may note an equivalent combination of *peace and fear*. Paul relies on "the God of hope who will fill you with all joy and peace in believing" (Rom 15:13), and he prays that "the peace of God . . . may guard your hearts and minds in Christ Jesus" (Phil 4:7). It may be significant that this peace is expressly said to "surpass all understanding" (*nous*); that suggests that the mind and reason are not reliable guides to reality. In any case, it is striking that Paul can make this prayer for others but still confess that his own mind is far from peaceful. He repeatedly tells the Corinthians of his fears (1 Cor 2:2; 2 Cor 7:11, 15), and he is anxious lest Satan overwhelm them (2 Cor 2:11) and is afraid lest the serpent that deceived Eve corrupt their minds (2 Cor 11:3). He has had no rest in his *pneuma* while he anxiously awaited news from Corinth (2 Cor 2:13; cf. 7:5), and at the climax of his list of trials (2 Cor 11:23–29) he emphasizes his daily constriction (*epistasis*) by his anxiety (*merimna*) for all the churches (2 Cor 11:28). Against every Stoic canon he appears to identify himself deeply and fully with the troubles of others: "Who is weak and I am not weak? Who is made to stumble and I do not burn with indignation?" (2 Cor 11:29). What happens to others clearly "gets to" Paul; he cannot and does not dismiss that as something ultimately someone else's business (*allotrion*). When he passes on the gospel, he gives also his own *psychē* (1 Thess 2:8), and the same self-donation continues in his spending of himself on behalf of his converts (2 Cor 12:15). In other words, Paul appears to have made himself vulnerable to a degree that would have appalled Epictetus, and if this is not merely surface rhetoric, we need to enquire if this corresponds to a different sense of human sociability than that required by Epictetus's Stoicism.

## Paul's Vision of Mutual Dependence

At the beginning of 2 Corinthians Paul describes his role as a mediator of the "comfort" (*paraklēsis*) of God in Christ: just as he shares Christ's sufferings, so he shares his comfort—and this so that he can pass on that comfort to the Corinthians ("for the sake of your comfort and salvation," 2 Cor 1:6). The relationship seems one-sided, as for Epictetus's socially committed Stoic. But then Paul recounts a crushing near-death experience "in Asia," when he despaired of life (1:8), an experience which taught him to put his confidence "not in ourselves but in the God who raises the dead" (1:9). He expresses confidence that this God will rescue him again, but then adds a very significant rider: "with you also helping on our behalf by prayer, in order that thanksgiving may be made on our behalf by many people for the gift that has come to us through many."[15] In this final statement Paul suggests that the relationship is, or at least should be, two-sided, that he wants, and even needs, them to play their part on his behalf, at least through prayer and in thanksgiving. This would match his pleas throughout 2 Corinthians, that his converts in Corinth renew their relationship with him, that they "open their hearts" to him as he has opened his to them (2 Cor 6:13; 7:2). He strongly desires a *mutual* relationship and is moved to anger, appeal, scolding, and bitter irony in order to effect this end. This would also match other requests he makes in his letters for support in prayer: he appeals to the Romans to "wrestle with me in your prayers on my behalf to God" that his visit to Jerusalem may be successful and safe (Rom 15:30–31) and tells the Philippians that he is confident things will turn out for him safely (*eis sōtērian*, "through your prayers and the provision of the Spirit of Jesus Christ" (Phil 1:19). In all such cases, others appear to have an instrumental role in bringing about the "safety" or "rescue" for which Paul hopes: his "security" depends on God but *also* on the cooperation and support of fellow Christians to whom he appeals for help.

Thus the mutual love that Paul takes to be integral to good community presupposes, as a structural necessity, a mutuality of *need*: believers not only have gifts to give to others but depend on the giving of others for their own fulfilment. The metaphor of the body is, of course, Paul's favourite means to portray this phenomenon. Having shown the necessity of diversity in the body (1 Cor 12:14–20), Paul turns to illustrate in particular the way that each part *depends on* the others: "The eye cannot say to the hand, 'I have no need of you,' nor again the head to the feet, 'I have no need of you.' On the contrary the parts of the body that seem to be weaker are indispensable" (*anankaia*, 1 Cor 12:20–21). This is a strong statement: it renders each part of the body *necessarily* dependent on others and *insufficient* on its own to operate as it should. Since Paul brings God into the discussion as the one who designed the body just so (12:24), he could not agree with Epictetus's pronouncement of the divine law, that "If you wish for any good, get it from yourself" (*Diatr.* 1.29.4). For all the vulnerability and uncertainty that it entails, the members of the body need each other to supply real "goods."

The body metaphor evokes a concept of mutuality that runs through very much of Paul's social ethics. Members of the body should exhibit the same care (*merimnaō*) for one another (1 Cor 12:25) and are exhorted elsewhere to "bear one another's

---

15. The construal of this sentence is difficult, and commentators differ in their alignment of its phrases. I here take *ek pollōn prosōpōn* to qualify the final verb *eucharistēthē* with *dia pollōn* qualifying *to eis hēmas charisma*.

burdens, and so fulfil the law of Christ" (Gal 6:2). With regard to love, the principle goes so far as to suggest "being slaves to one another" (Gal 5:14), an expression that Epictetus, who placed a premium on freedom, would have regarded as deeply unfortunate. This love that seeks others' interests *rather than* one's own (Phil 2:4) suggests a form of self-sacrifice that is only bearable in a community where *others* are looking out for your interests, just as you are looking out for theirs. The mutual support operates not just in practical, external matters but at the psychological level as well. If one suffers, all should suffer together (1 Cor 12:26); the strong are exhorted to support the weak, especially those who are faint-hearted or feeble-minded (*oligopsychoi*, 1 Thess 5:14). Timothy needed to have his mind set at rest (*anapepautai*) by the Corinthians, just as Paul hopes that his mind will be rested or refreshed in the company of the Romans (*synanapausōmai*, Rom 15:32). That suggests that we need one another even for our peace of mind.

The one passage where Paul speaks about self-sufficiency (*autarkēs*) might appear to point in another direction (Phil 4:10–20). Here Paul, while thanking the Philippians for their gift, declares that he has learned to live in all kinds of circumstance, in both prosperity and need: "in any and all circumstances I have learned the secret of facing plenty and hunger, abundance and want. I can do all things in him who strengthens me" (Phil 4:12–13). This might suggest that he is dependent solely on God and can take the support of others as an additional, but non-essential, benefit when it occurs. Even on this reading, the *koinōnia* of the Philippians would be an ideal scenario that would clash with Epictetus's ideal of the Stoic who needs nothing in the category of "the good" from others. However, I think Paul's point is otherwise. What he is indifferent about here is his material condition, the supply or nonsupply of material things; he is not indifferent as to whether or not he enjoys fellowship with others. He has learned how to be abased and how to abound; he can be content in want or plenty. But, we cannot imagine him saying that he has learned how to enjoy *koinōnia* and how to do without it: he does not mind if the *koinōnia* does not, because it cannot, take material forms (4:10), but he does mind very much that he has always shared some form of *koinōnia* with the Philippians from the very beginning (1:7). Mutual encouragement, mutual struggle, and mutual dependency are for Paul *core constituents* of life in Christ; it is only by this means that his joy can be complete (Phil 2:2). The God on whose encouragement he relies supplies his needs *through others*, and he is desperately at a loss when they fail to play their part.

One can imagine Epictetus raising loud objections to this strong Pauline notion of mutual dependency. By making himself so vulnerable Paul has placed his happiness and self-fulfilment at stake. He may be fortunate enough that others will play their part for his sake, but in making himself dependent on others he is risking his own fulfilment as a human being and making himself, in effect, a slave of others. More fundamentally, he is bringing into question God's providence, since a benevolent God could hardly make our lives so subject to others and to chance. If others fail to play their necessary part, Paul will go to his grave frustrated and incomplete, and God will be ultimately to blame for arranging the world so poorly. If only, Epictetus would say, Paul had expanded his partial appreciation of self-sufficiency (*autarkeia*), and if only he had recognized that God had given him complete freedom in control of his volition, none of these appalling consequences would have ensued.

How may we imagine Paul's reply? Only a superficial Paul would have accused Epictetus of lacking any basis for social ethics, and we may credit Paul with more understanding than that. A more perceptive reply would be that, deeply vulnerable as it may be, human flourishing is constituted by God to be double-sided, dependent for its fulfilment on receipt as well as gift. *Koinōnia*, in the strong Pauline sense of mutual *dependency* in mutual love, is thus a necessary trait of human well-being, however much it may be subject to inadequacy, distortion, and failure. Such *koinōnia* is enacted ideally in the body of Christ, although there too it is liable to stutter or fail. If Epictetus wonders how all this is compatible with a God of love, Paul would reply that the world is *not* presently well-administered and well-ordered but is the battleground between forces much bigger than ourselves, on which there will inevitably be victories and losses on both sides. The frustration which Epictetus works so hard to eradicate is for Paul an *inevitable* feature of "the present evil age" (Gal 1:4). For as long as Christ is putting all his enemies under his feet, and for as long as death, the last enemy, is undefeated (1 Cor 15:20–28), there is no security in this world.

In other words, it is only on the eschatological horizon that Paul sees the well-ordered universe that Epictetus takes for granted as the present condition of life. Where Epictetus therefore expects and finds the possibility of human fulfilment, so long as correct judgments are made in accordance with the reason we have been given, Paul is prepared to defer that fulfilment to a future that is only partially and inadequately adumbrated in the present.[16] If he can make the Stoic-sounding claim

---

16. For this reason I am disinclined to follow Joel Willits who considers that Paul and Epictetus follow different roads to the same goal, "a present experience of peace, freedom, and a life lived in the light of an assured sense of ultimate security in the face of present uncertainty." The first part of this is Stoic (and not Pauline) if it is understood in the sense of psychological peace and freedom; the second part is Pauline (and not Stoic) if "ultimate" is heard in the Pauline sense of eschatological change. In this

that "in everything God works for good for those who love him" (Rom 8:28), this is only against the backdrop of a radically disordered creation, which will not be released from frustration and decay until the eschaton (Rom 8:18–25). In the light of that hope we may tell each other to be "steadfast, immoveable, always abounding in the work of the Lord, knowing that in the Lord your labour is not in vain" (1 Cor 15:58). But in the present that work is not at all guaranteed to be successful: frustration, disappointment, and failure are unavoidable. What sustains us through these troubles is not the inner security of knowing that we have rightly used and controlled what is "up to us," as we sit loose to outward conditions, but the support and encouragement of others, as expressions of the comfort of Christ. Crucial as they are, even these, of course, will let us down, and we *will* go to our graves unfulfilled and frustrated in small or large part. It is only because he believes in "the God who raises the dead" (Rom 4:17) that Paul can live with this unsatisfactory scenario. It is in the promise of ultimate security that he can and must live with the deep insecurity of the present.

---

respect we need to break from a long tradition of Christian Stoicizing if we are to be true to the Pauline vision of community and history.

# RESPONSE TO BARCLAY

## *Joel Willitts*

The planners of this year's theme, I am sure, had no idea just how *apropos* the topic of "security" would be in light of the recent instability of the financial markets in the United States and around the world. So insecure was the United States government about the future of the financial market it has undertaken the biggest government bailout in United States history. Against this very contemporary background John Barclay has provided a brief and useful reflection on St. Paul's perspective on the issue of security and self-sufficiency by putting the Apostle into conversation with the first-century Stoic philosopher Epictetus.

Barclay is interested in discovering what these two figures think to be the remedy—if there be one—to what he calls "psychological insecurity," that is, the *feeling* of insecurity and vulnerability. He asks,

> Can this psychological insecurity, with all its debilitating consequences both individual and social, be treated? If so, how? Or is it an ineradicable feature of the human condition, for which we may seek mitigation or compensation, but no satisfactory cure?

Barclay's thesis is that when Epictetus's and Paul's respective answers to these questions are placed side by side the conclusion is clear: Paul is not a Stoic, at least on this issue, and Christianity is irreconcilable with the Stoic ideal of imperturbability.

There is much to commend in Barclay's reflection. At least three points can be made by way of commendation. First, at the level of methodology this paper reveals the usefulness of Greco-Roman comparative study for illuminating the perspectives of NT ideas. While it is fashionable to compare Paul with Jewish sources, it seems scholars are far less convinced of the usefulness of Greco-Roman comparative studies. While the goal of such comparisons must be realistic and chaste, Barclay has shown here how useful they can be.

Second, the choice of Epictetus is appropriate and interesting on a number of levels. I would only mention that his *Discourses* was composed by his student Arrian in Koine Greek early in the second century. Thus, the proximity in both time and language to the literature of the NT makes Epictetus's work an important, albeit oft-overlooked, comparative source. Furthermore, NT readers will feel at home in Epictetan literature and will find it accessible.

Third, Barclay's thesis that Paul is not a Stoic and Christianity is not a form of Stoicism is surely right, although it is true that there are Stoic sounding ideas in both Paul and Christianity, as Barclay concedes.[1] However, Barclay is quite right to highlight the central difference between Epictetus and Paul (and by extension Christianity) by exposing Paul's distinctive vision of human sociability, i.e., Paul's conviction that mutual dependency is basic to God's created order for humanity. Paul seems to have taken the creation story of the Jewish Scriptures as foundational for his anthropology: humanity, 'ādām, was created male and female and they were created, according to Paul, with an inherent mutuality and interdependency (1 Cor 11:8–12). Barclay says it well when he wrote: "Mutual encouragement, mutual struggle, and mutual dependency are for Paul core constituents of life in Christ; it is only by this means that his joy can be complete."

My quibbles, if you can even characterize them as such, are related to his treatment of Paul in comparison to Epictetus on the one hand and the implications of Paul's "vulnerability" on the other hand.

As for the former, whereas Barclay places Epictetus within the context of Stoicism, his treatment of Paul is solitary. For example in discussing Epictetus's Stoic view that the cosmos is a well-ordered sphere over which a benevolent power is exercising control ensuring that all things will ultimately turn out for the good, Barclay states, "Epictetus draws on the long tradition of Stoic reflection on Fate and Providence," and elsewhere, "Like Socrates, we should love our children, but remember that our first duty is to love the Gods."

There is no doubt from where Paul's perspective on issues of security and self-sufficiency derive. Paul's anthropology, theology, and eschatology are rooted in and fashioned by Jewish Scripture and tradition. Hence, placing Paul's perspective on the issue of psychological insecurity within a Hellenistic-Jewish, first-century worldview would have been useful in illuminating what road Paul is on. Yet Barclay does not attempt to address this. Instead he more vaguely writes of a "different road, with a different concept of human flourishing and human social relations," which leaves me with the notion that perhaps Paul was blazing his own trail. However, it seems more likely that Paul's perspective represents at the very least a variation of one or more Jewish perspectives.

---

1. This is a point echoed by the historian of ancient philosophy A. A. Long, *Epictetus: A Stoic and Socratic Guide to Life* (Oxford: Oxford University Press, 2002), 3.

In addition, while Barclay is right in his assertion that Paul's letters contain a pervasive dialect of confidence and insecurity, nevertheless his assertion that Paul is "far less concerned with stability and serenity as essential virtues" may be overstated. Does Paul, as Barclay maintains, "live with the deep insecurity of the present"? Or better, what does it mean that Paul lives in this state of insecurity? Is that "living" really so much different from Epictetus's outlook?

Paul and Epictetus are no doubt on fundamentally different roads, but it seems to me that the goal of their journeys is the *same*: a present experience of peace, freedom, and a life lived in light of an assured sense of ultimate security in the face of present insecurity. They both encourage their respective audiences to live a life free from fear, anxiety, anger, envy, lust, ambition, grief, and distress.[2] I think Paul would have affirmed what Barclay credits to Epictetus. I quote Barclay with some revision:

> In normal waking life [Paul] is confident that [believers in Jesus] have the capacity [by the power of the Spirit and a discipline and renewed mind] to control our evaluations of life and thus to pass serenely through any and all circumstances, up to and including death . . . This means no one and nothing can *truly* harm me, not even the ill-will of a close family member or the cruelest treatment by a tyrant: they may harm my property, my reputation, or my body, but they cannot harm me.

This Pauline mindset is evinced in many places in his letters. Indeed it is the tenor of such passages as Phil 4:4–9 and Rom 8:28–39. The practice of assessing life and controlling one's reaction to it by proper judgment, the use of what Epictetus terms one's "volition" is comparable to Paul's command in Phil 4:8, "to think on these things" and 2 Cor 10:5 to "take every thought captive to obey Christ" (see also Col 3:1–2). Moreover, Paul asserts that believers have "crucified the flesh with its passions and desires" (Gal 5:24) and should produce the "fruit of the Spirit" (Gal 5:22–23). Elsewhere Paul exhorts believers in Jesus not to "grieve as others who have no hope" (1 Thess 4:13).

One text that perhaps best captures this attitude and yet reveals the fundamental differences between Epictetus and Paul is Rom 12:18–21:

> If it is possible, *so far as it depends on you*, live peaceably with all. Beloved, never avenge yourselves, but leave room for the wrath of God; for it is written, "Vengeance is mine, I will repay, says the Lord." No, "if your enemies

---

2. The list of items comes from Barclay's characterization of Epictetus's philosophy. These same items could be drawn from Paul's own lists (see for example 2 Cor 12:20; Gal 5:20; Eph 4:31; and Col 3:8).

are hungry, feed them; if they are thirsty, give them something to drink; for by doing this you will heap burning coals on their heads." Do not be overcome by evil, but overcome evil with good.

Several important points can be highlighted. First, the phrase "as far as it depends on you" sounds very much like the key phrase of Epictetus, what is "up to you." There is a similar perspective between Epictetus and Paul that there is an essential distinction between what is up to us and what is out of our control, the latter being left up to God.[3] Second, basic to Paul's outlook is his concept of God, the God of Israel.[4] His understanding of YHWH's righteous intervention in the affairs of the world forms the basis for his security—seen here in Paul's reference to God's wrath. Third, Paul's source text for his outlook is the Jewish Scriptures quoting from the Law (Deut 32:35) and the Writings (Prov 25:21–22). Finally, Paul contends, much like Epictetus might, believers in Jesus should never allow themselves to be overtaken by evil and instead to overcome evil with the good they have the capacity to emit.

What makes Paul's perspective much more radical than Epictetus's, however, is that while Epictetus believed the cosmos to be a well-administered sphere governed by a benevolent power leading to the real possibility of psychological security through self-discipline, Paul believed that humanity was inherently marred and the world was presently controlled by evil and hostile forces. What is more, Paul believed apart from the God of Israel's direct intervention there was no capacity for true security. Paul's twin convictions of human mutual dependence and the present condition of humanity and the world not only would have made his call for psychological security astonishing to Epictetus but is also astonishing to us. Hence, the fundamental dissimilarity notwithstanding, Epictetus's Stoicism and Paul's Jewish apocalyptic messianism represented competing worldviews on the landscape of the first-century Greco-Roman world that promised to deliver "an admirable and thoroughly satisfying life."[5]

---

3. This seems to be in slight tension with what Barclay asserted: "Paul cannot rest content that he has at the least *tried* to do the right thing for them, reckoning that it is up to them now how to respond" (emphasis his). Romans 12:18 at the very least reveals a complexity to Paul's perspective that cannot be drawn with such stark characterization.

4. Troels, Engberg-Pedersen agrees that the respective conceptions of God underlie the difference between Epictetan Stoicism and (Pauline) Christianity. See his "Self-Sufficiency and Power: Divine and Human Agency in Epictetus and Paul," in *Divine and Human Agency in Paul and His Cultural Environment* (ed. John M. G. Barclay and Simon Gathercole; London: T. & T. Clark, 2006), 117–39, 135–37.

5. Phrase borrowed from Long, *Epictetus*, 18; see also Engberg-Pedersen, "Self-Sufficiency and

In sum, I think the comparison between Epictetus and Paul is useful and illuminating. It revealed the uniqueness particularly of Paul's anthropology but also of his theology and eschatology. However, perhaps in contrast to Barclay, I think that Epictetus and Paul hoped for similar outcomes for life in the present, although the worldviews that undergirded their common hope were significantly dissimilar.

---

Power," 139, who writes "While they are both more or less explicitly rejecting the other position, they also in fact make basic claims that are fundamentally similar."

# MARTIN LUTHER'S TEACHINGS ON SECURITY IN THE PSALMS AND THEIR SIGNIFICANCE FOR THE ART OF READING SCRIPTURE

## G. Sujin Pak

Many scholars have pointed to the quest for certainty amongst the Protestant reformers. Especially in the midst of what they saw as a church that propagated uncertainty of salvation for its own financial gain, the Protestant reformers—Luther and Calvin in particular—argued that a person can be certain of his or her salvation and often equated faith with this very assurance and certainty.[1] Indeed, Protestant reformers aimed to soothe and assure the "terrified consciences" of Christians with this teaching of the certainty of salvation—providing a kind of security, you might say. Yet, be not misled; the word "security" does not carry for Martin Luther, at least, so positive an import as that of "certainty."

Indeed, one could also understand much of Martin Luther's reformation program, particularly the early years of his reforming work, as precisely addressing the idolatry of security that he found himself surrounded by in the church of his time. For example, one of the key themes in his attack on indulgences in *The Ninety-Five Theses* (1517) is that indulgences do not accomplish what they promise and thus provide the people with a false security.[2] Luther argues that these indulgences dull consciences so that Christians fail to seek true contrition and practice proper godly fear.[3] Likewise, the heart of many of Luther's early attacks on the Roman Church is exactly the false securities it teaches and provides, such as trust in the Mass, monasticism, or a human priest, instead of providing the true foundation of security, which according to Luther is faith in the promises of God.[4]

---

1. See, for example, Susan Schreiner, "'The Spiritual Man Judges all Things': Calvin and the Exegetical Debates about Certainty in the Reformation," in *Biblical Interpretation in the Era of the Reformation* (ed. Richard A. Muller and John L. Thompson; Grand Rapids: Eerdmans, 1996), 189–93.

2. See, for example, thesis thirty-two. LW 31:28.

3. See theses forty and forty-nine. LW 31:29, 29–30.

4. There are a plethora of examples to be found here. As an initial example, see Luther's *On the Babylonian Captivity of the Church* (1520), specifically LW 36:50, 75, and 84. See also LW 36:143–44.

In much of Luther's numerous statements concerning the topic of security five basic themes arise. First, in the vast majority of his writings he spends significant time naming false securities and revealing the idolatry contained therein. Secondly, he aims to define the right kind of security—*godly* security—and demonstrate its true foundation. Not surprisingly, the foundation of true security according to Luther is God the only true refuge, which contains the gospel promise of justification by faith alone. He warns Christians about the very danger of the desire for security to the true worship of God and points to the good function that a kind of godly *in*security effects. Third, Luther cautions his readers concerning the various entrapments of the desire for and practice of false securities, including apathy, blindness, and the inability to recognize and name sin. Fourth, he reminds his readers that God often speaks and acts through the experiences of affliction and that in many ways the struggles and hardships involved in abandoning one's false securities are necessary to following the Christian path of righteousness. Finally, Luther maintains that both the godly insecurity that may be found in the abandonment of false securities and the virtue of humility are necessary elements to the faithful practice of reading Scripture.

This essay concentrates upon Luther's teachings on security in his commentaries on the Book of Psalms. There is good reason to focus on the Psalms for the subject of security because themes of comfort, assurance, and refuge are all key concepts in the Psalms, and each has its own relation to the larger topic of security. I will use Luther's writings on the Psalms to provide examples of his criticisms of false security and his definition of true security and its proper foundation. Luther's 1532 sermon on the second psalm is a clear case in which he demonstrates the danger of false securities to the true worship of God, while his earlier lectures on Psalm 69 (1513–1515) enumerates the various snares and dire consequences of false securities. Next, I will explore Luther's argument for the necessity of the virtue of humility and a kind of godly insecurity for faithful and proper readings of Scripture. The essay will conclude with some suggestions of what Luther's teachings on security and the practice of biblical interpretation have to offer us today.

## True and False Security

Luther's basic definition of false security is faith or trust in something other than God—trust in one's own efforts or works and trust in finite, created persons or things. One of the key mistakes of the ungodly, he argues, is that they are secure in their own power and efforts and lack the fear of God. They place their faith in their own works, the help of princes, and their experience of prosperity and fail to see that they are actually in great danger, for they do not recognize their idolatry before God.[5] On the contrary, true security is found in God alone, as the psalmist's appeal to God as one's only refuge teaches.[6] Thus, when the psalmist writes in Ps 90:1, "Lord, you are our dwelling place from generation to generation," Luther comments that this is the same as calling God our refuge, in whom solely we may be secure and safe.[7] Similarly, he employs Ps 147:13 ("For he strengthens the bars of your gates") to teach that only God can provide real security and so security is, in actuality, a gift from God.[8] Of course, for Luther, at the heart of the statement that God is our refuge is the fact of justification by faith alone: God is a refuge of mercy, from whom humans receive salvation that is not dependent on them or anything they do but upon the sure foundation of God's promises fulfilled through Jesus Christ, God's character of mercy and forgiveness expressed in the gospel message, and the gift of faith.[9]

In his 1530 commentary on Ps 118:8–9, Luther also draws a contrast between true and false security, specifically concerning a misplaced trust in princes. These verses read, "It is better to take refuge in the Lord than to put confidence in humans. It is better to take refuge in the Lord that to put confidence in princes." He employs this text as an opportunity to answer some accusations of his critics that he himself has placed his trust in princes (specifically, Frederick the Wise) and depended on their protection. Yet, his larger purpose is to provide a teaching concerning the idolatry involved in placing one's trust in humans and, specifically, human rulers. He writes,

> It remains a rare and remarkable skill not to trust in men or princes. The world is and remains the same and trusts and relies on men and princes, and thus it rejects God and tramples [God's] First Commandment underfoot. [People] are willing to trust all sorts of false gods, but not the one true and faithful God. . . . God does not, should not, and cannot tolerate it. It is idolatry that would rob God of [God's] divinity.[10]

---

5. LW 10:250; 11:372; 12:29, 74; 14: 75, 200, 292.

6. See, for examples, LW 10:396–97; 13:83–84; 12:93, 14:191, 256. Key verses in the Psalms where the psalmist speaks of God as our refuge include Ps 9:9, 14:16, 46:1, 7, 11; 48:3; 57:1; 59:16; 62:7,8; 71:7; 91:2, 9; 94:22; 104:18; and 142:4, 5.

7. LW 13:83–84.

8. LW 14:112–13.

9. See, for examples, LW 18:190, 250; 36:84; 40:276, 294, 296.

10. LW 14:66, 67. I have revised for inclusive language.

Hence, misplaced trust in someone or something other than God is ultimately idolatry, that is, a violation of the first commandment, while the foundation of lasting security is precisely the proper keeping of the first commandment—namely to place one's trust in God alone.

Luther further comments on Ps 118:8–9 in order to draw a distinction between trust and use—a distinction that both works toward a defense of his own actions and provides a larger teaching for the church. He writes,

> We should use and enjoy the princely office and temporal government for food, protection, and peace on earth, as God instituted it. But we should not rely, trust, hope and boast in them. We must use other temporal goods, money, cattle, houses, homes; but we must not place our trust, hope, and confidence in them. To trust and to use are two different things. The former is appropriate to God; the latter is appropriate to creatures.[11]

Thus, Luther understands himself as not having placed his trust in princes but as having used what they had to offer. On the contrary, he knows very well that it is only by placing his trust in God alone that he can have true security. These princes, he writes, cannot provide the comfort needed either for him or for anyone else: "For men do not have the right word or spirit to comfort and uphold a sorrowful heart. Nor do princes have a fist strong enough to help a wretched man and to suppress his enemies. God alone has the word of comfort and the fist for help."[12] In the end, proper security can come from no other place than God, the promises of the gospel, and the gift of faith; any other source leads to idolatry.

### Danger of Security to the True Worship of God: Psalm 2:11–12

Luther's interpretation of Ps 2:11–12 focuses upon the dangers false securities—and even the desire for security—can pose to the practice of the true worship of God. The verses read: "Serve the Lord with fear, with trembling; kiss the Son, lest he be angry and you perish in the way; for his wrath is quickly kindled. Blessed are all who take refuge in him." While he first applies these verses to the uprising of the nations and kings against Christ,[13] his exegetical import falls upon instructing the church

---

11. LW 14:68–69. Note that this echoes St. Augustine's teachings on the distinction between the love of use (*uti*) and love of enjoyment (*frui*), except that Luther speaks of this in terms of faith or "trust," rather than love.

12. LW 14:66.

13. LW 12:69–70, 73.

concerning what is the true worship of God. Both of these verses, Luther points out, contain the two necessary elements of the true worship of God: godly fear and properly placed trust. "Serve the Lord with fear [and] with trembling," along with the warnings against God's anger and wrath, alert the believer to the necessity of godly fear, while the commands to "kiss the Son" and "take refuge in him" provide instruction for the proper placement of godly trust. Thus, true worship, Luther maintains, involves proper godly fear, humility that recognizes that all glory belongs to God alone, and faith and trust in Jesus Christ.[14]

He contends that both false security and even the desire for security interfere with this true godly worship. When people rely upon their false securities—their works, their own power, or other human powers, they become presumptuous and proud and fall into idolatry. In the seeking of security they tend to seek it in the wrong ways or in the wrong things and forget the constant necessity of godly fear. That is to say, even when they try to seek the proper security that lies in God alone, the problematic temptation is to forget the proper fear of God that must always be part of a holy disposition toward their Creator.[15] Thus, Luther exhorts Christians toward a life of holy tension, a life of a subtle balance between the fear of God and trust in God:

> For God does not want us to be either up in the clouds or flat on the ground, but in the middle. Our feet reach downward, but our head reaches upward. And although we live on earth, yet we are commanded that our "conversation should be in heaven" (Phil 3:20). In short, we who are Christians are not entirely fearful nor entirely happy. Joy is joined with fear, hope with dread, laughter with tears, so that we may believe that we shall then at last be perfectly joyous, when we have put away this flesh. For just as the flesh cannot rid itself from fear, so it serves a purpose for it to be in fear, in order that we may not become smug. In this manner the present psalm has described the service of God. For to fear God and to trust God alone is true religion. Where these two are in correct balance, there the whole life is righteous and holy.[16]

The point is that *both* trust and fear belong to God alone. Just as trusting in something or someone other than God leads to idolatry and destroys the proper

---

14. LW 12:73–76, 80–83, 85, 92–93.

15. Here Luther expounds on a distinction between servile fear (a fear that despairs) and filial fear, such as the fear a child has toward a loving parent. See LW 12:75–78.

16. LW 12:81.

worship of God, so does fearing something or someone more than one fears God also lead to idolatry and destroys the proper worship of God. Thus, Luther argues for a proper balance between trust and fear, rendering a kind of godly *in*security; namely, Christians must never forget the radical distinction between themselves as finite creatures and God as infinite Creator, even in the midst of the assurance and security of salvation through faith in Jesus Christ and the great mercy of God.

Indeed, Luther applies these verses in Ps 2 to critique the promotion of false worship that he sees in his own sixteenth-century context. He argues that the religious leaders of his day—instead of advancing the true worship of God, which entails above all trust in God alone and not in human efforts—teach trust in human ceremonies and good works.[17] These religious leaders have not only taught trust in the wrong things, they have also misled the people on the other vital element of the proper worship of God, the necessity of godly fear. Luther insists that when the Roman Church of his day implies that only priests and monks can truly and fully embody a life of worship to God or, at least, that they do so at a higher level than a lay person, they give that lay person a false security that such a high calling is beyond them and rob that same lay person of the godly fear involved in being answerable for *not* having pursued this true worship of God.[18] Hence, Luther wisely discerns the two poles around which true worship of God rotates—trust and fear—and how the neglect or wrong use and placement of both of these lead to idolatry.

## The Entrapments of Security: Psalm 69

Luther uses his first lectures on Ps 69 to expound upon the various snares of false securities and even the desire for security. As with Ps 2, he first interprets Ps 69 as a description of Christ's sufferings on earth;[19] yet, the weight of his exegesis falls upon his application of this psalm to the story of the church and her experience of suffering. For Luther the psalm describes three ages of the church's suffering: the age of the martyrs, the era of the heretics, and his current time, in which he sees a large

---

17. LW 12:71, 73, 80, 81, 85, 88, 90. Note that in Luther's 1532 comments on Ps 2 justification by faith alone is a prominent theme, while in his 1513–1515 comments on Ps 69 humility is the key theme. Of course, Luther did not arrive at the full expression of his doctrine of justification by faith alone until after his first lectures on the Psalms, but many scholars note the importance of his emphasis on humility in these first lectures as a preparatory step. See, for example, Martin Brecht, *Martin Luther: His Road to Reformation, 1483–1521* (Minneapolis: Fortress, 1985), 128–37.

18. LW 12:71, 72–73, 75, 81, 85, 86, 88, 89, 90, 91. See especially LW 12:89.

19. LW 10:351, 354, 381.

presence of lukewarm and evil Christians.[20] Throughout his reading of Ps 69, Luther offers cautions against five entrapments of the desire for security and trust in false securities. He warns that the desire for security and false securities lead Christians to (1) become apathetic and lukewarm, (2) become blind to the devil's tricks and the true calling of how the church lives faithfully on earth, (3) fall into economic abuses, (4) become ineffective in preaching and prayer, and (5) become unable to recognize, name, and confess sin.

Luther first maintains that the desire for security and the trust in false securities leads Christians to become lukewarm and apathetic. He sees this as the particular state of Christians in his time, and he offers them a prophetic challenge:

> ... there is much worship of God everywhere, but it is only going through the motions, without love and spirit, and there are very few with any fervor. And all this happens because we think we are something and are doing enough. Consequently, we try nothing, and we hold to no strong emotion, and we do much to ease the way to heaven, by means of indulgences, by means of easy doctrines, feeling that one sigh is enough.[21]

Indeed, Luther points out that indulgences actually have two fatal effects that lie on opposite extremes—not only to terrify some consciences (that they are not doing enough and, thus, a wrong kind of fear) but also to give them a false security (and, thus, a wrong kind of trust and a lack of *godly* fear) that this is all they need to do. False securities can produce presumption and smugness and a lack of the proper fear of God. Furthermore, a lukewarm Christian who lacks proper fear of God will also fail to be watchful. He warns,

> ... the eyes fail more from sleepiness than from adversity. Indeed, they are stimulated by the latter, but they get sleepy and they fail because of the former, and they fall asleep with a certain smugness ... For one who does not fear everything from all sides does not look around. But he who is afraid will neglect nothing, because he is thoroughly alert ... Therefore, to fight that failure the Lord so anxiously commands us to be watchful and always to have open eyes and wait for his coming.[22]

Indeed, Luther cautions Christians against forming a habit of going easy on themselves, which begets not only an apathy and lack of discipline in fighting the

---

20. LW 10:351. Luther uses this pattern throughout his interpretation of the psalm.
21. LW 10:351.
22. LW 10:360–61.

"desires of the flesh," but also a kind of blindness that includes an inability to recognize their own sin.[23]

Thus, secondly, he argues in his reading of Psalm 69 that the desire for security has a blinding effect. First and foremost, it causes Christians to fail to recognize the tricks of the devil, for, Luther asserts, the devil "does not fight us with adversity . . . but with prosperity, security, and peace."[24] Likewise he declares, "Thus the devil now fights the church with the greatest persecution because he fights with no persecution, but rather with security and idleness."[25] In this way Luther points to the false assumptions of his day that the church is supposed to be in a place of security and that such an experience of security is a good thing. On the contrary, he contends that the expected and proper and faithful experience of the church in the world is not one of security and power but one of hardship and affliction. Adversity, writes Luther, is an expected and even good thing for a Christian, for adversity keeps the eyes open, keeps the heart and mind watchful, and guards against smugness and apathy. Indeed, adversity is a loving tool of discipline, while relaxing in security leads to destruction:

> So you see how truly dangerous the times of this peace and security are, as the apostle describes them to Timothy (II Tim 3:2f). For everything he mentions there arises from peace and security, "lustful, puffed up, lovers of pleasure, etc." Therefore consider this a sign that God is extremely angry and be not deceived because you do not feel [God's] jealousy over you. And note that as the primitive times were happy times because they were times of discipline and affliction, when the church made its greatest progress, so these last times are unhappy ones, because they are and will be times of peace and security, when the church is and will be most deficient. And the ultimate in persecutions for the church will be peace and security.[26]

A church that becomes blinded by a life of ease and security, says Luther, falls easily prey to false securities and the abandonment of the proper fear of God. Thus, it draws away from the proper worship of God and falls into the vices of pride, apathy, and carnal contentment.

Closely related to the blinding effects upon the Christian life of the desire for security, Luther hones in upon the dangers of seeking and relying specifically upon

23. LW 10:381–82.

24. LW 10:352.

25. LW 10:361.

26. LW 10:373–74. See also LW 12:24–25, 28–29.

economic security or prosperity. He warns lukewarm Christians that the Antichrist will "kill the majority of people not through poverty but through an abundance of everything."[27] Indeed, he calls prosperity a "double adversity," for it dulls the senses and causes one to rely upon a false idol.[28] Luther criticizes the economic abuses of the church of his day, in which they amass for themselves profit for the church rather than glory to God, and he speaks of the "abomination of guzzling and high living"—what I might rename as the "abomination of consumerism"—that abounds in his time.[29]

Fourth, Luther cautions that the desire for security and the reliance upon false securities have dire effects upon specific Christian practices, particularly the practices of preaching and prayer. He maintains that if Christians become apathetic and lukewarm, particularly through their desire for and reliance upon false securities, they can no longer properly hear God's Word, preach God's Word, or pray. He expounds upon Ps 69:3 ("I have labored with crying; my jaws have become hoarse"):

> Indeed, according to blessed Augustine, the voice of the preacher is hoarse when he who hears it listens to it poorly, but it is clear and bright when it is heard clearly and brightly. For appearances and addresses are regularly depicted in Scripture according to the disposition of those to whom they were made. Second, prayers were offered, but so languidly and hoarsely that the neighbor can scarcely hear them. For a prayer is truly hoarse when it is uttered rough and hard and dry and without earnestness ... For that reason this verse briefly depicts the labored, dry, and irreverent prayer of the church in our time.[30]

In other words, Christians who lack proper godly fear and godly trust not only become blind, they become deaf and dumb. They cannot properly hear prayers or sermons, and by consequence, the ineffectiveness of these prayers and sermons has a detrimental effect upon the larger community and the one who delivers these prayers and sermons.

Finally, through his reading of Ps 69:16 ("Answer me, O Lord, for your steadfast love is good; according to your abundant mercy, turn to me"), Luther discerns that the seeking of security and reliance upon false securities hinders the church and the Christian's abilities to recognize, name, and confess sin. He argues that people can-

---

27. LW 10:353.
28. LW 10:361.
29. See LW 10:377–78.
30. LW 10:358–59.

not rightly see the mercy of God when they seek false securities or rely upon these false securities. The reason for this is that these very false securities eclipse the reality of the human condition as one of enslavement to sin. Instead, when people rely upon false securities, they are smug, lazy, apathetic, and content with themselves, when what they are really called to do is "magnify and aggravate [their] sins and thus always to accuse them more and more." As Luther writes, "The more deeply a person has condemned himself and magnified his sins, the more he is fit for the mercy and grace of God."[31] Since the desire for and reliance upon false securities are so rampant in his day, he provides a map for his readers on how to acknowledge and confess sin. He imparts eight instructions, which include considerations of various sins of omission and commission. His seventh instruction specifically takes up the danger of security to the practices of the confession of sin:

> Consider that the peace and security of our time is the greatest hindrance and reason why God's mercy is not often good or great, for it does not permit evils to appear as many and great, although, if one would think about it, it would be so much greater.[32]

In other words, giving into the idolatry of security hinders the mercy of God from reaching persons because they can no longer recognize and name the evil and sin in their midst or the magnitude of that evil and sin, and so they also do not recognize the magnitude of their own need for God's mercy.

## The Need for Humility and Godly Insecurity for Proper Biblical Interpretation

In several places in his interpretations of the Book of Psalms Luther applies his teachings concerning the dangers of false securities and even the desire for security to the practices of reading and interpreting Scripture. Time and again he stresses that the proper disposition of the faithful interpreter of Scripture is the practice

---

31. LW 10:368.

32. LW 10:370. The eight instructions are the following: (1) consider the sins of omissions in regard to natural things (i.e., whether you have thanked God for the basic things that sustain your daily life), (2) consider the sins of omissions in regard to the gifts of grace you have received (e.g., spiritual blessings of God, sacraments, the church), (3) consider the sins of omission concerning the commandments of God (e.g., loving God and neighbor), (4) consider the neglect of zeal of correcting and admonishing the sins of others, (5) consider sins of commission and transgression, (6) consider the sins of others that you ought to assume as your own, (7) consider the peace and security of our time (and its related idolatry and snares), and (8) weep over your hardness of heart that you are not moved by the gravity of these things laid out in the first seven instructions. See LW 10:368–71.

of embodying the virtue of humility. First and foremost this humility entails the recognition that the interpretation of Scripture is a spiritual act that must be guided by the Holy Spirit for its correct practice and in order to attain faithful readings. Thus, the first action a faithful reader of Scripture must do is to surrender his or her will and control to the guidance and wisdom of the Spirit. Indeed, on every page of his 1532 commentary on Ps 2, for example, Luther makes constant appeal to the Holy Spirit as the author of Scripture and as the teacher and guide of faithful readings of Scripture.[33] Elsewhere, he writes that one must pray for God's gift of the Holy Spirit, for it is the Spirit that leads and enlightens one's reading and provides understanding.[34]

Secondly, this virtue of humility is practiced in the reading of Scripture by the recognition that the parameters and basic content of Scripture have already been outlined by the divine author to guide faithful readings and delimit unfaithful readings. This is the next way in which the Christian is called to submit and surrender his or her own will and control in the faithful practice of reading Scripture. In this way Luther maintains that all of Scripture points to the God revealed in Jesus Christ; that is, Christ is the content of all Scripture. In this way Luther holds to a christological center as the guiding principle for his reading of Scripture. In reference to the Psalms particularly, Luther understands the chief sense of the Psalms to be the *sensus Christi*—its christological sense.[35] He maintains,

> Because in all the words of the Law and the Prophets truth is the chief and head, so all the words of the Law are directed, as members to the Head, to faith or to the truth done in Christ . . . that is, in the chief and literal sense, which always shows Christ. For as Christ is the Head of the church, so Scripture is also in the Head, that is, it speaks of Him [Christ] before all things.[36]

Indeed, when Luther applies this head-member analogy of Christ's relationship to the church to his understanding of Scripture, it not only points to this christological center but also to the larger task and formative purposes of reading Scripture for Christians. Namely, the story of Christ found in Scripture is the chief sense that

---

33. For Luther's appeals to the Holy Spirit as author, speaker, guide and teacher of Scripture on Ps 2:11–12, see LW 12:74, 75, 76, 81, 87, 89, 90, 91, and 92. See also LW 10:391; 12:405.

34. LW 34:285–86.

35. LW 11:517.

36. LW 11:517.

specifically acts as a guide for the life of the church and its participation in the life of Christ.

Luther sees in the story of Christ as revealed in Scripture the story of the church as a whole. The story of Christ acts as a guide by which the church may read her own story and participate in the life of Christ, just as members of the body are led, taught and guided by its head.[37] Hence, in his comments upon the fourth Psalm, Luther directly relates the participation of the church in the life of Christ with her practice of reading Scripture:

> For if they [the saints] participate with Him in grace and inherit all things from Him, then also the words of Scripture which speak of Christ participate with Him in a similar way and inherit the same words of praise and description from Him and with Him and in Him, "who is blessed."[38]

Furthermore, it is not solely the christological center—the story of Christ—that is the guiding principle for Christian reading of Scripture for Luther, but more broadly the narrative of the triune God's work of salvation, in which Christ is central. For example, in his 1532 comments on Psalm 51, Luther expounds upon the proper subject of theology and its relation to the reading of Scripture:

> The proper subject of theology is [humanity] guilty of sin and condemned, and God the Justifier and Savior of [humanity] the sinner. Whatever is asked or discussed in theology outside of this subject is error and poison. All Scripture points to this, that God commends [God's] kindness to us and in [God's] Son restores to righteousness and life the nature that has fallen into sin and condemnation ... The issue is ... the God who justifies, repairs, and makes alive and [humanity], who fell from righteousness and life into sin and eternal death. Whoever follows this aim in reading the Holy Scriptures will read holy things fruitfully.[39]

Thus, Luther argues that the guiding principle of reading Scripture is the narrative of the Triune God's gift of salvation through the person of Christ, which includes proper self-knowledge of oneself as a sinner.[40]

---

37. For example, Luther says explicitly in Ps 54, "This first happened to Christ, the Head of all the righteous, and then to all His members" (LW 10:248).

38. LW 10:52.

39. LW 12:311.

40. This is what many have named as the "Rule of Faith." See Treier, 57–59; Paul M. Blowers, "The *Regula Fidei* and the Narrative Character of Early Christian Faith," *Pro Ecclesia* 6/2 (1997): 199–228; and Kathryn Greene-McCreight, "Rule of Faith," in *Dictionary for Theological Interpretation of the Bible*

For Luther, then, one of the central goals of reading Scripture is both the personal (i.e., of each Christian) and communal (i.e., of the church) "appropriation of the christological content" of the text.[41] Such an appropriation, by which one participates in the life of Christ, conveys with it a significant ethical dimension. In Luther's practices of reading Scripture this appears in his considerable emphasis upon the tropological sense.[42] If the faithful reading of Scripture involves the appropriation of the christologial content through an ethical life lived through participation in the life of Christ, then, for Luther, it is not so much that the reader *interprets* Scripture as it is that Scripture transforms its readers. He explains,

> And note that the strength of Scripture is this, that it is not changed into [the person] who studies it, but that it transforms its lover into itself and its strengths.[43]

This is the third dimension of the role of humility in the interpretation of Scripture; ultimately, faithful interpretation of Scripture for Luther entails the abandonment of the impulse to make Scripture say what one wants it to say and the surrender to Scripture's power and authority over one's character formation and personal and communal practices. Thus, the humility involved in reading Scripture, according to Luther, specifically means that a reader learns to embody the virtues of Scripture, which are the virtues of Christ himself:

> Now set forth the virtues of Scripture: It is light, and therefore the souls are enlightened; it is truth, and therefore they are truthful; it is wisdom, and therefore they are wise; it is discipline, and therefore they are disciplined

---

(ed. by Kevin J. Vanhoozer et al.; Grand Rapids: Baker Academic, 2005), 703.

41. John R. Wilch argues for the more individual version of this statement: "Luther's unique emphasis on the *sensus tropologicus* was prompted by his conviction that the goal of interpretation is the personal appropriation of the Christological content of Scripture" (found in "Luther as Interpreter: Christ and the Old Testament," *Consensus* 9/3 [1983]: 5). I believe that there is a communal dimension to Luther's exegesis, but it is true that it is not as explicit in his descriptions and practices of reading Scripture as one might hope. Indeed, for the importance of the community for the practice of reading Scripture, John Calvin arises as a much more clear and helpful example. However, Luther is certainly reading with others in his community, whether they are patristic sources (such as Augustine, Lyra, or Bernard of Clairvaux) or contemporaries.

42. See, for example, LW 10:265, 379–80; 11:12. This is especially true of Luther's first lectures on the Psalms, the *Dictata super psalterium*. See Gerhard Ebeling, "Luthers Psalterdruck vom Jahre 1513," *Lutherstudien*, Vol 1 (Tübingen: J. C. B. Mohr, 1971), 127–30; Scott Hendrix, "Luther Against the Background of the History of Biblical Interpretation," *Interpretation* 37 (1983): 230; and Wilch, "Luther as Interpreter," 5.

43. LW 10:332. I have revised for inclusive language.

... Because you will not change me into what you are, but you will be changed into what I am. Nor will I be designated by you, but you by me.[44]

For Luther, the reading of Scripture (and the preaching of Scripture) involves an encounter with God through Christ, from which one cannot emerge unchanged.

Contained within this very emphasis upon encounter is Luther's conviction that using Christ's story as a guide by which Christians understand their own story entails a pursuit of "what the Spirit says to the church" of one's own time and place.[45] He reads with the confidence that the larger salvation narrative guides Christians concerning how to live faithfully in their current contexts. He writes, "You must keep an eye on the word that applies to you, that is spoken to you."[46] Indeed, he specifically cites his experience of those he believed to be heretics as crucial to helping him read Scripture more faithfully—namely, the circumstances of the idolatrous practices of the Roman Church led him to realize the true nature of salvation as a gift of God rather than a result of human works.[47] Hence, Luther firmly believed that the word the Spirit had to say to the church of his day was the message of justification by faith alone, and he found this teaching in numerous passages of Scripture.

Yet, it also needs to be clear that Luther does not believe that any one reading of Scripture stood for all time. On the contrary, he affirms the "infinite potential" of Scripture.[48] Hence, he cautions, "Therefore, no matter how much you understand,

---

44. LW 10:333. See also Hendrix, "Luther Against the Background of the History of Biblical Interpretation," 236.

45. Indeed, Luther has been rightly described as a kind of contextual reader of Scripture. See Eric W. Gritsch, "The Cultural Context of Luther's Interpretation," *Interpretation* 37 (1983): 266–67, 276. Gritsch writes, "One could say . . . that [Luther's] expository sermons, lectures, and meditations always related what he understood to be the word of God to the issues of his day. In this sense, Luther's interpretation of Scripture was always contextual" (276).

46. LW 35:170.

47. Luther writes, "The reading of the Bible would never have led me to the understanding I have unless I had been instructed by the actions of my adversaries. In the beginning I defended the Mass and monasticism with my life and body, but the circumstances taught me otherwise" (LW 54:274). Likewise, Luther writes in the preface to his German writings, "I myself am deeply indebted to my papists that through the devil's raging they have beaten, oppressed, and distressed me so much. That is to say, they have made a fairly good theologian of me, which I would not have become otherwise" (LW 34:287).

48. Luther writes, "But every Scripture passage is of infinite understanding" (LW 11:433). Luther's emphasis upon seeking and hearing the word that the Spirit has to say to the church of one's own day, combined with the principle of the infinite potential of Scripture, holds much potential fruitfulness. It can be fruitfully used to call Christian readers to recognize that they all read from a particular location and with particular cultural lenses and not to presume that one culture's reading is more true than an-

do not be proud, do not fight against another, do not withstand, because they are testimonies, and perhaps [another] will see what you do not see . . . Therefore it is always a matter of making progress in the understanding of Scripture."[49] In this same passage, Luther describes this very progress in terms of virtue—that a reader must progress from "act to act, from virtue to virtue," and in the end one must guard against all smugness and security, which brings us back to where we began. Thus in order to be a faithful reader of Scripture, the fourth aspect of the embodiment of the virtue of humility is the abandonment of false securities, which includes the security and pride of claiming that one has *the one and only* correct interpretation of Scripture.

In sum, Luther finds three rules in Psalm 119 for the practice of reading Scripture that aids one from falling into the temptations of pride, presumption, and security. These are the rules of *oratio*, *meditatio*, and *tentatio* (i.e., prayer, meditation, and affliction). All three involve both the performance of humility and the abandonment of false securities. The first step in reading Scripture, counsels Luther, is to despair of one's own understanding, for such presumption will only lead to destruction. Rather, one should "kneel down in your little room and pray to God with real humility and earnestness, that [God] through [God's] dear Son may give you the Holy Spirit, who will enlighten you, lead you, and give you understanding."[50] Prayer is the first step of reading Scripture, for its sets the right disposition of humility and recognizes the necessary aid of the triune God. Secondly, Luther directs Christian readers of Scripture to meditate with "diligent attention and reflection." It is only in this practice of meditation that a Christian reader learns to hear the Spirit and discern the meaning intended by the Spirit. He warns that one cannot be a good theologian if he or she wearies from just meditating on the words once or twice. It takes perseverance, concentration, and attentiveness.[51]

---

other's. In other words, these principles could act as a kind of protection from what post-colonial theorists might call the "colonizing of the text." See, for example, essays in *The Postcolonial Bible* (ed. by R. S. Sugirtharajah; Sheffield: Sheffield Academic, 1998), Fernando F. Segovia, *Decolonizing Biblical Studies: A View from the Margins* (Maryknoll, N.Y.: Orbis, 2000), R. S. Sugirtharajah, *The Bible and the Third World: Precolonial, Colonial, and Postcolonial Encounters* (Cambridge: Cambridge University Press, 2001), and *Voices from the Margin: Interpreting the Bible in the Third World* (ed. R. S. Sugirtharajah; Maryknoll, N.Y.: Orbis, 2006).

49. LW 11:433.

50. LW 34:285-86.

51. LW 34:286.

Finally, Luther believes that the experience of affliction has a role to play in making a good and faithful reader of Scripture. This experience of affliction is part of the call to participate in the life of Christ or, more specifically, the cross of Christ. Time and again in his writings on the Psalms, Luther insists that one must go through the process of learning to despair of one's own works, abilities, or efforts in order to grasp the reality that faith is wholly a gift from God and not an item earned.[52] Thus, affliction might be this crucial process of despairing of one's own self, but it is also for Luther more largely a kind of trial in which one learns to grasp the promises of God with faith despite all evidences to the contrary, such as in the case of Abraham's faithfulness in the sacrifice of Isaac.[53] More personally, Luther felt that it was through his experiences of *Anfechtung* as a monk, in which he felt the despair of never being able to do enough, that he himself came to understand the profound freedom and release that the proper understanding of the righteousness of God as that which freely justifies rather than judges brings to the believer.

Affliction not only helps the individual Christian to abandon false securities and rightly trust in the promises and gifts of God, but Luther also reminds the church that she as a community must understand that she cannot expect a life of ease and security in this world; rather, more often than not the world offers the church adversity and affliction.[54] While there is good reason to take caution about an emphasis on the *necessary* role of affliction in the church's life, there is also something to be said for the fact that Luther's rules of scriptural reading ends not on a note of triumphalism but encourages a constant cycle of humility and complete surrender to God. Thus, Luther contends that the temptation to security is dangerous to being a faithful interpreter of Scripture because of the tendencies toward pride and presumption, but perhaps even more so because it obscures the call of the church and each Christian to be willing to bear the cross of Christ in the world.

---

52. Luther's first lectures on the Psalms (*Dictata super psalterium*, 1513–1515) is full of this theme, which Martin Brecht calls Luther's theology of humility. See Brecht, 128–37.

53. See Luther's comments on the trial of Abraham in Gen 22 (LW 4:93–124). For Luther, the trial of Abraham is a model for all Christians, in which Abraham experiences the contradiction between the Law and the Gospel, between the despair felt with the contradiction of God's command and the faith in God's promise despite this apparent contradiction.

54. See, for examples, LW 12:24–25, 28–29.

## What Does Luther Offer Us Today?

Luther's teachings on security are very much embodied in his practices of reading Scripture. The starting point for the true worship of God is also the starting point of faithful Christian reading, namely, proper humility and the giving up of false securities, which involves proper knowledge of God and proper knowledge of ourselves. For, is not the church's reading of Scripture a way in which she seeks to worship God? In the faithful practice of biblical interpretation our starting point as Christians is the humility that recognizes our complete reliance upon the guidance and wisdom of the Holy Spirit and the necessary patience and forbearance needed to discern the Spirit together. Secondly, it is the humility that acknowledges that Christian readers do not ultimately decide the content of Scripture; Scripture itself has provided the core story and parameters that guide and delimit faithful and unfaithful readings of Scripture. Third, it is the humility that understands that the end goal is not to change Scripture into ourselves or what we want it to say but that we ourselves are transformed by Scripture to embody more faithfully the virtues of the Christian life in the world.

Furthermore, the very story that guides faithful Christian readings of Scripture, at least according to Luther, is a narrative centered upon *insecurity* and humility. It is the story of a God who in humility takes on the insecurities of human flesh, who bears the terrors of sin and death, who partakes of the sufferings and afflictions of this world, who—as a kind of paraphrase of Paul's words in Philippians 2—empties himself of all divine securities in order to "become obedient to the point of death, even death on a cross" (Phil 2:7–8). The call for Christians to participate in the life of Christ is, first and foremost, the participation in this grand narrative of *in*security, in which we surrender all our false securities and become willing to bear the insecurities of a suffering world.

Moreover, Luther teaches us some very practical lessons that aim to protect against false securities that arise in the very practice of reading Scripture. The first of these is the recognition that we do not so much *interpret* Scripture but that God's intention in our reading of Scripture is the opportunity for Scripture to mold and shape and form and transform us—to allow the Potter to mold the clay and unveil the treasure hidden in these vessels of clay (2 Cor 4:7). The second key practical lesson is the warning that no one of us can ever have the absolute, correct reading of Scripture for all time. Thus, we should proceed with humility and charity for our fellow Christians, as we learn to discern together what the Spirit says to the churches of our day. A third lesson is that our readings of Scripture should not lead us to a triumphalist stance but, rather, more deeply into the virtue and fruits of humility.

Though I have emphasized the positives that Luther has to offer us in his teachings on security in the Psalms and, specifically, how these relate to the art of reading Scripture, this is not to say that Luther was himself a perfect embodiment of the virtues and practices he espoused. Even as he claimed that there was no one right interpretation of Scripture, he was quite certain that his own readings of Scripture were better than his contemporary Roman Catholics' readings and better than Jewish readings.[55] This leads to a serious question for Christian readers today. What is the faithful way to address differences in interpretation or even "heresies" and "enemies" in our midst? On the one hand, Luther's example reveals that admitting that there is no one right interpretation of Scripture for all time does *not* mean that one has to give up a strong sense of conviction; it does not mean that we give up on the importance of naming sin and even heresy. On the other hand, it should be conviction tempered with humility, a humility that recognizes we are all trying to "make progress in the understanding of Scripture."[56] In the end, perhaps the best thing we

---

55. Indeed, one of the aspects of Luther's biblical exegesis that most concerns me is how anti-Jewish it tends to be. Luther more often than not reads the Jews in the biblical texts as the crucifiers of Christ who have rejected Christ and thus are abandoned by God. In this way he has effectively excised the Jews from any possible participation in the grand salvation story of the triune God. It is my contention that this kind of anti-Judaism is one of the first "sins of security" committed by early Christians and perpetuated still to this day: namely, in seeking the security of "the truth" over and against Jews and Judaism, many Christians have promulgated a history of exegesis that condones various kinds of violence and denigration of persons, beginning with the Jews and moving broadly outward from that. This is not the faithful exegesis that begins with the virtue of humility and participates in the virtue of the self-giving love of Christ that seeks the end of all forms of violence and terror.

56. LW 11:433. Here I find Rowan Williams's article, "The Literal Sense of Scripture" (*Modern Theology* 7 [1991]: 121–34) extremely helpful. Williams appeals for a diachronic reading of Scripture that envelops the processes of the "history of counter-claims and debate," in which there are limits set to pluralism. As Williams so eloquently states, "What I am suggesting is that it is 'diachronic' reading of Scripture that gives us the 'interiority' of the text, and that this interiority is not a point of hidden clarity or security but a complex of interwoven processes; a production of meaning in the only mode available for material and temporal creatures.... Christ is 'produced' by the history of the covenant people in a way that is both continuous with, even internal to, the history of its conflicts; yet, as the focal point for the unity of a new people with a new history, he is also for the believer a gratuitous and unpredictable moment in the whole process. This double perception is one way of stating the basic Christological duality behind the classical formula of Chalcedon ... We are not spared the cost of conflict or promised a final theological resolution; rather, we are assured of the possibility of 're-producing' the meaning that is Christ crucified and risen, through our commitment to an unavoidably divided Church—not by the effort to reconcile at all costs, but by carrying the burdens of conflict in the face of that unifying judgment bodied forth in preaching and sacrament ... what matters is not our ability to finish our business or to secure consensus, as if Christ would be 'audible' only in this mode, but our readiness to decide, to

can ask is, "What fruits does my reading of Scripture bear?" Does it bear the fruit of humility? Does it teach and embody the true worship of God, in which I rightly give both my trust and my fear to God alone? Does it call and assist the church to embody Christ in the world, or on the contrary, does it lead to pride, presumption, apathy, or triumphalism? Is it not more important that our readings of Scripture deeply form us in the virtues of humility, charity, peace, faith, hope, and justice than that we be so-called "right"?

In conclusion, I also want to point out that Luther's specific teachings on security also suggest some important wisdom needed for the particular political, economic, and social contexts in which we find ourselves today. Christians in the United States, particularly, are surrounded on all sides with the temptation toward security: the temptation toward prosperity, economic security, and consumerism; the temptation to trust in the power of "princes" to secure our borders and protect our land; the temptation to a life of ease and convenience; and the temptation to trust in our own selves and our own devices and technologies. Luther cuts to the chase to demonstrate most clearly that all of these are idolatry before God. Furthermore, he reminds us that *both* our trust and our *fear* belong rightfully to God alone. Letting fear guide our actions is just another form of idolatry. While Luther may not adequately challenge issues of state and political security (I leave that to the other essays in this volume), he does prophetically remind the church that it must resist all of these temptations and instead seek to live faithfully in the world by embodying the virtues of humility, godly fear, and proper faith and trust in God alone. In these things is found the true worship of God, by which we can learn to resist our temptations toward idolatry. Luther warns that giving in to the temptation of security inhibits the church's zeal for God, ability to see truly, effectiveness in preaching and prayer, and ability to name and confess sin. Finally, he unveils for the church that seeking security is dangerous to faithful readings of Scripture both because of its tendencies toward pride and presumption and also because, while it is not the church's call deliberately to seek suffering, it is also not her call deliberately to avoid it. Indeed, to participate in the life of Christ and his offer of salvation to the world always involves in some way a willingness to participate in his suffering and to bear the sufferings of others.

---

take sides, as adult persons, and to live with the consequence and cost of that within the disciplines we share with other Christians of openness to the judgment of the Easter mystery" (129–30, 132). In this way, for example, it does not so much matter if we agree with Luther that the key teaching of Scripture is justification by faith alone (or if we even think this is a correct doctrine). What matters is that in the larger history, Luther is one of the important conflicting voices in the church's attempt to discern the truth of Scripture.

# RESPONSE TO PAK

## *Jo Ann Deasy*

This past month the International Federation of Evangelical Free Churches met in Germany. On the agenda was the issue of women's roles in the church, including women's ordination. As with most debates in the evangelical world, the debate over women's ordination generally focuses on the correct interpretation of Scripture. Both sides seek to prove that their interpretation is more biblical or historical, often charging the opposing camp with holding to a lesser view of biblical authority. One could only be "secure" in his or her position when one was sure one had the "right" interpretation of Scripture. Evangelical books published on both sides of the issue seek to prove that they are the ones that have the true interpretation. One side seeks to "recover biblical manhood and womanhood" while the other argues for "biblical equality."

Students are left feeling they must be able to exegete a text like a biblical scholar in order to feel secure in their position. The debate itself raises significant issues about the interpretation of Scripture, in particular the role of history, tradition, practice, translation, and exegesis. More importantly, though, the debate raises significant questions about the relationship between security and biblical interpretation, a central theme in Prof. Pak's paper.

Prof. Pak explores Luther's three different responses to security: an argument against the false security offered by the church and sought after by the people of his day, an argument for a definition of true security grounded in God as our refuge and Christ as our high priest, and a caution about seeking security and expecting security as the normal state of the church. Prof. Pak then begins to consider the relationship between security and biblical interpretation in Luther's work. She focuses her conclusion on Luther's contention that "the temptation to security is not only dangerous to being a faithful interpreter of Scripture because of the tendencies toward pride and presumption but also because some of life's most important lessons can only be learned through affliction." I would like to propose, however, two additional points raised in her paper regarding the relationship between security and the interpretation of Scripture that I believe warrant further exploration, and then I want to raise a point of clarification.

As Prof. Pak begins her section on Luther's approach to the interpretation of Scripture, she places it in a Trinitarian framework, beginning with the Holy Spirit, moving on to Luther's christological focus, and grounding it all in the idea of God as our refuge. She begins by stating, "First and foremost, Luther views the interpretation of Scripture as a spiritual act, as an act that must be guided by the Holy Spirit for its correct practice and in order to attain faithful readings." Luther calls us to seek the guidance of the Holy Spirit as the only source of security in the interpretation of Scripture, but to do so with humility, recognizing that the Holy Spirit is not someone we can control or possess but is a gift from God. This begs the question as to how one seeks the Holy Spirit and how one might recognize when the Spirit is present.

Within the Pietist tradition the presence of the Holy Spirit was linked to pious living. In *Pia Desideria* Spener draws on the work of John Gerhard who wrote:

> "Those who are wanting in love of Christ and who neglect the practice of piety do not obtain the fuller knowledge of Christ and more abundant gift of the Holy Spirit. Hence to obtain a genuine, living, active, and salutary knowledge of divine things it is not enough to read and search the Scriptures, but it is necessary that love of Christ be added, that is that one beware of sins against conscience, by which an obstacle is raised against the Holy Spirit, and that one earnestly cultivate piety."[1]

Such piety was often defined by a personal morality but also included acts of compassion that were an expression of love of God through love of neighbor. Within the evangelical world today, piety is still tied to personal morality but also often includes one's position on such matters as abortion, women's ordination, and homosexuality. I raise these questions not to debate these particular issues but to suggest that issues of morality have become deeply entwined with the evangelical understanding of security, particularly as it relates to the interpretation of Scripture. Having right beliefs about a certain set of moral principles is equated with having a right interpretation of Scripture. Is it possible that the desire for the right interpretation of Scripture has become a false idol of security promised by the church in our day?

Regardless, Prof. Pak's work suggests a connection between ethics and morality and the interpretation of Scripture in Luther's work. As she points out, for Luther one of the central goals of reading Scripture is the personal appropriation of the christological content of the text. She writes, "for Luther, it is not so much that the

---

1. *Pia Desideria* (Eugene, Ore.: Wipf and Stock, 2002), 106.

reader *interprets* Scripture as it is that Scripture transforms its readers." Ethics and morality then provide both the prerequisite for, as well as the result of, a true reading of Scripture. One must approach Scripture with a sense of insecurity, knowing that while you have attempted to live in obedience and love of Christ, in the reading of Scriptures you will be convicted, challenged, and transformed to reflect more fully a life in Christ.

Appealing to the Holy Spirit in the interpretation of Scripture has often destabilized and provided insecurity within the established church while providing a type of security for reform movements seeking to challenge the status quo. Appealing to the Holy Spirit has also served to challenge the morality and authority of the established church, particularly challenging historical interpretations of Scripture. It seems though that Luther, rather than appealing to the Holy Spirit to destabilize the authority of the church, appealed to Christ. As Prof. Pak points out, Luther's head-member analogy of Christ's relationship to the church is also central in his interpretation of Scripture. Luther's appeal to Christ as the only head and the only high priest shifted the understanding of the church and the priesthood away from the sacramental and towards the functional. In doing so it elevated the status of the laity and empowered them to participate in the interpretation of Scripture. A christological focus destabilized the authority of the church and provided security for the laity in the interpretation of Scripture.

While Luther's christological focus is crucial, it also led to a strident anti-Jewish sentiment that polluted much of his interpretation. Prof. Pak contends that Luther's anti-Jewish sentiment arises from his "rather flat reading of the salvation narrative when he reads the Psalms concerning the literal-historical events of the crucifixion . . . rather than reading it through a much grander and broader salvation narrative that would . . . identify *ourselves* as the crucifiers of Christ." In a sense Prof. Pak is arguing that Luther failed to apply his own concept of humility, recognizing salvation as a gift from God, to his own interpretation of Scripture. It may be outside the scope of the paper, but I would have been interested in hearing further reflections on how Luther's understanding of security related to his understanding of the "other." In this case Luther's security in Christ comes at the expense of the Jews. It seems that often in seeking security in our interpretations of the faith we must also create an other who is "insecure" or outside. For Luther, the "other" took on many forms, such as the Roman Catholic Church, the Jews, or the peasants who revolted against the government. The more we seek security in our own positions, the more we characterize the "other" as less than, outside the scope of salvation, not fully in the image of God, not fully human.

So far I have addressed the pneumatological and the christological in Luther's interpretation of Scripture. There is focus on the third person of the Trinity in the first half of the paper, but more may be merited. I would also raise one further question for discussion and clarification. Up to this point I have been using the term security without providing much of a definition of the term. For the most part, I have been referring to a sense of confidence in one's position, an assurance that one is in the right or has found the truth. As Prof. Pak points out, Luther uses security in a variety of ways referring to assurance of truth, assurance of salvation, physical safety and financial well-being. I am unclear how the various aspects of security relate to one another in Luther's theology. Luther speaks strongly against the dangers of prosperity and of the role of adversity in keeping the eyes open and the heart and mind watchful, which suggests a link between economic security and the interpretation of Scripture. Prof. Pak suggests that this is not a call for the church to seek such adversity but rather a call to be open to participating in Christ's suffering and to bear the suffering of others. While I do not think that the church is always called to pursue suffering, I do believe that in the United States many churches have made economic security into a false idol and the pursuit of adversity, a sacrificing on behalf of others, might be exactly what is needed for eyes that are open to the formative work of Scripture in our lives.

# "ONE WHO TRUSTS WILL NOT PANIC"
## Providence and the Prophet of Desecuritization

## *Jill Carlson Colwell*

*Imagine: you are the king of a small country. To the north are two other small kingdoms, one of which had at one time been joined with yours. On their own neither of these nations might seem to represent much of a threat. But now they band together and attack your city, your kingdom, in the hopes of overthrowing your government and deposing you. You are terrified. What can you do? Your army is small, your resources are few, and, despite the similar limitations of your opponents, two against one hardly puts the odds in your favor.*

*But beyond the borders of these enemy nations, further north, lies a great and powerful empire, with military might surpassing anything you or your attackers can imagine. Perhaps you can appeal to this empire for protection—send a tribute, pledge your allegiance—so that they will intervene on your behalf and abolish the threat. Security for you and your people seems to depend on your finding some way—any way—to obtain the military power to defeat your enemies, whatever the cost or consequences.*

King Ahaz of Judah may have lived nearly three thousand years ago, but the fear and desperation which overcame him in 734 BC bear an uncomfortable similarity to the prevailing sentiments that have hovered over the fragile dawn of the twenty-first century. For many people around the world threats to life, livelihood, and self-determination constitute the daily realities of existence, but those of us who live in the United States have not always been as acutely aware of our own vulnerability. Since September 11, 2001, however, "security" has become the catchword for American anxiety in the face of international instability, religious and cultural conflicts at home and abroad, and the changing face of the global economy. Political rhetoric is dominated by the demand for "security," and candidates and policies are evaluated by both the media and the public in terms of whom or what is most likely to make us "secure."

What "security" actually means, and to what extent it should be valued, are questions that are rarely voiced in this political climate. It is generally assumed that we know what we mean when we talk about "security." As international relations scholar James Der Derian puts it, "We have inherited an *ontotheology* of security, that is, an *a priori* argument that proves the existence and necessity of only one form of security because there currently happens to be a widespread, metaphysical belief in it."[1] Der Derian notes that, contrary to the implicit meaning and value we habitually ascribe to it, the word "security" has not always carried positive connotations. In addition to its more familiar usage to signify a condition of safety or protection, "security" at one time had alternate meanings that have since slipped from conventional usage. Der Derian cites numerous sermon texts from the sixteenth through nineteenth centuries in which "security" was condemned as "a careless, hubristic, even damnable overconfidence,"[2] and also recalls that it was with this sense that Shakespeare used it to describe the fault which brought about the downfall of Macbeth: "And you all know, security/Is mortals' chiefest enemy."[3] The Westminster Confession draws upon similar implications when declaring that the reason that the Day of Judgment remains unknown to believers is so "that they may shake off all carnal security."[4] Even those who use the customary definition have not always presumed that security is an unqualified good. Nietzsche, for one, saw security in terms of a need to protect ourselves by control and conformity from all that is different, uncertain, and unknown; from this he concludes, "And has not the world lost some of its charm for us because we have grown less fearful?"[5]

The lost charm of an uncertain world was certainly not what troubled King Ahaz of Judah when Israel and Aram (Syria) banded together to attack Jerusalem in the eighth century B.C. As the book of Isaiah records it, "the heart of Ahaz and the heart of his people shook as the trees of the forest shake before the wind" (Isa 7:2).[6] Here, as elsewhere, the prophet counsels the leaders of Judah not to fear but rather to trust God for their protection. However, Ahaz does fear and acting upon his fear he pursues an alliance with Assyria that goes against the prophet's counsel. Seeking security at the expense of following the will of God leads to disasters far worse than Ahaz had initially dreaded. In almost the next breath, and repeatedly throughout the

---

1. James Der Derian, "The Value of Security: Hobbes, Marx, Nietzsche, and Baudrillard," in *On Security* (ed. Ronnie D. Lipschutz; New York: Columbia University Press, 1995), 24–45, 25.

2. Ibid., 28.

3. William Shakespeare, *Macbeth*, 3.5.32–33.

4. *Westminster Confession of Faith* 33.3.

5. Friedrich Nietzsche, *Daybreak,* 551; quoted in Der Derian, "The Value of Security," 36.

6. All biblical references are from the New Revised Standard Version.

text, Isaiah makes it clear that Ahaz and the people of Judah have very good reasons to tremble in the face of the one power that truly can bring them harm: God. The only real threat to Ahaz or his people is from the Lord who controls all of history, who will punish their faithlessness by causing the safety they seek from Assyria to redound on them as peril. As Walter Brueggemann puts it, for Isaiah God is both our only real problem and our only real possibility.[7]

The fear of the Lord, as Isaiah portrays it, has the potential to displace all other fears and reorient our desire for security towards its proper object and ends. But, how can we both fear God and trust God—that is, how can we trust for our security a God who gives us such cause to fear? In this paper I will examine the import of God's providential governance of the world for how we should value security and what we should do in its name.[8] The relationship between divine governance and political action is foregrounded by the book of Isaiah through its presentation of God's absolute dominion over history. This is a theme that was also vital to John Calvin, who, perhaps more than any other theologian, worked rigorously to explicate the details and difficulties to which belief in divine sovereignty gives rise. Calvin's nuanced understanding of God's governance will be used here both to elaborate the theological motifs found in Isaiah and to begin framing a providential ethic of security and risk. To begin, however, I will examine some recent critiques of the traditional notion of security which have emerged from the subfield of "Security Studies" within International Relations. Borrowing the speech-act conceptualization of security developed by the scholars of "New Security Studies," I will argue that the doctrine of providence can be seen as a resource for "desecuritization," by which "threats" are converted into "challenges" and our responses to such threats are brought faithfully into line with our deepest beliefs and values.

---

7. Walter Brueggemann, *Isaiah 1–39* (Louisville: Westminster John Knox, 1998), 77–80.

8. I use the first person and make specific reference to contemporary situations here merely in order to engage the reader in considering with me the resonances of the text's themes of fear and trust for our time (and, indeed, for any time). It is not my intention to equate Judah—or Assyria, though this may in some ways be more fitting!—with the United States, or with the church, or with any other modern entity. Reading ourselves or others too easily into the text by means of such an analogy is deeply problematic for both historical and hermeneutical reasons, and it is because of this that I have adopted a theological interpretation as most appropriate for addressing the issues. In other words, I consider that it is precisely by turning to the theological questions evoked by the text—that is, what does it say about who God is, and how God acts in the world, and what God requires of those who seek right relationship with God—that such pitfalls can be avoided, or at least mitigated.

## From Insecurity to "Desecuritization"

According to the classic formulation by Hobbes, life without security would be "solitary, poore, nasty, brutish, and short."[9] In this view security underlies all other values and is their prerequisite; consequently, the pursuit of security is the primary task and motivation of states. This is the position which has dominated the study of international relations and politics since World War Two through its leading schools of thought, realism and neo-realism. Prominent neorealist Kenneth Waltz based his argument for the preeminence of security on the anarchical nature of the international system, that is, the fact that there is no formal government at the international level that regulates the interests and activities of states. "In anarchy," he claimed, "security is the highest end. Only if survival is assured can states seek such other goals as tranquility, profit, and power."[10] Order and security are preserved in an anarchic system through the balance of power and through war; war is seen as necessary to both preserve the balance and to resolve conflict. For realism and its variations military power is privileged as the means by which states assert and defend their interests on the global stage. The Cold War provided the resonant backdrop for the ascendancy of realist thought; international relations in this context was all too easily viewed as inherently dangerous, defined and determined by the fear and insecurity which were seen as its enduring features.[11]

Although neorealism still retains much of its primacy, especially in the United States and among policy makers, the fall of the Berlin Wall and the changes in the international order at the end of the twentieth century sparked a renaissance in "Security Studies" in which multiple critiques and alternatives began to surface. The assumption that the state is both the agent and "referent object" of security has been challenged in light of both the rising significance of nonstate actors on the international stage—from corporations and nongovernment agencies to terrorists—and the recognition that, in many cases, the state represents more of a threat to its own citizens than do external forces.[12] Some security scholars have also challenged the field's focus on military and strategic concerns, noting that environmental (e.g., global warming), social (immigration, loss of cultural identity), and economic

---

9. Thomas Hobbes, *Leviathan* (London: Andrew Crooke, 1651), part 1, chapter 13.

10. Kenneth Waltz, *Theory of International Politics* (Reading, Mass.: Addison-Wesley, 1979), 126.

11. See Chris Brown, *Understanding International Relations* (2d ed.; New York: Palgrave, 2001), 99–100.

12. For the latter argument, see Caroline Thomas, *In Search of Security: The Third World in International Relations* (Brighton: Harvester Wheatsheaf, 1987).

(unemployment, resource scarcity) issues may present greater perils than invasion or military attack.[13] Others have noted that security defined in the traditional way is an essentially conservative concept, as under its purview the *status quo* is defended—regardless of its merits—against the instability of change. These and other arguments have led to a reintroduction of normative concerns into the discourse of international relations, as theorists and practitioners dispute *who* or *what* is to be secured, against *what, by whom,* and *with what means*?

The Copenhagen school, also known as the proponents of "New Security Studies," began their work as a response to the problems raised by attempts to broaden the agenda of security studies. Traditional security theorists objected to the inclusion of nonmilitary issues on the security agenda, arguing that the concept became incoherent once security began to encompass such disparate concerns.[14] More sympathetic critics argued that to speak of things such as environmental degradation as security threats might entail uncritically importing the state-centric, militarist assumptions of security discourse into an arena where such approaches could be inappropriate and counterproductive.[15] The Copenhagen School has sought to address these challenges by defining security in such a way as to make it applicable across various categories ("sectors") of threats.[16] Rather than describing security as an ontological state or value, the Copenhagen scholars adopt a constructivist approach by focusing on the act or process of "securitization" through which an issue is formulated as a security threat and granted an urgency that legitimizes responses exceeding the bounds of what would normally be considered acceptable. "Securitization," in their view, is "inter-subjective and socially constructed": something does not become a security threat until we identify and grant it validity as such.[17] This is not to say that there is no objective reality to the problems or enemies that might be branded as

---

13. See, for example, Jessica Tuchman Mathews, "Redefining Security," *Foreign Affairs* 68 (1989): 162–77; Barry Buzan, *People, States and Fear: An Agenda for International Security Studies in the Post-Cold War Era* (2d ed.; Boulder, Colo.: Lynne Rienner, 1991); and, from a policy perspective, United Nations Development Program, *Human Development Report 1994: New Dimensions of Human Security* (New York: Oxford University Press, 1994).

14. See, for example, Stephen Walt, "The Renaissance of Security Studies," *International Studies Quarterly* 35 (1991): 211–39.

15. See, for example, Daniel Deudney, "The Case Against Linking Environmental Degradation and National Security," *Millennium* 19 (1990): 461–76.

16. The analysis of various threats to security in terms of "sectors" was first taken up by Buzan in *People, States and Fear.*

17. Barry Buzan, Ole Waever, and Jaap de Wilde, *Security: A New Framework for Analysis* (Boulder, Colo.: Lynne Rienner, 1998), 31.

security threats, but it does mean that there is a subjective element with regard to how threats are classified and measured. Security, after all, is about the future, "about alternative futures—always hypothetical."[18] It involves the examination of possibilities: what will happen if we do (or do not do) X about Y? To apply the security label is thus always a choice: it may have causes, but it also has alternatives, and it has consequences.

Borrowing from language theory, "new security" theorist Ole Waever describes security as a "speech act":[19] as with making a promise, naming something as a security issue is a performative utterance. When an actor (for example, a state representative or government official) claims that an issue is of such priority and urgency that it must be dealt with immediately and by extraordinary means, this declaration itself *makes* the issue a matter of security. "Securitization" is thus the process, by which something is "presented as an existential threat.[20] An act of securitization involves claiming a right to break the rules—to be exempted from the usual constraints and debate involved in political decisions in order to defend against something that is considered too threatening to be subjected to the laws and mores of less urgent times. The use of force, the expansion of executive powers, and the resort to secret or otherwise illegal tactics are among the means that a securitizing actor seeks to justify or claim a right to use in combating the threat. Military conflicts almost invariably are securitized,[21] but there is nothing about the logic of securitization that suggests that environmental or social challenges cannot also be elevated to the mode of "security," if proper legitimization is obtained through a successful securitizing speech act.[22]

What is somewhat unique about the approach of the Copenhagen school among security scholars is that they do not presume that security is always an unqualified good. In fact, they argue that "security should be seen as a negative, a failure to deal

---

18. Ibid., 32.

19. Ole Waever, "Securitization and Desecuritization," in *On Security*, ( ed. R. D. Lipschutz; New York: Columbia Univeristy Press, 1995), 55; see also Buzan, Waever, and de Wilde, *Security*, 26.

20. Buzan, Waever, and de Wilde, *Security*, 23–24.

21. Buzan, Waever, and de Wilde argue that securitization becomes institutionalized in cases such as national defense; that is, the issue remains securitized and a new security speech act is not needed for it to retain its status as such: "It is implicitly assumed that when we talk of *this* (typically, but not necessarily, defense issues), we are by definition in the area of urgency: by saying 'defense' (or, in Holland, 'dikes'), one has also implicitly said security and priority" (ibid., 27).

22. Buzan, Waever, and de Wilde note that securitizations do not always succeed. In order to be successful a security speech act must not only be uttered but must also be accepted by the relevant audience. Acceptance, however, may entail a certain amount of coercion (ibid., 25).

with issues as normal politics."[23] To deal with an issue politically is to make it open to debate and subject to the constraints of what a community considers to be the moral and legal limitations on its actions and reactions. Since securitizations tend to be enacted by the elite and powerful, security can be used to silence opposition, maintain or enhance political power, and suspend democratic principles.[24] While the Copenhagen scholars grant that securitization may in certain instances have tactical advantages and in others be unavoidable, they nevertheless emphasize that political actors need to weigh the costs of this decision and be responsible for its outcomes.[25] "Desecuritization"—moving issues out of this "threat-defense sequence" and restoring them to the public sphere—is "the optimal long-range option."[26]

## "Do Not Call Conspiracy..."

In the midst of the Syro-Ephraimite crisis, after the king has refused the prophet's counsel and sought military reinforcements from Assyria, Isaiah receives a word from God that is addressed directly to him for his comfort or perhaps correction. It begins with the admonishment "not to walk in the way of this people" (Isa 8:11). What this "way" is becomes apparent from the exhortations that follow: Isaiah is to resist the "panic politics"[27] that have swept through Judea filling the people with terror and driving them to seek and approve drastic measures in the hopes of securing their salvation from harm. "Do not call conspiracy all that this people calls conspiracy," says the Lord, "and do not fear what it fears, or be in dread" (Isa 8:12). To "call conspiracy" is an act of naming; by it, the treachery of the "conspirators" is labeled and their nefarious intent declared, and the kingdom is implicitly accorded a certain status as that which is jeopardized.[28] Such a declaration can be seen as

---

23. Ibid., 29. It might also be worth noting the similarities between the Copenhagen School's critical analysis of the process of securitization and Carl Schmitt's defense of dictatorship, which entailed the argument that the defining feature of sovereignty was the ability of the executive to declare the "state of exception" and suspend the rule of law. Without this authority, according to Schmitt, the state would be incapable of effective action. See *The Concept of the Political* (Chicago: University of Chicago Press, 1932). Whatever his other contributions to political philosophy, Schmitt is perhaps best known for using this argument to champion Hitler and the Nazi regime.

24. Buzan, Waever, and de Wilde, *Security*, 29.

25. Ibid., 211.

26. Ibid., 29.

27. Buzan, Waever, and de Wilde assert that to make something a security issue is "to transfer it to the agenda of panic politics" (ibid., 34).

28. Clements and Seitz both interpret "conspiracy" to refer, not to the collusion of Israel and Aram

a security speech act, performed initially by Ahaz or his representatives, with the "people" filling the role of the accepting and enabling audience. God's instruction to Isaiah is, in effect, to resist the public securitization of this threat.

The divine injunction not to fear is offered as consolation and assurance elsewhere in the biblical testimony—think, for example, of the angel telling Mary and the shepherds not to be afraid, but in this context it can hardly be seen as comforting. God does not tell Isaiah, "Do not fear, for all will be well"; rather, God offers the far more disquieting suggestion, "Do not fear *this*; rather fear *me*." Isaiah's terror is not discouraged, but redirected: "But the LORD of Hosts, him you shall regard as holy; let him be your fear, and let him be your dread" (Isa 8:13). To regard God as holy is to reverence God, and it is with this sense that we usually construe "the fear of the Lord." The emphasis here, however, is on God's absolute power and sovereignty. As the "Lord of Hosts" God inspires fear, not in the sense merely of awe, but of representing a real and concrete danger to God's people before which they should, in fact, tremble. The Lord of Hosts is the only one truly capable of the devastation the Judeans fear,[29] and it is God's declared intention to inflict this upon them! God may be their only refuge against the storm they face, but the refuge is far more fearsome than the storm: "He will become a sanctuary, a stone one strikes against; for both houses of Israel he will become a rock one stumbles over, a trap and a snare for the inhabitants of Jerusalem" (Isa 8:14–15).

How has the sanctuary of God's protection, the rock of God's faithful preservation, turned into a trap and a snare? The message which the prophet delivers to the people alternates purposefully between comfort and condemnation, between promise and threat. Ahaz is given assurance that the coalition that assaults him will not succeed (Isa 7:7); this is an implicit reminder of the promise made to David that God will uphold the monarchy for his descendants (2 Sam 7:16). The prophet warns him, "If you do not stand firm in faith, you shall not stand at all" (Isa 7:7), but Ahaz refuses to trust in the promises given by God and out of fear turns elsewhere for

---

against Judah, but rather to accusations of treason made against the prophet himself. However, this seems unintelligible as something regarding which the prophet would stand in need of divine correction. Moreover, this rendering does not cohere with the subsequent clauses; that is, why would the prophet be at risk of wrongly fearing himself? For these reasons I have followed Brueggemann in accepting the more obvious meaning of the text, which is that the "conspiracy" refers to the imminent peril of Judah at the hands of the Syro-Ephraimite coalition. See Brueggemann, *Isaiah 1–39*, 78; R. E. Clements, *Isaiah 1–39* (Grand Rapids: Eerdmans, 1980), 99; Christopher B. Seitz, *Isaiah 1–39* (Louisville: Westminster John Knox, 1993), 82.

29. As Brueggemann puts it, "What if Yahweh is the only 'conspiracy,' and all else is paranoia?" (*Isaiah 1–39*, 80).

security. The prophecy that Aram and Israel will fall and no longer pose a threat to the kingdom of Judah is fulfilled, but by rejecting Isaiah's counsel and God's protection Ahaz sets in motion a greater catastrophe than the one he sought to avert. The armies of the Assyrians which he summoned will indeed come, but they will not stop with Judah's enemies. God will use Assyria to punish Ahaz and the people for their faithlessness.

These circumstances are recapitulated through an evocative but enigmatic metaphor: the people have refused "the waters of Shiloah that flow gently" and instead "melt in fear" before their adversaries (Isa 8:6). Most commentators understand the "waters of Shiloah" to refer to a conduit or stream that brought water into Jerusalem from a nearby spring. This stream would have constituted the water supply for the city, nurturing the inhabitants and providing fortification in times of siege.[30] Seitz interprets these waters as symbolizing "indigenous sustenance,"[31] which for the people of Judah depended upon their unique covenantal relationship with God. The protection and promise of God might have seemed to them like a slow and steady stream, adequate and almost invisible in times of peace, but far too sluggish and mild to inspire confidence in a moment of crisis. In panic, the people look longingly towards the "mighty river," which symbolizes "external power and might," and they seek to secure themselves by appeal to a massive display of force. The actual river of Assyria, the Euphrates, was prone to ruinous floods, and the metaphor is extended to signal just such a disaster: "it will rise above all its channels and overflow all its banks; it will sweep away Judah as a flood, and, pouring over, it will reach up to the neck" (Isa 8:7–8). It is precisely when under attack that the gentle stream that feeds the city becomes most vital, but the city scorns its true source of sustenance and is consequently overwhelmed by the ferocity it sought to unleash in its defense.

The text makes it clear, however, that this flood is not a natural disaster: it is *God* who brings up the mighty waters to destroy the city and its inhabitants. Assyria, says the Lord, is "the rod of my anger—the club in their hands is my fury!" (Isa 10:5). God is the one who inflicts the harm performed by the violence of the invading armies who are but God's instruments. This invocation of a menacing Almighty is consistent with the understanding of God's relationship to creation which prevails throughout the prophet's testimony. For Isaiah God is in absolute control of the world and the events of history, both in terms of its blessings and its perils. Therefore, faithlessness, the refusal to trust God, amounts to denying that God is sovereign over all

---

30. See, for example, Clements, *Isaiah 1–39*, 96.

31. Seitz, *Isaiah 1–39*, 81.

of history. The theological affirmation of God's providential governance results in practical, concrete obligations with regard to how life is lived and decisions made, regardless of the circumstances. The faith to which the people are called, and for the lack of which they are punished, is not merely a matter of cognitive assent. Faith means, as Brueggemann puts it, "to entrust one's security and future to the attentiveness of Yahweh—to count God's attentiveness as adequate and sure, thereby making panic, anxiety, or foolishness unnecessary and inappropriate."[32] It is not that Ahaz has made a strategic mistake by underestimating the imperial designs of Assyria, though this may also have been the case. Ahaz's error is to have underestimated the sovereignty of God over all plans and all nations and to have put his trust in something other than this divine governance.

Divine wrath and retribution is not, of course, the end of the story. The oracles of the prophet return again to proclaim words of consolation: the Lord promises to break "the rod of their oppressor" (Isa 9:4) and to usher in a time of "endless peace for the throne of David and his kingdom" (Isa 9:7). Such reassurances may not suffice for modern readers who are unaccustomed to a worldview in which God causes suffering and inflicts devastation both on God's own chosen people and on other nations. Does this not make God the author of evil? Moreover, does this mean that all misery and torment is indicative of divine wrath against the sinful, faithless, or arrogant? In other words, are we to blame the victims and justify their oppressors, since both affliction and achievement are ordained by the hand of God?

To have faith in God's providential governance of history means at the very least that we cannot live and act as if securing ourselves were up to us, to accomplish in whatever manner seems most expedient. Submitting our quest for security to the faithful acknowledgement of God's governance of the world is therefore a powerful act of *desecuritization*. Since the only power that can truly harm or save us is God, all other "threats" are turned into "challenges"[33] to be faced with the full confidence that there is no need which abrogates the law and command of God and no true protection apart from obedience to God's call. By revealing God's providential rule of history in the context of an international political crisis and calling his people to a deep trust in God's promise and power, Isaiah positions himself as a prophet of desecuritization, providing reasons and resources for resisting the agenda of "panic

---

32. Brueggemann, *Isaiah 1–39*, 67.

33. Waever borrows this characterization from Egbert Jahn in explicating the process of desecuritization. See "Securitization and Desecuritization," 55.

politics" and restoring the relevance of our most sacred values and norms for even the most ominous moments of life.

The difficulties raised by assertions of divine sovereignty in a world of sin and suffering are neither exhausted nor resolved by Isaiah's treatment of divine governance. For these reasons it is tempting to abandon the idea of a sovereign God and rely on ourselves to insure our own security. In his commentary on Isaiah, John Calvin noted that "there is nothing of which it is more difficult to convince men than that the providence of God governs this world."[34] Calvin himself was an exile; he had fled the country of his birth in fear and watched streams of refugees follow him to Geneva without ever knowing whether his homeland would be a place of safety again. For us as well as for him, to think of history in terms of God's providential care is both unnatural and countercultural, and it raises numerous theological difficulties even, or perhaps especially, for Christians who believe in a loving God. But, it is precisely the radical claim that this doctrine[35] makes on us that gives it the potential to transform our fears and revive our faith, reorienting ourselves and our actions towards the will of God.

## "The Deep Labyrinth of Secret Providence"

It is difficult to imagine a more zealous advocate of divine providential governance than the reformer who made the sovereignty of God the cornerstone of his writings, sermons, and civic and ecclesiastical polity. In keeping with the Isaiah tradition and often with specific reference to it, Calvin denied that fortune or chance play any part in human affairs,[36] insisting instead that God "governs all events," such that "nothing

---

34. From *Commentary on the Book of the Prophet Isaiah* (trans. William Pringle, 4 vols.; Grand Rapids: Eerdmans, 1948), 13:1. References to this commentary are hereafter abbreviated using *Comm. on Is*. Brueggemann echoes Calvin's claim in his assertion that "It is easy (easier!) to perceive reality in terms of practical politics than it is to situate a decisive Yahweh at its center. According to the prophetic tradition, however, such a construal of reality is deeply misjudged and will never bring security, well-being, or joy" (Brueggemann, *Isaiah 1–39*, 90).

35. By "doctrine," I do not mean a rigid theological truth-claim but rather a locus of theological inquiry. The doctrine of providence is the arena wherein Christians have traditionally discussed how it is that God remains involved in the world postcreation. There are many ways in which this can and has been conceived. I have considered Calvin's rather exhaustive treatment of the issue in order to elucidate some of the possible implications of providential thinking for the question at hand. Calvin's is not the only way to frame these questions, yet I think that aspects of his reasoning provide resources for thinking through how any assertion of God's providential governance of the world can help to reorient our thinking on security.

36. With regard to Isa 7:4, Calvin asserts that "Nothing takes at random or by chance, but that

happens except what is knowingly and willingly decreed by him" (*Inst.* 1.16.3). Not content to assert that God merely sustains the created order or only occasionally intrudes in miraculous ways, Calvin contended that God is the active, controlling, and determinative agent and cause of everything that exists and happens in the world. This divine control applies to the rise and fall of kingdoms, but no less to the rising and setting of the sun; the latter is as dependent on a specific act of God as is the former. Calvin was willing to speak of an "order of nature" which God established at creation and sustains through universal providence,[37] but this "order" is at every instant governed by God's determination. Special providence in its most meticulous sense thus applies to even the most everyday of occurrences: "It is certain," Calvin wrote, "that not one drop of rain falls without God's sure command" (*Inst.* 1.16.5).[38]

Calvin was well aware of the most serious objections that this position raised for his contemporaries, namely, that it seems to make God the author of evil and suggests that human beings have no free will and hence no responsibility for their actions. Still, he resisted what he seemed to view as the untenable evasion that God merely permits evil but does not cause it. For Calvin the omnipotence of the sovereign God meant, not that God is merely capable of doing whatever God wants, yet instead sits idly in heaven and observes what goes on below, but rather that God causally determines everything that happens.[39] Providence "pertains no less to

---

everything is governed by the hand of God." (*Comm. on Is.* 7:4). Elsewhere he echoes this theme: "God so attends to the regulation of individual events, and they all so proceed from his set plan, that nothing takes place by chance." See *Institutes of the Christian Religion* (ed. J. T. McNeill; trans. Ford Lewis Battles; 2 vols., Library of Christian Classics, vols. 20 and 21; Philadelphia: Westminster, 1960), 1.16.4. References to "The Institutes" are hereafter abbreviated using *Inst.* Calvin also states that "nothing happens by chance, but only in accordance with His counsel and judgment. And He is sorely angry whenever we think that these things occur by other means or whenever we fail to look up to Him, recognizing Him not only as the principal cause of everything, but also as the author, whom by His counsel disposes as He wills." See "Against the Libertines" in *Treatises Against the Anabaptists and Against the Libertines* (ed. and trans. Benjamin Wirt Farley; Grand Rapids: Baker, 1982), 244. References to this treatise are hereafter abbreviated using TAL.

37. See, for example, TAL, 243.

38. Also, "no wind ever arises or increases except by God's express command" (*Inst.* 1.16.7).

39. "For he is deemed omnipotent, not because he can indeed act, yet sometimes ceases and sits in idleness, or continues by a general impulse that order of nature which he previously appointed; but because, governing heaven and earth by his providence, he so regulates all things that nothing takes place without his deliberation" (*Inst.* 1.16.3). Also: "*The will of God* is the one principal and all-high *cause* of all things in heaven and earth!" From "Defence of the Secret Providence of God," *Calvin's Calvinism* (trans. Henry Cole; Grand Rapids: Eerdmans, 1950), 246. References to this treatise are hereafter abbreviated using DSPG.

[God's] hands than to his eyes" (*Inst.* 1.16.4).⁴⁰ Even in the midst of calamities which seem to call into question the goodness of God, God's providential governance is active and absolute. With regard to Isaiah's depiction of Assyria as "the rod of [God's] anger," Calvin reflects, "Whether, therefore, we are attacked by tyrants or robbers, or any other person, or foreign nations rise up against us, let us always plainly see the hand of God amidst the greatest agitation and confusion, and let us not suppose that anything happens by chance" (*Comm. on Is.* 10:5).

Yet, if God is in control of even the most severe tribulations and unimaginable horrors of life and history, does this not mean that God commits evil? To defend the goodness of God, Calvin turned to the notion of secondary causality as a way to explain how God works through human sin without being sullied by it. All things are caused by God, Calvin alleged, but God uses intermediaries as instruments of his providence. This is true not only for the blessings and benefits that God confers but also for the afflictions which God uses to test, chastise, and punish even the faithful. "Thieves and murderers and other evildoers are the instruments of divine providence," Calvin claimed, "and the Lord himself uses these to carry out the judgments that he has determined with himself" (*Inst.* 1.17.5). This, Calvin insisted, does not mean that God perpetrates evil. God's will is the ruling cause, but not the only cause, of what occurs: "Satan and evildoers are not so effectively the instruments of God that they do not also act on their own behalf."⁴¹ To explain how God remains guiltless in the sin his intermediaries commit, Calvin made a distinction between the motives of the evildoer and those of God. "Every work," he argued, "is qualified by the intention of the one who performs it" (TAL, 247). The evildoer is motivated by greed or cruelty or selfishness, whereas God's motive is to use the evil deed to serve good purposes.⁴² When Joseph's brothers sold him into slavery, they acted out of jealousy

---

40. And elsewhere; see, for example, "That Providence, therefore, which we ascribe to God, pertains as much to His operating hands as to His observing eyes" (DSPG, 224).

41. "For we must not suppose that God works in an iniquitous man as if he were a stone or a piece of wood, but He uses him as a thinking creature, according to the quality of his nature which He has given him. Thus when we say that God works in evildoers, that does not prevent them from working also in their own behalf" (TAL, 245).

42. We must note "the enormous diversity between God's work and that of an evil man's [*sic*] when God makes use of it as an instrument. For the wicked man is motivated either by his avarice, or ambition, or envy, or cruelty to do what he does, and he disregards any other end. Consequently, according to the root which motivates his heart and the end towards which he strives, his work is qualified and with good reason is judged bad. But God's intention is completely different. For His aim is to exercise His justice for the salvation and preservation of good, to pour out His goodness and grace on His faithful, and to chastise those who need it" (TAL, 246).

and malice, but God ordained this to happen in order that later Joseph could be the means of deliverance for his father and family in a time of famine and need.[43] This is what allows Joseph to say to his brothers, recalling the crime that had been committed against him, "It was not you who sent me here, but God" (Gen 45:8). Elsewhere Calvin compared the relationship between God and the evil instruments God uses with the striking image of the sun that shines on carrion, causing it to rot. The purity of the sun's rays "is not the cause of the carrion's stench and infection. God also so truly performs His works through evildoers that His sanctity does not justify them nor does their infection contaminate anything in Him" (TAL, 247). The goodness of God's purposes is what accrues to God, while the evildoers are condemned by their own quite different motives. "Those things which are vainly or un-righteously done by man are, rightly and righteously, the works of God" (DSPG, 233).

A significant consequence of this view is that God's purposes remain *hidden* to us: "All inferior and secondary causes . . . veil like so many curtains the glorious God from our sight" (DSPG, 231). The "secret" providence of God thus remains a mystery; human perception cannot penetrate the reasons and ends of God's will as enacted through creaturely instruments. Since "God's providence does not always meet us in its naked form, but God in a sense clothes it with the means employed" (*Inst.* 1.17.4), belief in providence is always a matter of faith.[44] Providence, as one Calvin scholar has put it, is not an empirical doctrine;[45] it is something that we assert in spite of the evidence available to our perceptions. Furthermore, since the purposes for which God determines particular events are concealed from us, we cannot equate God's *will* with God's *favor*. If someone does something, it is because God willed it, but this does not mean that the success God granted to the second-

---

43. "Joseph was sold by his brethren; for what reason, but because they wished, by any means whatever, to ruin and annihilate him? The same work is ascribed to God, but for a very different end; namely, that in a time of famine the family of Jacob might have an unexpected supply of food. . . . Whence it appears, that although he seems, at the commencement, to do the same thing as the wicked; yet there is a wide distance between their wickedness and his admirable judgment." See *A Commentary on Genesis* (trans. and ed. John King; reprinted from the Calvin Translation Society edition of 1847; Edinburgh: Banner of Truth, 1965), 45:8. References to this commentary are hereafter abbreviated using *Comm. on Gen.*

44. "Since the order, reason, end, and necessity of those things which happen for the most part lie hidden in God's purpose, and are not apprehended by human opinion, those things, which it is certain take place by God's will, are in a sense fortuitous. For they bear on the face of them no other appearance, whether they are considered in their own nature or weighed according to our knowledge and judgment" (*Inst.* 1.16.9).

45. Susan E. Schreiner, *The Theater of His Glory: Nature and the Natural Order in the Thought of John Calvin* (Durham, N.C.: Labyrinth, 1991), 113.

ary actor counts as an endorsement of the act or of the purposes for which this intermediary committed it. Thus, we cannot assume that victory indicates divine favor, nor that failure or misery is a sign of God's rejection. "Even though nothing in this world is active except as directed by God's secret providence, it is an intolerable blasphemy," Calvin contended, "to pretend that therefore nothing happens except by his approval."[46]

It is precisely this reasoning that Calvin used to explicate the providential will of God as enacted through the Assyrian (and later the Babylonian) empires and to illustrate more broadly human accountability for sin under the absolute sovereignty of God. The Assyrians may have been subject to the providential "command" of God (Isa 10:6), but this did not excuse them from culpability for the evil they committed. "There are two ways in which God *commands*;" Calvin contended, "by his secret decree, of which men are not conscious; and by his law, in which he demands from us voluntary obedience."[47] Elsewhere, Calvin made the same point by means of a distinction between God's *will* and God's *precept*. When a wicked deed is committed, the commandment of God is broken, even if the act is in accordance with the providential will of God in that particular instance. Human beings are subject to the law of God and are liable when they break it, even if God decrees for God's own purposes that they do so. "While God accomplishes through the wicked what he has decreed by his secret judgment, they are not excusable, as if they had obeyed his precept which out of their own lust they deliberately break" (*Inst*. 1.18.4). The results of our actions are in God's hands, but we are nevertheless judged responsible based upon the purposes for which we commit these acts and by whether they are done in obedience to God: "The deeds of men," according to Calvin, "are not to be estimated according to the event, but according to the measure in which they may have failed in their duty, or may have attempted something contrary to the divine command, and may have gone beyond the bounds of their calling" (*Comm. on Gen.* 45:8).

Trusting God's providential care does not, therefore, for Calvin, provide believers with a blueprint for ethical or appropriate behavior in response to the vicissitudes of life and history. The hiddenness of God's purposes means that we cannot discern the will of God by examining world events or personal circumstances. The emphasis upon absolute divine sovereignty in Calvin's theology thus forbids any

---

46. John Calvin, *Commentaries on the Epistle of Paul the Apostle to the Romans* (trans. and ed. John Owen; Grand Rapids: Eerdmans, 1947), on 8:7. Hereafter this work is referred to as *Comm. on Rom.*

47. "When the Lord reveals his will in the law, I must not ascend to his secret decree, which he intended should not be known to me, but must yield implicit obedience" (*Comm. on Is.* 10:6).

kind of messianism or triumphalism; God does not turn over the reins of the world to human agents who are somehow enabled to discern or enact God's own purposes in God's stead. While reflection on God's providential governance does not itself offer us moral guidelines, it makes possible the obedience to the command of God to which we are called. "What folly it is," Calvin asserted, "to seek the distinction between rectitude and iniquity, which the law places before our eyes so openly and distinctly, in the deep labyrinth of secret providence!"[48] To put it another way, providence does not supply us with rules or norms for ethics, but it provides the *ground* for ethical behavior: by faith in God's governance we are enabled to act righteously in the world without fear of the consequences. Since God rules over all of history, we are not truly capable of acting against God's providence, but we are responsible for following the revealed will of God which is set before us in God's word and by the example of Jesus Christ.

### "The Effect of Righteousness Will Be Peace"

The impact of this view of providence on the question of security becomes apparent in Calvin's analysis of those later chapters of Isaiah wherein Judah faces another crisis with similar temptations; in this case, to oppose the onslaught of the Assyrian forces by appealing to Egypt for military aid. Again the prophet decries the people's refusal to trust God for their protection and denounces the furtive and desperate plans that they make which are in opposition to the will and command of God (Isa 30:1–2). Calvin's commentary on this point is worth quoting at length:

> The prophet condemns the presumption of those who attempt unlawful methods, and think that they will succeed in them, when they labor, right or wrong, to secure their safety, as if it could be done contrary to the will of God. It is certain that this proceeds from unbelief and distrust, because they do not think that God alone is able to protect them, unless they call in foreign though forbidden assistance. Hence come unlawful leagues, hence come tricks and cheating, by which men fully believe that their affairs will be better conducted than if they acted towards each other with candor and fairness. There are innumerable instances of this unbelief in every department of human life; for men think that they will be undone, if they are satisfied with the blessing of God, and transact all their affairs with truth and uprightness. But we ought to consider that we are forsaken, rejected,

---

48. *Comm. on Rom.* 8:7. Also, "we ought not to inquire into His providence, which is a secret to us, since we know what he wants of us and what He approves and condemns" (TAL, 253).

and cursed by God, whenever we have recourse to forbidden methods and unlawful ways. In all our undertakings, deliberations and attempts, therefore, we ought to be regulated by the will of God. We ought always to consider what he forbids or commands, so as to be fully disposed to obey his laws, and to submit ourselves to be guided by the Spirit, otherwise our rashness will succeed very ill. (*Comm. on Is.* 30:1)

Judah has again "securitized" an impending threat by seeking a solution which is in violation of the covenant to which the people ordinarily consider, or should consider, themselves subject. Fearing that the urgency of the threat requires emergency measures and cannot be addressed within the bounds of the law that has been given to them, the people resort to "tricks and cheating" rather than relying on God and pursuing a course of upright action. The prophet's public protest is an attempt to *desecuritize* the situation, not by denying the reality of the armies which are mustered against them, but by recalling to the people the true source of both their safety and their peril. As Calvin points out, distrust in God's providential care leads to a disavowal of God's authority and decree. It is not that we are forbidden to act in our own defense or to take reasonable precautions when confronted with potential dangers,[49] but we are never justified in rejecting the commandment of God in order to secure our safety. Regardless of the circumstances, we are "not to undertake anything but what we know to be pleasing and acceptable to God" (*Comm. on Is.* 30:1). The belief in God's providential governance makes this a practical as well as a moral concern: if God is in control of all that happens, seeking to save ourselves by opposing God can only result in failure, and trusting and obeying God is our surest path to true security.

The association between divine providence and righteous action is a consistent theme of the prophetic testimony. Isaiah charges the leaders of Judah with not one, but two, faults. First, as we have already seen, he denounces the faithlessness by which they refuse to trust God for their protection, driven by what the Copenhagen scholars would call "existential fear" to doubt the efficacy of God's sovereignty and promise. The prophet also repeatedly condemns the injustice of their way of life: "Ah, you who make iniquitous decrees, who write oppressive statutes, to turn aside the needy from justice, and to rob the poor of my people of their right" (Isa 10:1–2).[50] The laws which exist for the protection of the innocent and vulnerable, all the provisions of public policy which ensure the integrity of the nation and the fair and just treatment

---

49. See *Comm. on Is.* 8:8; 31:1.
50. See also, for example, Isa 1:16–17, 23; 3:14–15; 5:8, 20–23; et al.

of all its citizens, are—in the case of Judah—derived from Torah, and hence from the spirit and command of God. This is the "normal politics" which is abandoned or corrupted by the avarice of the powerful who seek to secure themselves at the expense of others. Isaiah's desecuritization of the situation of imminent threat thus involves not only asserting the sufficiency of God for protection against any danger and the futility of attempting to seek refuge elsewhere, but also the reminder to the people of who and what God has called them to be in joining with them in covenant. The only path to security is through righteousness, that is, through right relationship with the Lord who is our only problem and our only hope.

The future consolation which Isaiah foretells depicts a world in which trust in God and just political and socio-economic practices insure the blessings of divine protection and prosperity for the people of Israel. Security cannot come by circumventing the demands of the law, but only through submission to the authority and sovereignty of God in all things, including the structures and practices of domestic and international relations. "The effect of *righteousness*"—not of superior military might, or of clever strategic maneuvers, or of unjust or illicit exercises of power—"will be peace, and the result of righteousness, quietness and trust forever" (Isa 32:17, emphasis mine).[51] To take this leap of faith in the midst of a situation of dire peril may seem like foolishness, but the real risk lies in not leaning on the one who alone controls both the present and the future. The cornerstone that will be the foundation of the people in the renewed time to come is symbolically named "One who trusts will not panic" (Isa 28:16). This is Isaiah's call: not to fear, not to "call conspiracy," but rather to "live in determined and unflinching anticipation that Yahweh will enact another, alternative, new thing."[52] Rather than attempting to read the will of God off of history or to read history apart from the ruling will of God, Isaiah's call is to live by faith, by what is not seen. This "deep trust in the midst of risk, so deep that it redefines the situation"[53] is quite different from the "realism" that insists that the use of force is the essential means of achieving that security which is the prerequisite for any other attainable good. No good can come from abandoning faith in the sovereign God, and any "securitization" which seeks to justify such faithlessness and sin can only be an idol.

---

51. Also, "Zion shall be redeemed by justice, and those in her who repent, by righteousness" (Isa 1:27).

52. Brueggemann, *Isaiah 1–39*, 79.

53. Ibid., 68.

## Conclusion: Providence and the Process of "Desecuritization"

Writing at the close of the twentieth century, the Copenhagen School cites the impact of desecuritizing movements on the collapse of the former Communist Bloc and the renewal of relations between east and west. From the perspective of the end of the twentieth century, they note optimistically that "the prospect now exists for a more widespread dissolving of borders, desecuritizing most kinds of political, social and economic interaction."[54] This, of course, was before September 11, 2001. Although it has been the military more than other "sectors" that has been the most prominent in this regard,[55] the "war on terror" has done much to reinvigorate the rhetoric of security, and the United States has made significant strides in the direction of multiplying and intensifying its securitizations. In the past few years security speech acts have been used in the United States to legitimize torture, spying on citizens without a warrant, preemptive war, and suspending the right of *habeas corpus* for those declared to be enemy combatants. In these cases and others security has been assumed to trump all other values (e.g., freedom, human rights, international cooperation, diplomacy), and the "security" designation has been used to justify actions that would otherwise contradict the ideals and laws (e.g., the Constitution, the Geneva Conventions, privacy statutes) of the nation. The "New Security" analysis would seem to have been startlingly prescient in its delineation of this process, if not in its hope for its decline, were it not that such situations and responses have been all too commonplace in human history, both ancient and modern.

For Christians, it may seem appropriate at times to suspend a human law, if it is unjust or inconsequential, for the sake of an overriding need to protect from harm. Putting restraints on the free market or limiting the purchasing options of consumers may be worthwhile in the face of threats to the environment such as global warming or the extinction of endangered species. But, what if the securitization in question involves an attempt to override a *moral* law? In such cases "desecuritization" would seem to be, not just an eventual ideal, but a present necessity. As the text of Isaiah and the analysis of Calvin contend, fear and urgency do not justify the disregard of God's law or command. While Christians today may find it more difficult than Calvin or Isaiah acknowledged to determine what constitutes divine

---

54. Buzan, Waever, and de Wilde, *Security*, 209. With regards to Europe, where the successful expansion of the European Union has occurred despite fears of economic collapse and national/cultural identity loss, this prospect seems to have borne more fruit.

55. Though it is worth noting that, since this paper was originally presented (September 2008), economic security may be said to have risen to the forefront of the national agenda in the United States.

law or even Christian values, or to agree on what prescripts are inviolable and which are *adiaphora* (indifferent things neither mandated nor forbidden), even this dispute can be part of a desecuritizing movement. After all, desecuritization does not mean that an issue is disregarded as unimportant or that there are no available means of addressing it which might be warranted by the situation. Rather, it entails the recognition that the seriousness of a problem or threat does not automatically justify emergency measures which would be unacceptable in less urgent circumstances. Disputes regarding the legality or morality of a proposed response are precisely the kinds of conversations that are promoted when an issue is brought back into the political sphere of open debate and dialogue through a process of desecuritization.

What does this process entail; that is, how are issues repoliticized, and what can be done to further this goal? Despite the ultimate preference they profess for desecuritization, the "new security" theorists focus more on the descriptive task of analyzing potential and actual securitizations than on the prescriptive one of suggesting options or means for facilitating the downgrading of security issues.[56] In describing historical examples of desecuritization,[57] however, Waever offers some hints as to how political discourse and action might be reclaimed from the space dominated by fear and force. Notable among these is the observation that desecuritization can be achieved by means of a speech-act *failure*.[58] In other words, an attempted securitization or resecuritization of a previously securitized subject may not be successful, which could lead to the issue losing its security status and consequently its legitimizing power.

What might cause such a speech act to fail? The most likely response is that the audience refuses to accept the proposed securitization. This could happen because the securitizing actor loses the authority to make a securitizing claim, or because the hazard is actually diminished, or because new information regarding the urgency or severity of the threat emerges. Such possibilities may indeed occur, but they would

---

56. One of the most significant criticisms of the Copenhagen School comes from those who are committed to defining security as an emancipatory ideal, serving those who are made most insecure by the prevailing order. See, for example, Richard Wyn Jones: *Security, Strategy, and Critical Theory* (Boulder, Colo.: Lynne Rienner, 1999), 118. These advocates of "Critical Security Studies" argue that the Copenhagen School, by insisting that security is a political construction and refusing to address the issue of whether a security speech act is valid with reference to the reality of the threat it names, is incapable of speaking to concrete situations of insecurity and in this way largely evades normative concerns.

57. Waever, "Securitization and Desecuritization," 55.

58. Ibid., 55–56.

seem to depend rather tenuously on circumstances and would be difficult to orchestrate as part of a deliberate desecuritizing agenda. But, what if the audience itself were to change, not in its composition, but in its worldview, its expectations, and its vulnerability to fear? What would happen if the people who were the addressees of a securitizing speech act, even a small number of them were to acknowledge the sovereignty of God over all situations of extremity, trusting God for their security in such a way as to constrain their efforts at self-protection within the bounds of the ethics and values of the heavenly kingdom?

It is along these lines that the doctrine of providence may offer theological resources for desecuritization. Isaiah pleads with Ahaz and the people who "call conspiracy" to view the situation they face in the light of the sovereign God's promise and command. Calvin uses the concept of secondary causality to explicate the hiddenness of God's purposes and the distinction between God's providential will and revealed command and in this way rescues providential thinking from any messianic presumption and demonstrates its efficacy as the ground for obedience to the word of God in all things. Not all faithful Christians, of course, will necessarily agree with the rigorous notion of providence advocated in Isaiah or by Calvin. Many, indeed, will find such a meticulous view of divine causality to be problematic or unconvincing, especially with regard to the attribution of suffering and evil to God. However, even a more modest theology of providential governance which trusts in the *ultimate* fulfillment of God's purposes, I would contend, is capable of resisting securitizations which call us to abandon the will of God in the face of worldly dangers. Such dangers may indeed do us harm; faith in divine providence does not insure our prosperity or guarantee our safety in this world.[59] The providential ethic thus necessarily entails an element of risk. It is not a naive confidence that God will make everything work out just as we want it but rather a sober assessment that not even protection from immediate harm is worth sacrificing all other principles which fidelity to God commends. By assuring us of God's ultimate sovereignty over all of history, the doctrine of providence frees us to act boldly and righteously in the face of fear, aligning our practices and policies with the values of God's kingdom and trusting that God will honor this risk and will conform it to God's good purposes in the end.

---

59. As Calvin put it, "whomever the Lord has adopted and deemed worthy of his fellowship ought to prepare themselves for a hard, toilsome, and unquiet life, crammed with very many and various kind of evil" (*Inst.* 3.18.1).

# RESPONSE TO COLWELL

## *Darrell Cosden*

I would like to begin by saying that I am personally quite sympathetic to the political conclusions called for by this paper. I too believe that political conclusions like these can and should ultimately grow out of theological reflection that builds from both the biblical narratives themselves and specifically constructive doctrinal formulations. To be more specific, I too am committed to letting the narratives of Scripture inform and give shape to a public and political theology where the biblical text (here Isaiah) is allowed on its own terms to challenge and critique, for example, current United States' policy and practice relating to "security." Further, I too believe that the way the United States is currently handling and being perceived to handle security and securitization is troublesome and in need of public debate and challenge. Theology, including a doctrine of providence, has prophetic, political ramifications for the current United States and international security contexts, and making theology a part of the wider public discourse now would be good for all, whether American or not and whether Christian or not.

Thus, my critique and remarks, as direct as they may be, should be taken as my attempt to enter sympathetically into this project and to open up this conversation to other thoughtful contributions. This is both for the sake of what is at stake regarding life together at this moment in history and to sharpen further the significant contribution made in this paper. My intention is to be a sympathetic critic.

## Comments of Appreciation and Critique

This paper has helped me immensely on several fronts. Generally, it has helped me to see more clearly the issues and to dig deeper into hermeneutical questions and concerns that I have had and have been wrestling with for quite some time. First, what really are the hermeneutical pitfalls and the responsible hermeneutical procedures for transposing the stories that we tell as nations, cultures, communities, and individuals so that they come "within the world" of the biblical texts? Second, how are our cultural stories to be absorbed by and subsequently reshaped through the scriptural narratives, particularly stories relating to the pressing public and ethical issues that concern all people, not simply Christians? That is, how do we actually use a narrative hermeneutics for a public political theology relating to issues like security?

It is my observation that the first part of this paper undertakes a narrative hermeneutical method and reading of the text of Isaiah and does so by reading Isaiah in the light of, and in attempt to absorb and then reshape and redirect, the narrative currently embodied by the United States' security policy and practice. Yet, it concerns me that I do not think the paper makes clear the hermeneutical steps necessary, nor follows critically such necessary hermeneutical procedures, for doing precisely this, i.e., getting from the text of Isaiah to "us." The paper begins by juxtaposing Judah's theo-political context with that of post-9/11 United States. This is a classic narrative hermeneutical procedure and as such is perfectly acceptable. However, early in the paper the horizons change from Ahaz/ Isaiah/Judah to "we"/"us," but what is never really clear throughout the rest of the paper is who "we" are or are supposed to be. Are we the United States? (The early narrative juxtaposition of texts suggests possibly so). Or, are we Christians generally? Or, are we Christian Americans? Such questions arise despite the fact that the qualifier "For Christians" is later mentioned in moving toward the conclusion of the paper. This is still too vague and imprecise for what is needed.

This matters considerably since it is these hermeneutical decisions and steps that determine the coherence of, and drives the conclusions for, the whole paper. How do we move from the ancient Judean context to the contemporary United States and its national security policy particulars? In Isaiah God's people were a specifically chosen political entity for a particular global transformative and restorative purpose. Judah is in a particular covenantal relationship with God, so all notions of law and command therein need to be first understood as specifically covenantal conditions—"rules of the game" rather than some general abstract moral or universal law, even if some points do seem transcultural. America does not have the same promise from God "sovereignly" to orchestrate world events on her behalf, nor to defend her, nor to punish her, nor the promise to use "us" until his universal redemptive purpose is accomplished through us. The church might have such a covenant, but this is my point. Who are the "we" in the paper? The church is a new trans-national religious and political entity. What exactly is or should be her relationship to the nation of the United States? How even would promises and commands to the church apply to the "We the people" of the national entity and how could they inform United States' security policy?

Let me not labor this point, for there is another hermeneutical area I would like to address. This paper has helped me in a similar fashion to see more clearly and dig deeper into my other questions and concerns. From a hermeneutical standpoint how should we proceed from particular narrative portions of Scripture to more general overarching doctrinal claims and formulations? How should constructive theology, for example, build its doctrines, such as a doctrine of providence, using a narrative text like Isaiah? This is a significant question given that we will subsequently use such doctrines for the purposes of spiritual formation, ethical motivation and orientation, and ultimately for a political theology. One way would be to use the methodology of systematic theology, but is this legitimate, or will it prove a hermeneutical dead end and liability? Can generalized "abstract" systematic theology be the bridge for the hermeneutical gap in which we find ourselves? Or, is it actually the problem?

Personally, I tend to view theology—and here I do not mean "systematic theology"—as a hermeneutic for taking us from Scripture to belief and practice. As I see it, we need to formulate doctrine for ourselves that remains coherent and broad enough to help us and yet avoid the problem of abstraction that the "systematization" of theology poses. Here I am with Barth. In relation to this paper specifically, is it appropriate and responsible to use the very "systematic" method that narrative hermeneutics so reacts against—the "find the wider more abstract biblical principle within the text" method—to develop a universal doctrine about God's providential control over all of creation and all events therein? From this very specific narrative concerning God's promised relationship at this moment with the nation of Judah, can we, given her unique role in God's eschatological purposes, really extract a more general and thus abstract principle about how God must therefore providentially "control," even currently, all of the actions and events taking place within creation?

By appealing to and making use of Calvin's doctrine of providence as he developed it in at least some dialogue with Isaiah, this paper offers a paradigmatic example of a long standing hermeneutical approach for building theology, one in considerable tension with the narrative approach used earlier. For me this is problematic since I do not think that God's statements to Judah can be used as universal abstract principles that can at our behest be reconcretized and reapplied to any and every situation in the whole universe. This is simply to me moving too far from what the text actually says. As the paper acknowledges, Isaiah does not say that God is against war *as such*, alliances *as such*, or the like. He says that God controls history, but not abstractly. Rather, God does so concretely with reference to his promise to and for his current and future use of Judah. God's specific purposes cannot ultimately be thwarted, and he will make sure of this. Thus, Judah need not fear anyone but God, for God will ultimately (perhaps eschatologically?) bring about his purposes for her one way or another.

This is a far cry from abstracting statements like "The Lord of Hosts" from this context and saying that this means that God exercises "absolute sovereignty over history" and by this meaning that God causes, either directly or indirectly, everything in creation that happens to everyone and everything everywhere. In making such claims Calvin does something like a "systematic" theology. He moves from the specific to the abstract to the universal and then back to a new specific. In doing so he has made some rather large and not fully acknowledged, nor do I think circumspect, hermeneutical leaps. These are leaps that not only moderns struggle with, but also ones that many of his contemporaries thought problematic. So too thought many of his predecessors, for there were those in medieval theology who had already come to reject almost identical notions of providence to those of Calvin, notions which had earlier been developed in scholasticism.

The problems with Calvin's doctrine of providence are not unique to, or caused by, our "modern" context as readers. They are problems brought about by his hermeneutical method. That Calvin has to defend God and qualify his comments by building a protective system around them—hidden will versus revealed will, notions of secondary causation and the like—and that he has to resort to arguments along the lines that "we need to assert [this belief] in spite of the evidence available to our perceptions" should make us look again at his method of doing theology, his hermeneutical steps in getting from Scripture to doctrine to application. I personally find the suggestion in the paper that *the* doctrine of providence, as if there were only one, undergirds a kind of "duty based" proto-Kantian, if not full-orbed Kantian, ethic of "obedience despite appearances" to be quite troublesome. Nor do I find this as an abstract and general approach to theological ethics to be in any way the direct and necessary teaching of the book of Isaiah. There are just too many covert hermeneutical maneuvers and steps to convince me of the paper's overall thesis, even if I do tend to agree with its politics and want to acknowledge that it has provided us with rich material for discussion.

## Conclusion

In summary and in relation to hermeneutics I want to raise questions and concerns about two areas. First, we need to consider carefully our use of narrative hermeneutics and methods for getting from narrative texts to contemporary public and political action, i.e., for a public and political theology. Second, we need to examine the issue of appropriate hermeneutical methods for developing doctrine from scriptural narratives that will be used as the basis for a public and political theology, specifically here the use of an abstraction/systemization method (usually regarded as antithetical to narrative approaches) to develop a doctrine of providence and thus ethics.

# THE RADICAL INSECURITY OF IDOLATRY?
# OR OF FAITH?

## *Randall C. Zachman*

The need for security lies at the very heart of human existence. In large part the quest for security stems from the finitude of human life. We know that our lives are bounded with the certainty of death, though we remain uncertain of the hour of death's arrival. The shadow of death not only lurks over our lives, but it threatens all that we hold near and dear. We are anxious lest we be deprived of food, water, and air, without which our lives are not possible. We are anxious lest disease or cancer eat our lives from within. We are anxious lest fire or earthquake or flood should sweep us away. We see how floods can destroy an entire city, how a tsunami or hurricane can obliterate entire communities, how an earthquake can flatten major cities, and we know that we could face the same fate. We know that we might not only lose our own lives at any minute, but we might also lose the lives of those we love, including those who care for us in this life. We might lose our possessions, we might lose our income, we might lose our home, we might lose our ability to support our families, we might lose our reputation, we might lose our investments, and we might lose our savings or pension. We also know that the power of death can be dramatically aided by human agency, as we become aware of those who seek to harm or destroy our lives. We are anxious when the stranger approaches on the street and when the plane flies over our city buildings. As Calvin notes, "Amid these tribulations must not humans be most miserable, since, but half alive in life, they weakly draw their anxious and languid breath, as if they had a sword perpetually hanging over their necks?" (*Inst*. I.xvii.10).

Our anxiety over finitude and death leads us to seek security from the depths of our existence. We seek some kind of refuge that will keep us safe from the power of loss and death, a fortress that will keep us secure in light of the threat other human beings pose to our existence, a rock that cannot be moved, on which we can stand when the floods rise up around us or the ground shakes beneath us. We want to secure our lives from the power of death, loss, and destruction. We seek refuge in health insurance to guard us from illness and disease, life insurance to secure us from the loss of any ability to care for others, home insurance to prevent the loss of our shelter, car insurance to prevent us from losing our mobility, and property insurance to keep us from the irrevocable loss of our possessions. We invest in securities and pensions to keep from being destitute in the future and in savings to provide for the loss of our livelihood. We pay taxes to support police departments to secure us from the harm that others inflict on us and the military to keep us safe from the attacks of those who wish to destroy us. Yet all the while the anxiety remains, as we become aware that the power of death still threatens all we hold dear, and we can feel our own lives and all that we care about slipping through our fingers into the void. We fear that what Job says of his life may one day be true of our own: "Truly the thing that I fear comes upon me, and what I dread befalls me. I am not at ease, nor am I quiet; I have no rest; but trouble comes" (Job 3:25–26).

The Hebrew Scriptures have much to say about the human quest for security in light of the deep anxiety over death and loss. According to these writings the only haven for security that we can have is to be found in God alone. "For God alone my soul waits in silence, for my hope is from him. He alone is my rock and my salvation, my fortress; I shall not be shaken. On God rests my deliverance and my honor; my mighty rock, my refuge is in God" (Ps 62:5–7). One of the favored ways of speaking about the security we are to find in God alone is to describe God as our sole refuge. To take refuge means to find a safe and secure shelter from danger or trouble, from the destructive forces that threaten our existence. When the dark forces of death and destruction threaten our lives, we should take refuge in God alone, for only in God is there safety from death. "Be merciful to me, O God, be merciful to me, for in you my soul takes refuge; in the shadow of your wings I will take refuge, until the destroying storms pass by" (Ps 57:1).

The godly are not free from the threat of the power of death but rather feel its power in the depth of their existence. "My heart is in anguish within me, the terrors of death have fallen upon me. Fear and trembling come upon me, and horror overwhelms me" (Ps 55:4–5). Thus the godly seek refuge in God when the powers of death threaten to annihilate them, not when they are already feeling secure. "I cry to you, O LORD; I say, 'You are my refuge, my portion in the land of the living.' Give heed to my cry, for I am brought very low" (Ps 142:5–6). Since the faithful feel the power of death drawing them down, they know that God is the only source of help, and so do not seek refuge or security anywhere else. "For my soul is full of troubles, and my life draws near to Sheol. I am counted among those who go down to the Pit; I am like those who have no help, like those forsaken among the dead, like the slain that lie in the grave" (Ps 88:3–5). God is the only refuge in trouble because God alone has the power to preserve life in the midst of death. "The Lord will keep you from all evil; he will keep your life" (Ps 121:7). Those who take refuge in God, and who trust in God to keep them safe and secure, know that God can keep them safe no matter how the powers of destruction are arrayed against them. "You will not fear the terror of the night, or the arrow that flies by day, or the pestilence that stalks in darkness, or the destruction that wastes at noonday" (Ps 91:5–6).

The godly take refuge in God by crying to God when they are afflicted by suffering and death. "The cords of death encompassed me; the torrents of perdition assailed me; the cords of Sheol entangled me; the snares of death confronted me" (Ps 118:4–5). They know they cannot secure their lives in the face of these forces, which gives their cry to God a heart-felt earnestness. "The snares of death encompassed me; the pangs of Sheol laid hold on me; I suffered distress and anguish. Then I called on the name of the Lord; 'O Lord, I pray, save my life'" (Ps 116:3–4). Our only security is thus to call on God to deliver us from death, and yet this very act of calling already begins the process of bringing safety from the forces of death. "Therefore let all who are faithful offer prayer to you; at a time of distress, the rush of might waters shall not reach them. You are a hiding place for me; you preserve me from trouble" (Ps 32:6–7). Yet God must in fact freely answer this prayer, revealing to the godly that not even their prayer guarantees their safety, but only God. If God refuses to hear our cry, there is no hope left. "To you, O Lord, I call; my rock, do not refuse to hear me; for if you are silent to me, I shall be like those who go down to the Pit" (Ps 28:1).

The freedom of God to answer prayer does not mean that the faithful call on God with doubt that God will hear. Rather, they know that the very nature of God is to hear the cries of the afflicted when they take refuge in God. "For the Lord hears the needy, and does not despise his own that are in bonds" (Ps 70:33). The fact that God hears the prayer of others when they are afflicted should encourage us to call upon God when the terrors of death surround us. "This poor soul cried, and was heard by the Lord, and was saved from every trouble" (Ps 34:6). Indeed, God appears to have an ear for the cries of the afflicted and attends to them above all others. "For he who avenges blood is mindful of them; he does not forget the cry of the afflicted" (Ps 9:12). In spite of the fact that all others may flee in horror from the afflicted and may be utterly deaf to their calls for help, God will not abandon them or be deaf to their cries, for the face of God is turned towards the afflicted in particular. "For he did not despise or abhor the affliction of the afflicted; he did not hide his face from me, but heard when I cried to him" (Ps 22:24).

The confidence that God hears the cries of the afflicted is reinforced by their conviction that God already sees their affliction before they cry. "I will exult and rejoice in your steadfast love, because you have seen my affliction; you have taken heed of my adversities, and have not delivered me into the hand of the enemy" (Ps 31:7–8). This is vividly seen in the case of Hagar when she first flees from Sarai. She does not even cry to the Lord, but the Lord sees her affliction and sends an angel to comfort and deliver her. "And the angel of the LORD said to her, 'Now you have conceived and shall bear a son; you shall call him Ishmael, for the LORD has given heed to your affliction'" (Gen 16:11). The afflicted are poor and needy, for they have no other help apart from God. Yet the godly know that the Lord watches over the poor and needy above all others and beholds their afflictions. "But you do see! Indeed, you note trouble and grief, that you may take it into your hands; the helpless commit themselves to you; you have been the helper of the orphan" (Ps 10:14). Indeed, God wishes to be a refuge and source of security especially for the poor and needy, for they have no other help besides God. "For he stands at the right hand of the needy, to save them from those who would condemn them to death" (Ps 109:31). Those in the human community who have no other source of safety, such as widows and orphans, can therefore be certain that God sees and cares for them. "The LORD watches over strangers; he upholds the orphan and the widow" (Ps 146:9). The afflicted take refuge in God, therefore, because they know that God already sees their affliction and will hear their cry, because God is a refuge for the poor and needy who are in distress. "For you have been a refuge to the poor, a refuge to the needy in their distress, a shelter from the rainstorm and shade from the heat" (Isa 25:4). However, in the face of the destructive power of death, every human being is poor and needy, unable to secure her life. Thus all the godly who take refuge in God in the midst of their distress will do so as the poor and needy, whose only hope is in God. "As for me, I am poor and needy, but the LORD takes thought for me. You are my help and my deliverer; do not delay, O my God" (Ps 40:17).

It is important to note that the godly cry to God to deliver them from death in *this* life, without any thought of a life after this one. The only future beyond this life is the grave, the Pit, Sheol, which is "the land of gloom and deep darkness, the land of gloom and chaos, where light is like darkness" (Job 10:21–22). The faithful take refuge in God in order to be made secure from this future as long as God wills, for they feel the power of Sheol and the Pit pulling their lives down, and cry to God to be delivered from death. "Turn, O Lord, save my life; deliver me for the sake of your steadfast love. For in death there is no remembrance of you; in Sheol who can praise you?" (Ps 6:4–5). Thus, when Hezekiah hears from Isaiah that he will die, he cries to the Lord, "O Lord, I am oppressed; be my security!" (Isa 38:14). God answers his prayer, and tells him through Isaiah, "I have heard your prayer, I have seen your tears; I will add fifteen years to your life" (Isa 38:5). God answers the cry of the afflicted by delivering them from the power of death in *this* life and by giving them in this life the safety and security for which they long, but which they cannot provide for themselves. "'Because the poor are despoiled, because the needy groan, I will now rise up,' says the Lord. 'I will place them in the safety for which they long'" (Ps 12:5). The godly take refuge in God, for they know that only God can give them the security for which they long, to be freed of the power of death. "O Lord my God, I cried to you for help, and you have healed me. O Lord, you brought up my soul from Sheol, restored me to life from among those gone down to the Pit" (Ps 30:2–3). God delivers the godly from all the destructive forces that threaten them, so that they may walk in safety in this life. "For you have delivered my soul from death, my eyes from tears, my feet from stumbling. I walk before the Lord in the land of the living" (Ps 116:8–9).

God's nature as the source of refuge from all destructive power, as the One who hears the cry of the oppressed and sees their affliction, as the One who frees the afflicted from all their fears and gives them the safety and security for which they long, is revealed with particular clarity in the exodus from Egypt. When God first speaks to Moses from the midst of the burning bush, the Lord says, "I have observed the misery of my people who are in Egypt; I have heard their cry on account of their taskmasters. Indeed, I know their sufferings, and I have come down to deliver them from the Egyptians, and to bring them up out of that land to a good and broad land, a land flowing with milk and honey" (Exod 3:7–8).

The Hebrew Scriptures are especially focused on the fact that God saw the oppression of the Hebrews in Egypt and upon seeing their affliction and oppression came down to deliver them and lead them to the promised land where they were to be safe and secure. "The people believed; and when they heard that the Lord had given heed to the Israelites and that he had seen their misery, they bowed down and worshipped" (Exod 4:31). In the book of Deuteronomy, the people of Israel are to rehearse these acts of God—hearing their cry, seeing their affliction, delivering them from the power of death and bringing them to safety—when they present the first fruits of the land to the Lord. "When the Egyptians treated us harshly and afflicted us, imposing hard labor on us, we cried to the LORD, the God of our ancestors; the LORD heard our voice and saw our affliction, our toil, and our oppression. The LORD brought us out of Egypt with a mighty hand and an outstretched arm . . . and he brought us into this place and gave us this land" (Deut 26:6–9). The Israelites may take refuge in God, for they know through the Exodus that the Lord answers those who cry to him when the powers of death take them captive, for God sees their affliction and delivers them from the bonds of destruction to bring them to a safe and secure place.

Once delivered from affliction and death, the godly should continue to pray to God, only this time not with cries for help, but with songs of thanksgiving, praising God for seeing their affliction, hearing their cry, delivering them from death, and leading them to a place of safety. This is the major theme of Psalm 107, which details the many ways God frees those who cry to him in their distress, when the power of death threatens them, either by hunger in the midst of the wilderness, or in prison, or in illness, or in storm on the sea. God hears their cry and brings them to a place of safety. In light of this response the psalmist makes this constant exhortation, "Let them thank the LORD for his steadfast love, for his wonderful works for humankind. And let them offer thanksgiving sacrifices, and tell of his deeds with songs of joy" (Ps 107:21–22). Over and above thanking God and testifying of God's works of deliverance, the godly are to mirror the character of God in their own lives. Since they know that God looks upon their afflictions, they also should be aware of the afflictions and suffering of their neighbors. Since they know that God hears the cry of the poor and needy, they also should attend to the cry of the poor and needy in their midst, especially the stranger, the widow, and the orphan, who have no one to look out for their safety and security. "Give justice to the weak and the orphan; maintain the right of the lowly and the destitute. Rescue the weak and the needy; deliver them from the hand of the wicked" (Ps 82:3–4). Though this is true for all the godly, this is especially true of their judges and rulers. They are to mirror the concern of God for the cries of the poor and needy by attending to these cries themselves, to deliver them from affliction and death. "For he delivers the needy when they call, the poor and those who have no helper. He has pity on the weak and the needy, and saves the lives of the needy. From oppression and violence he redeems their life; and precious is their blood in his sight" (Ps 72:12–14).

Those who hear the cry of the poor and needy, and who act to deliver them, are the righteous who mirror the righteousness of God in their own lives. The godly therefore remain in the security given to them by the Lord by securing the lives of the poor and needy in their midst. "Happy are those who consider the poor; the Lord delivers them in the day of trouble. The Lord protects them and keeps them alive; they are called happy in the land" (Ps 41:1–2). The righteous are assured that God hears their prayers in the same way that God hears the cries of the poor and needy. "The eyes of the Lord are on the righteous, and his ears open to their cry" (Ps 34:15). If the righteous fall into affliction again, they know that God attends especially to them to deliver them, just as God delivers the poor and needy. "Many are the afflictions of the righteous, but the Lord rescues them from them all. He keeps all their bones; not one of them will be broken" (Ps 34:19–20). Thus, once one has been delivered from the power of death and placed in safety, the way to remain secure is to watch after the most vulnerable in one's midst. "For the righteous will never be moved; they will be remembered forever. They are not afraid of evil tidings; their hearts are firm, secure in the Lord. Their hearts are steady, they will not be afraid; in the end they will look in triumph on their foes. They have distributed freely, they have given to the poor; their righteousness endures forever" (Ps 112:6–9).

The book of Proverbs is especially interested in the way that the righteous attain security. Wisdom herself cries out, "Those who listen to me will be secure, and will live at ease, without dread of disaster" (Prov 1:33). Those who are righteous remain secure from the power of death, unlike those who live wicked and foolish lives. "One who walks in integrity will be safe, but whoever follows crooked ways will fall into the Pit" (Prov 28:18). The security of the righteous is found especially in the fact that they are not deaf to the cry of the poor and needy, for they honor God by mirroring God's character in their lives. The wicked, on the other hand, have no security because their oppression of the poor and needy is an assault on the character of God. "Those who mock the poor insult their Maker; those who are glad at calamity will not go unpunished" (Prov 17:5). However, the righteous do not attempt to secure their lives by their righteousness alone, for they know that only the Lord has the power to free them from affliction and death. Hence their security is founded on their trust in the Lord, for it is only God who can keep them safe. "Then you will walk on your way securely and your foot will not stumble. If you sit down, you will not be afraid; when you lie down, your sleep will be sweet. Do not be afraid of sudden panic, or of the storm that strikes the wicked; for the Lord will be your confidence and will keep your foot from being caught" (Prov 3:24–26).

Our only security, therefore, is to seek and call on God as the only refuge from the power of death and destruction, knowing that God sees our affliction and hears our cry and will come to deliver us from the power of death to place us in a land of safety and security. Once delivered to safety, the godly are to remain secure from the power of death by thanking God and proclaiming what God has done and by acting in a way that mirrors the nature of God, namely by hearing the cry of the poor and the needy, seeing their affliction, and acting to save them from death and destruction. Those who act in this way are righteous and know that their way is secure in God. "Trust in the Lord, and do good; so you will live in the land, and enjoy security" (Ps 37:3). If the righteous suffer affliction in the future, they know that God will hear them and will act yet again to deliver them, since they also have acted on behalf of the poor and needy. "When the righteous cry for help, the Lord hears them, and rescues them from their troubles" (Ps 34:17).

However, being delivered from affliction and being brought to a place of safety and security brings with it a whole host of new problems, which can render life radically insecure again. Those delivered from affliction might think the Lord only delivers from death but that other gods are responsible for keeping them in safety, especially the gods who appear to have blessed the land they have entered. They might come to trust in their newfound wealth and security and no longer trust in God. They might try to use this wealth to secure their lives against death, leading them to oppress the poor and to be deaf to the cries of the needy. They might look to their own security arrangements in the land and trust their rulers and princes to keep them safe and secure. Were this to happen, the only solution would be for God to allow the people to be afflicted yet again, so that they might seek refuge in the Lord and cry out to God for deliverance from oppression and death, so that God might hear their cry and free them from their affliction. This indeed is the nature of the relationship between God and Israel from the death of Joshua to the anointing of Saul. The Lord hands the people over to the power of their enemies because they worship other gods. The people cry out to God, and God sends judges to deliver them, "For the Lord would be moved to pity by their groaning because of those who persecuted and oppressed them" (Judg 2:18). However, when the judge dies the people relapse into their false sense of security, leading God to hand them over to their enemies to be oppressed, so that they would cry out to God to be delivered. The wisdom of this arrangement is that it continually reveals to the people that their only safety is in God, so that they are continually led to seek refuge in God alone, as their false efforts to secure their lives continually fail. There is in fact a major strand of Hebraic tradition that sees this arrangement as the best way to keep the people in safety. Thus, over against the people's request for a king, Samuel rehearses the cycle of Judges in the following way: "Then they cried to the Lord and said, 'We have sinned, because we have forsaken the LORD, and have served the Baals and the Astartes; but now rescue us out of the hand of our enemies, and we will serve you.' And the LORD sent Jerubaal and Barak, and Jephthah, and Samson, and rescued you out of the hands of your enemies on every side, *and you lived in safety*" (1 Sam 12:10–11). God sees the request for a king as the people's rejection of God as King over them, for God is the only one who can secure their existence in the land (1 Sam 8:4–9).

According to a different Hebrew tradition the cycle of idolatry, oppression, prayer, and deliverance means that the people are never really safe and secure in the land but are rather constantly harassed by their enemies and threatened with destruction. This contradicts the way God seeks to deliver the afflicted from their troubles so that they might live in safety. According to this tradition God sends the king to the people, initially in the person of Saul, to deliver them from their affliction as their cry rises up to God. "Tomorrow about this time I will send to you a man from the land of Benjamin, and you shall anoint him to be ruler over my people Israel. He shall save my people from the hand of the Philistines; for I have seen the suffering of my people, because their outcry has come to me" (1 Sam 9:16). After God rejects Saul as king, God does not abandon the monarchy as the solution to giving the people the security for which they long but rather turns to David. David is a person after God's own heart, and his desire to build a house for the name of God in Jerusalem leads God to promise David that he and his sons will be the ones through whom God will finally keep the people safe and secure in the land, in contrast to their insecurity in the time of the judges. "I will make for you a great name, like the name of the great ones of the earth. And I will appoint a place for my people Israel and will plant them, so that they may live in their own place, and be disturbed no more; and evildoers shall afflict them no more, as formerly, from the time that I appointed judges over my people Israel; and I will give you rest from your enemies" (2 Sam 7:9–11).

God's promise is in fact fulfilled during the reign of David's son Solomon. "During Solomon's lifetime Judah and Israel lived in safety, from Dan even to Beer-sheba, all of them under their vines and fig trees" (1 Kgs 4:25). Once Solomon builds the house for God's name, God increases the security of the people by promising to dwell in this temple forever. After Solomon consecrates the temple, God appears to him and says, "I have heard your prayer and your plea, which you made before me; I have consecrated this house that you have built, and put my name there forever; my eyes and my heart will be there for all time" (1 Kgs 9:3). According to this strand of Hebraic tradition, God abandons the plan to send judges when the people cry to

God in their affliction and seeks to keep the people safe and secure for all time both by the perpetuity of the Davidic monarchy, which will be blessed and protected by the steadfast love of God forever, and by the perpetuity of the temple in Jerusalem, in which God chooses to dwell forever. "For the Lord has chosen Zion; he has desired it for his habitation: 'This is my resting place forever; here I will reside, for I have desired it'" (Ps 132:13–14).

Israel's safety and security is now no longer founded only in God but also in Jerusalem, in the monarchy and the temple that God has chosen forever. God promises never to withdraw God's steadfast love from the descendants of David, as he withdrew it from Saul, even were they to fall into sin (2 Samuel 7, Psalm 89). God will hand the enemies of the king over to him so that he will keep the people safe from all who threaten them. "I have found my servant David; with my holy oil I have anointed him; my arm shall also strengthen him. The enemy shall not outwit him, the wicked shall not humble him. I will crush his foes before him and strike down those who hate him. My faithfulness and steadfast love shall be with him" (Ps 89:20–24). The king is not to trust in his own strength or in the strength of other rulers, for the Lord is the only refuge for the king. "It is better to take refuge in the Lord than to put confidence in mortals. It is better to take refuge in the Lord than to put confidence in princes" (Ps 118:8–9). However, when the king cries out to the Lord for help, God will in fact answer and give the king victory over all who threaten the security and safety of his kingdom. "All nations surrounded me; in the name of the Lord I cut them off! They surrounded me, surrounded me on every side; in the name of the Lord I cut them off! They surrounded me like bees, they blazed like a fire of thorns; in the name of the Lord I cut them off!" (Ps 118:10–12). The safety and security of the people therefore rest in the fact that the house of David rules in Jerusalem, to protect the Israelites from all their foes. "The Lord says to my lord, 'Sit at my right hand until I make your enemies your footstool.' The Lord sends out from Zion your mighty scepter. Rule in the midst of your foes" (Ps 110:1–2).

Reinforcing the security of Israel under the Davidic monarchy is the fact that God dwells on Mount Zion, in the temple that Solomon built for God's name. With God in the midst of the city, the people can dwell secure, for the presence of God will defend them. "Great is the Lord and greatly to be praised in the city of our God. His holy mountain, beautiful in elevation, is the joy of all the earth, Mount Zion, in the far north, the city of the great King. Within its citadels God has shown himself a sure defense" (Ps 48:1–3). Taking refuge in God now means taking refuge in the defense that God gives to Jerusalem by dwelling in its midst, even when the city is besieged by its enemies. "God is in the midst of the city; it shall not be moved; God will help it when morning dawns. The nations are in an uproar, the kingdoms totter; he utters his voice, the earth melts. The LORD of hosts is with us; the God of Jacob is our refuge" (Ps 46:5–6). God will fight for the city of God even without the Davidic king, even without a single soldier, no matter how powerful the adversaries of the city seem to be, for even the sight of the city of God sends its enemies into a panic. "The kings assembled, they came on together. As soon as they saw it, they were astounded; they were in panic, they took to flight; trembling took hold of them there, pains as of a woman in labor, as when an east wind shatters the ships of Tarshish. As we have heard, so we have seen in the city of the LORD of hosts, in the city of God, which God establishes forever" (Ps 48:4–8). The security of Jerusalem is therefore founded on God's unconditional promise to show the Davidic king steadfast love and to dwell in the temple on Mount Zion forever. "Pray for the peace of Jerusalem: 'May they prosper who love you. Peace be within your walls, and security within your towers'" (Ps 122:6–7).

The Israelites now have two distinct ways of remaining secure in the land. The first is to trust God alone and help the poor and needy. The second is the Davidic monarchy and the temple, which God promises will both last forever. The question now becomes which source of security serves as the foundation for the other. Will God continue to protect the city if the king leads the people to worship other gods? Will God continue to defend Jerusalem if the king oppresses the poor and needy? Will God be a sure defense of Jerusalem if the king seeks to insure the security of the city by making treaties with the powerful nations surrounding Israel? The prophets sent to Jerusalem appear to give differing answers to these questions. Isaiah seems to make the presence of God foundational to the security of Jerusalem, even though he gives a scathing indictment of the Davidic king regarding the treatment of the poor and needy. "The LORD enters into judgment with the elders and princes of his people: It is you who have devoured the vineyard; the spoil of the poor is in your houses. What do you mean by crushing my people, by grinding the face of the poor? Says the LORD God of hosts" (Isa 3:14–15). Isaiah also rejects Hezekiah's attempt to seek security in alliances with other rulers to defend Jerusalem from the Assyrians, calling such arrangements "a covenant with death" and an agreement with Sheol, which will not stand (Isa 28:15). For Isaiah, the king is above all to be still and trust in the Lord, and in God's promise to defend Jerusalem, no matter how powerful the enemies of Jerusalem appear to be. "Thus says the LORD, the Holy One of Israel: In returning and rest you shall be saved; in quietness and in trust shall be your strength" (Isa 30:15). The king is to trust that God will fight for Jerusalem in the same way that God fought against Pharaoh at the shore of the Red Sea, when certain death threatened the Hebrews on all sides. "But Moses said to the people, 'Do not be afraid, stand firm, and see the deliverance that the LORD will accomplish for you today; for the Egyptians whom you see today you shall never see again. The LORD will fight for you, and you have only to keep still'" (Exod 14:13–14). In spite of the fact that Hezekiah makes a covenant of death with Egypt to secure himself against Assyria, when King Sennacherib of Assyria finally lays siege to Jerusalem and all seems to be lost, God does in fact fight to defend the city, not because of the trust of the king and not because the king cares for the poor and needy but for the sake of God's unconditional promises to the temple and to David. "By the way that he came, by the same shall he return; he will not come into this city, says the LORD. For I will defend this city to save it, for my own sake and for the sake of my servant David" (Isa 38:34–35).

Micah and Jeremiah, on the other hand, think that the trust of the people in the promise of God to defend Jerusalem is conditional on their care of the poor and needy. There can be no security for the king or the city when the poor and needy are oppressed, no matter what promises God made to David and the temple. In fact, those who trust in the temple thinking they are safe from danger when they oppress the poor and needy are sadly mistaken, for God will destroy the temple. "Hear this, you rulers of the house of Jacob, and chiefs of the house of Israel, who abhor justice and pervert all equity, who build Zion with blood and Jerusalem with wrong! Its rulers give judgment for a bribe, its priests teach for a price, its prophets give oracles for money; yet they lean upon the LORD and say, 'Surely the LORD is with us! No harm shall come upon us.' Therefore because of you Zion shall be plowed up as a field; Jerusalem shall become a heap of ruins, and the mountain of the house a wooded height" (Mic 3:9–12).

Jeremiah follows the same line of approach, insisting that the promise of God to dwell in the temple and to protect the city is completely dependent on the righteousness of the rulers and people, manifested in the way they care for the poor and the needy. Thus he declares in the temple, "If you truly amend your ways and your doings, if you truly act justly one with another, if you do not oppress the alien, the orphan, and the widow, or shed innocent blood in this place, and if you do not go after other gods to your own hurt, then I will dwell with you in this place, in the land I gave of old to your ancestors forever and ever" (Jer 7:5–7). However, if the people keep oppressing the poor and needy thinking that they will nonetheless be safe and secure because God dwells in the temple, then God will destroy the temple in Jerusalem just as he did the temple at Shiloh (Jer 7:8–15). Such words directly threaten the security of Jerusalem as it was understood at the time, so it is not surprising that the king wanted to have Jeremiah put to death for saying such things about the temple. Jeremiah is only spared by an appeal to the precedent of king Hezekiah, who did not put Micah to death when he preached the same message (Jer 26:10–19).

Jeremiah makes the same move regarding God's promise always to be with David. Jeremiah makes the security of the Davidic king conditional on the righteousness of the king, especially in terms of his treatment of the poor and needy in the land. Jeremiah insists that David's security came from the fact that he helped the poor and needy. "He judged the cause of the poor and needy; then it was well" (Jer 22:16). If the king oppresses the poor, there can be no security for the king, even if he is a son of David. "To the house of Judah say: Hear the word of the Lord, O house of David! Thus says the Lord: Execute justice in the morning, and deliver from the hand of the oppressor anyone who has been robbed, or else my wrath will go forth like fire, and burn, with no one to quench it, because of your evil doings" (Jer 21:11–12). Because the kings ignore this warning, when King Jehoiakim asks Jeremiah if God will perform a "wonderful deed" to save Jerusalem from the Babylonians the way God saved the city from the Assyrians, Jeremiah responds by telling him that God will not fight for Jerusalem to save it, for God is now fighting against Jerusalem to destroy it. "I myself will fight against you with outstretched hand and mighty arm, in anger, in fury, and in great wrath. And I will strike down the inhabitants of this city, both human beings and animals; they shall die of a great pestilence" (Jer 21:5–6).

The destruction of the temple and the city of Jerusalem and the captivity and deportation of the Davidic king to Babylon is devastating and convincing proof that there can be no safety or security for the unjust who oppress the poor and the needy and who do not defend the orphan, the widow, and the stranger. After the return from Babylon, the people would never again make the mistake of thinking they could be secure while contradicting the very nature of God, who is the watcher and defender of the poor, the needy, the afflicted, and the oppressed. However, the post-exilic period brings with it a new and apparently insoluble problem, which raises serious questions about the security of the righteous. For in this period it began to become lucidly clear that the righteous are afflicted for their righteousness by the wicked, who seem to live in complete safety and security. The destruction of the Babylonian invasion and exile could be explained by Israel's oppression of the poor and needy in the land, but how could one now explain the suffering of those who trust in God and help the afflicted? "All this has come upon us, yet we have not forgotten you, or been false to your covenant. Our heart has not turned back, nor have our steps departed from your way, yet you have broken us in the haunt of jackals, and covered us with deep darkness" (Ps 44:17–19). God is not granting security to the righteous but is rather handing them over to be afflicted and destroyed by the wicked. "Because of you we are being killed all day long, and accounted as sheep for the slaughter" (Ps 44:22). One example of this dilemma is the suffering and death that took place in Judea during the time of Antiochus IV, Epiphanes, for it was precisely those who obeyed the law of God who were tortured and killed (2 Macc 6–7).

A more vivid example is the figure of Job. In spite of the fact that he helped the poor and the needy and did not trust in other gods besides the Lord, Job did not live in security but rather suffered the loss of his home, his possessions, his family, and his health. "Truly the thing I fear comes upon me, and what I dread befalls me. I am not at ease, nor am I quiet; I have no rest; but trouble comes" (Job 3:25–26). Job concludes that God is attacking and afflicting him, intentionally destroying the security he once had. "I was at ease, and he broke me in two; he seized me by the neck and dashed me to pieces" (Job 16:12). Making matters even worse, Job sees that God does not afflict the wealthy and powerful who plunder the poor and afflict the needy but rather gives to them the security that God denies to the righteous. "The tents of robbers are at peace, those who provoke God are secure, who bring their gods in their hands" (Job 12:6).

Far from being his refuge from all danger of death, God has become the source of Job's affliction, even though Job trusts God and does what is right. "Therefore I am terrified at his presence; when I consider, I am in dread of him. God has made my heart faint; the Almighty has horrified me" (Job 23:15–16). When Job cries out to God in his affliction, God does not respond. ""I cry out to you and you do not answer me; I stand, and you merely look at me" (Job 30:20). Job's experience of being abandoned to death even when he cries out to God is echoed in the psalms. In spite of the fact that the psalmist has no help from the power of death and the pit except God, God refuses to answer when the psalmist cries out to God for refuge. "But I, O Lord, cry out to you; in the morning my prayer comes before you. O Lord, why do you cast me off? Why do you hide your face from me? Wretched and close to death from my youth up, I suffer your terrors; I am desperate. Your wrath has swept over me; your dread assaults destroy me" (Ps 88:13–16). The psalmist receives no answer other than the silence of isolation and darkness (Ps 88:18). How can God afflict the afflicted who call upon God and seek refuge in God from the power of death and yet give security to those who trust in their wealth, their strength, and their false gods, and who oppress the poor? "They harm the childless woman, and do no good to the widow. Yet God prolongs the life of the mighty by his power; they rise up when they despair of life. He gives them security, and they are supported; his eyes are upon their ways" (Job 24:21–23).

This problem appears to be insoluble on the grounds of the Hebrew Scriptures. The revelation of the nature and character of God is revealed in the exodus from Egypt: God hears the cries of the people, sees their affliction, delivers them from the power of death, and brings them to a place of safety and security. The people will remain in safety in the land if they trust in God alone, and not in idols, or their wealth, or their princes; and if they hear the cry of the poor and needy in their midst. "Trust in the LORD, and do good; so you will live in the land, and enjoy security" (Ps 37:3). Even though it seemed for a while that the people would be given greater security than this with the temple and king in Jerusalem, the exile in Babylon reveals that trusting God and helping the poor is foundational to their security in the land. However, if the righteous who trust in the Lord and who defend the widow, the orphan, and the stranger are themselves afflicted and oppressed, while the wicked are given the security which the righteous are denied, then it seems as though there can be no security for the godly at all in this life.

This is exactly the answer given to this problem in the teaching of Jesus and the apostles. Far from being surprised or dismayed by the affliction of the righteous in this life, Jesus pronounces a blessing on those who are persecuted for righteousness' sake. "Blessed are you when people revile you and persecute you and utter all kinds of evil against you falsely on my account. Rejoice and be glad, for in the same way they persecuted the prophets who were before you" (Matt 5:11–12). To see how radically different this is from the Hebrew Scriptures, we only have to look at Jeremiah. When he was persecuted and reviled, he did not consider himself to be blessed, and he certainly did not rejoice. Rather, he cried out to God to deliver him from persecution and to destroy those who persecuted him. "Let my persecutors be shamed, but do not let me be shamed; let them be dismayed, but do not let me be dismayed; bring on them the day of disaster; destroy them with double destruction!" (Jer 17:18). Jesus, on the other hand, not only wants the faithful to rejoice in the blessing of persecution but also commands them to love their enemies and pray for those who persecute them (Matt 5:44). Far from delivering his followers from affliction, oppression, and death, Jesus assures them that suffering and death will come upon all who follow him. "Do not think that I have come to bring peace on earth; I have not come to bring peace, but a sword. For I have come to set a man against his father, and a daughter against her mother, and a daughter-in-law against her mother-in-law; and one's foes will be members of one's own household" (Matt 10:34–36). Indeed, Jesus assures his followers that there will never be a time of peace and security for them in this life, but only suffering, persecution, and affliction. "Then they will hand you over to be tortured and will put you to death, and you will be hated by all nations because of my name. Then many will fall away, and will betray one another and hate one another" (Matt 24:9–10). Only those who endure this affliction to the end will be saved.

Far from bringing the afflicted to a place of safety and security, Jesus goes out of his way to remove all such forms of security from his followers. He commands his followers to sell all their possessions and give to the poor, leaving them without any means of securing their lives in this world (Luke 12:33). His followers are forbidden to defend themselves when their enemies seek to destroy them and are commanded to give away even more of their possessions when thieves steal from them (Matt 5:38–42). Indeed, Jesus explicitly warns his followers that those who seek to secure their lives will lose them (Matt 16:25). Unlike the kings who reigned in Jerusalem, Jesus does not have power over his enemies but will rather be handed over to them to suffer and die. "See, we are going up to Jerusalem, and the Son of Man will be handed over to the chief priests and scribes, and they will condemn him to death; then they will hand him over to the Gentiles to be mocked and flogged and crucified" (Matt 20:18–19). Those who follow him will similarly be powerless against their enemies and will suffer and die at the hands of those who hate them. "Brother will betray brother to death, and a father his child, and children will rise against parents and have them put to death; and you will be hated by all because of my name. But the one who endures to the end will be saved" (Matt 10:21–22). The faithful of Israel cry out to God to free them from the power of death in this life. "Turn, O LORD, save my life; deliver me for the sake of your steadfast love. For in death there is no remembrance of you; in Sheol who can give you praise?" (Ps 6:4–5). Jesus promises those who follow him that they will be blessed when their enemies who hate them put them to death and assures them that their enemies will come from within their own families.

The situation is not any different for those who believe that God raised the crucified Jesus from the dead. In fact, in his defense of the resurrection Paul insists that he is in danger every hour. "I die every day!" (1 Cor 15:31). Paul describes those who have faith in Christ as afflicted in every way, perplexed, persecuted, and struck down (2 Cor 4:8–9). The faithful are sentenced to death, hungry, beaten, homeless, weary, reviled, persecuted, and slandered—indeed, they are "the rubbish of the world, the dregs of all things, to this very day" (1 Cor 4:10–13). Far from being freed of the afflictions that assail him, Paul commends himself to his readers by the afflictions he experiences for the sake of Christ, boasting of floggings, lashings, stoning, shipwrecks, hardships, calamities, beatings, imprisonments, riots, labors, sleepless nights, and hunger (2 Cor 6:4–5). The one time Paul asked the Lord to free him from affliction, his request was denied (2 Cor 12:8–9). Far from being brought to a place of safety and security, Paul claims he is exposed to "danger from rivers, danger from bandits, danger from my own people, danger from the Gentiles, danger in the city, danger in the wilderness, danger at sea, danger from false brothers and sisters" (2 Cor 11:26). Rather than being dismayed by this kind of affliction, Paul confidently declares, "I am content with weaknesses, insults, hardships, persecutions, and calamities for the sake of Christ" (2 Cor 12:10). Indeed, whereas the psalmist had complained that being subjected to the power of death contradicted the way God should treat those whom God loves, Paul confidently declares that such affliction is precisely what it means to be loved by God. "Who will separate us from the love of Christ? Will hardship, or distress, or persecution, or famine, or nakedness, or peril, or sword? As it is written, 'For your sake we are being killed all day long; we are accounted as sheep to be slaughtered'" (Rom 8:35–36). Instead of crying out to God to be delivered from suffering and persecution, Paul says that we are to "boast in our sufferings, knowing that suffering produces endurance, and endurance produces character, and character produces hope, and hope does not disappoint us, because God's love has been poured into our hearts by the Holy Spirit that has been given to us" (Rom 5:3–5). On the other hand, those who seek security in this life are setting themselves up for complete destruction. "When they say, 'There is peace and security,' then sudden destruction will come upon them, as labor pains come upon a pregnant woman, and there will be no escape" (1 Thess 5:3). For Paul the afflictions and persecution we experience prove the validity of our faith, not the fact that we dwell secure in the land. "For you, brothers and sisters, became imitators of the churches of God in Jesus Christ that are in Judea, for you suffered the same things from your own compatriots as they did from the Jews, who killed both the Lord Jesus and the prophets, and drove us out" (1 Thess 2:14–15).

In sum, the preaching of Jesus and the apostles solves the problem created by the suffering and affliction of the righteous by eliminating any and every thought that there could be anything like safety and security in this life. The removal of earthly security has other spiritual advantages as well. The godly will never be tempted to trust in their wealth instead of God, as they will be utterly impoverished. The faithful will never be tempted to trust in their rulers and princes, as they will be the very ones persecuting, torturing, and executing them. The godly will never oppress the poor and needy, for they will be more destitute than any of the poor. The godly will never be drawn to the worship of idols and false gods, for their worshippers will be seeking to put the godly to death. Their suffering and affliction will not cause them to despair but rather to rejoice, and they will not doubt the love of God when they are handed over to suffering and death but will be confident that this is exactly what happens to those who are loved by God in Christ.

# RESPONSE TO ZACHMAN

## Kyle J. A. Small

After I finished Prof. Zachman's essay, I began to wonder as a wealthy, American Christian, who faces trivial suffering, how we can live cruciform lives as God's people in *this life*? It appears that Prof. Zachman seeks to overcome the idolatry of security through an exploration into a cruciform doxology, a life of affliction and praise. He proposes a hermeneutical reading of Scripture for an American church that has too often coveted an overly realized eschatology and has forgotten about discipleship in *this life*. His hermeneutic reminds the church that resurrection was not an invitation to the world that we might rest *secure*.

Prof. Zachman creates a posture that is "this life" oriented. In a cultural milieu where "spiritual life" is too commonly an escape clause, Zachman offers the ethical reminder that God engages the here and now, especially through justice to the poor and needy. The pursuit of security in another life can too often reduce salvation to a fire insurance plan when Hartford Life and State Farm fail us and we end up anxious and "half-alive" in this life. Prof. Zachman actually seems to have very little concern for another life. He does not overcome anxiety and insecurity by searching for security in the Bible but by noting its insolubility and absence. The response to anxiety, fear, and insecurity is not security, from God or otherwise, but through cruciform doxology.

The essay surveys Scripture in ten performative acts (eight OT acts: Psalms, Proverbs, 1 Samuel, the prophets Isaiah, Micah, and Jeremiah, Job, and Exodus; and two NT acts: Jesus and Paul). He argues that security is only seemingly attainable in waiting upon the Lord, even if God continues to be absent and silent. If security is even seemingly attainable, it is only practiced through justice to the poor and needy through a dual agency, namely the crucified God and the suffering kingdom of Israel (and the church); yet again this is about dependence on and doxology toward God, not about stability and security. For example, the words of the psalmists (and even Job and the prophets) lavish praise on God even when, or maybe especially when, violence and destruction upset the comfort and sabbath rest that Israel (and the church, and Christians) enjoy. Prof. Zachman argues that if there is any reality to security in the OT it is conditional on a godly dependence and just practices for the poor and needy.

Prof. Zachman turns from the OT to the NT with the linkage, "it seems as though there can be no security for the godly at all in this life . . . This is exactly the answer given to this problem in the teaching of Jesus and the Apostles." The last two acts of this performance complete the claim that there is indeed no pursuit of security within the Christian life. Security is not a Christian virtue or practice. The pursuit is not security but doxology through a cruciform choir, the church. The lack of security in this life and the reckless abandonment within the cruciform life might push us to ask, "Can we love God and practice justice for naught?" We will suffer and die in this life.

Prof. Zachman captures within Scripture a new narrative identity, a cruciform identity that is fully alive in this life as it overlooks security all together. The paper is an invitation to a narrative identity, a suffering justice, and this cruciform hope makes little room, if not completely eclipses, the whole idea of security as a Christian perspective and practice.

There is a problem here if I hope to take Prof. Zachman or his thought home with me. My wife and I are pastors in a suburban congregation southwest of Minneapolis. We are a wealthy church, and our neighborhood has interesting neighbors. Paula Abdul's producer, Jimmy Jam, several Minnesota Twins and Vikings athletes, and the artist formerly known as Prince live within three miles of our church building. Single family homes begin at $400,000, and elderly who own their homes are moving because they cannot afford the taxes. The type of lifestyle embodied in our community presumes a world of financial security and family protection. To prove this point, two years ago our congregation engaged in a series of interviews with area politicians, social service agencies, and educators. We were trying to create a vision and ministry plan. We asked questions regarding values, recent changes, and growing concerns within the community as a whole. Several respondents stated that a core value was the preservation of safety and security. The second question regarded the recent changes in the neighborhood. Several responded that the potential rise in immigrant populations, more lower income residents, and growing crime are new changes.[1] We finally engaged the respondents on community concerns, and respondents stated (after noting the changes in the community) that personal safety, child safety, and identity security were increasingly under threat. Another respondent

---

1. This inquiry was occurring during the possible immigrant influx from Southeast Asia to the Minneapolis/St. Paul area.

said, "The community simply wants a safe place for our children to grow up." Given a cruciform ecclesiology, how does one preach the gospel and serve as a minister of reconciliation when the community is at threat level orange?

The gospel in the world has a "this life" orientation that is cruciform in practice, as Prof. Zachmann has expressed, yet for *faithful* and *lifelong* Christians in the suburbs of Minneapolis upholding security is at the core of their Christian discipleship. Unfortunately there has been little challenge to the security we/they have enjoyed. Cruciformity has been mentioned elsewhere in the conference papers and conversations, but the fact is that very few American theologians, pastors, and congregations will have to confront cross-bearing in any real or significant way. This is a moment of confession. I think Prof. Zachmann has offered a clear ethic that the very thing my community values cannot be conceived by faith in God, or in Zachman's words, "security is insoluble within the biblical witness." Obviously, I have a problem if I take Zachman home with me.

Even so, I would like to explore the reality of his proposal through two pastoral situations: the upcoming 2008 presidential election and the practices of investments and financial planning. First, as a pastor, I do not look forward to the upcoming presidential elections. Behind the trivial rhetoric of pitbulls and community organizers and the out-of-touch and the elite liberal news media is a campaign committed to the promotion of security. The promises made by each and every candidate are that they will make decisions, policy, and military action that will *protect* your household economy and your family. Every candidate runs on a platform of peace and prosperity through the rhetoric of security. I cannot blame them; this is the nation-state's value system, and this is what Americans seek from the government. Yet, this is a conflict with our discipleship. The conflict welcomes a conversation between Romans 13 and Revelation 13. Painfully, the Christian church in the United States continues to seek hope and promise in the presidential candidates, all the while forgetting the story of 1 Samuel 8, which provides the litany of all the things that the king (chosen by God or otherwise) will *take* from those he rules. To seek hope and promise in Washington D.C. is to walk "half-alive and weakly," citing Calvin. The very persons we hope to offer us security and protection by the sword are indeed those who have the power to hang an economic or military "sword around our necks."

Secondly, the narrative identity of cruciform doxology needs to understand how to live in a time that expects (and usually blesses) financial security through Wall Street investments and financial planning institutions. How do those of us who have an abundance live out a cruciform doxology with our financial wealth? What is a revised understanding for planning and saving in a cruciform life? Christians do not give to receive, nor do they practice generosity out of power and excess. Christian stewardship *can* reap an abundant harvest, albeit for participation in God's justice, not security or storing up treasures. This is to be distinguished from the common practice of the empires who plan and store up and even give from within a *benefactor* framework, or as Walter Brueggemann explains, a royal conscience.[2] Benefactors give for prestige, and they always hold to a remainder. They want to control benevolently and consume, and they give out of xenophobia to keep the enemies satisfied, as well as their quest for human immortality and freedom from anxiety. The benefactor must store and give away resources in order to squelch their inherent fear of loss. Disciples are not *benefactors* (Luke 22:25–26). If I understand Prof. Zachman's implications, planning and stewardship are not washed away in cruciform doxology, but instead cruciform generosity is a participation in the atonement through the practices of Jubilee (the economics of Leviticus 25). The narrative identity from Prof. Zachman radically reorients a person and the church to new life in a cruciform economy.

Therefore, when AIG, Lehmann Brothers, and Bear Stearns collapse, Christians rejoice: "This is the day the LORD has made, let us rejoice and be glad in it." We echo the Passover liturgy: "We should have been content." Doxology is the language of resurrection. Despite Prof. Zachman's seemingly intentional inattention to the resurrection, his call for praise and rejoicing is a reminder and the traditional ecclesial practice signifying that new life is indeed here and coming.[3]

Prof. Zachman's essay welcomes a new narrative identity. The ethic he offers argues that a presidential race rooted in protecting your security, or an economy rooted in excess and remainder is contrary to a life rooted in cruciformity. It has no doxology but only self-praise. When the Christian life looks to security versus looking over it (focused, instead, on the in-breaking reign of God), we fall into a life of idolatry.

All of this said, I conclude with two questions and a statement. First, the image of suffering and affliction is agreeable, yet in the western world which is rich with

---

2. See Frederick W. Danker, *Benefactor: Epigraphic Study of a Graeco-Roman and New Testament Semantic Field* (St. Louis: Clayton, 1982). See also Walter Brueggemann, *Prophetic Imagination* (Minneapolis: Fortress, 2001).

3. See Mark Noll's essay, "Evangelicalism at its Best" in *American Evangelical Christianity: An Introduction* (Oxford: Blackwell, 2001).

idolatry and insecurity, money and position, how do we conceive of an ecclesiology centered in a cruciform doxology? Second, I am a father of a fifteen month-old son, Micah, named after a bold prophet who rebuked idolatry and security. How do we understand your proposal of a cruciform doxology for those who are called to the vocation of parenting?

My church is happy when I say nothing about politics or their money, and if I question the pursuit of security, indeed I will be crucified. Besides, I enjoy my middle-class lifestyle, my home, and my professional security; I too am idolatrous.

# HOMELAND INSECURITY
## The Spiritual Lust for an Escape Clause

## Ben Witherington III

In perilous times religious people look to their religion for succor and reassurance that things, though they now appear to be going all wrong, will in the end turn out all right. This desire or anxiety for something more than just assurance, for some kind of theological guarantee of eternal security or at least eternal safety from the most outrageous forms of the slings and arrows of fortune, is understandable in a world full of trouble and tribulation. Two of the theological ways these sorts of anxieties have been manifested and dealt with in the Protestant movement have been through the emphasis on eternal security when it comes to the matter of salvation proper and timely safety when the "final tribulation" comes, which some of the faithful expect at the end time. This essay focuses on the second of these artful attempts to dodge reality, not least because in America rapture theology had its major birthplace right here in our host city, Chicago.

As church historians have noted, since the Protestant reformation it has been especially during times of war and depression and stock market crashes that these sorts of theologies of eternal security or heavenly rescue have played to good effect and have been most zealously embraced. One can see this in modern dispensational circles especially. Among conservative Christians during the Gulf War and the Iraq War there was a spike in sales of books such as John Walvoord's *Armagedon, Oil, and the Middle East Crisis*[1] or of novels like the "Left Behind" series.

Looking for the spiritual equivalent of comfort food, many people have consumed such notions in large quantities. Of course the irony and paradox has been that while at the same time the larger culture was placing more and more emphasis on Homeland Security through political means this has only ramped up the fears of many, including those already most prone to think apocalyptically about our times. The rhetoric of empire, however well coordinated with certain kinds of theological reflections "that all will be well and all manner of things will be well," has not suc-

---

1. Grand Rapids: Zondervan, 1990.

ceeded in quieting the spiritually disquieted, and as we shall see, it did not do so in Paul's day either.

Our task in this essay is to examine in somewhat cursory fashion the rhetoric of "rapture" set over against the "rhetoric of empire," using 1 Thessalonians 4–5 as a context for a discussion of theological safety or security during tribulation. We will discover that "the assurance of things hoped for" did not entail a guarantee of either eternal security or of an escape clause should things go bump in the night on planet earth.

## Head in the Clouds—The Theology of Rapture

I have elsewhere chronicled at some length the amazing story of that modern phenomenon known as Dispensationalism or in England as Darbyism.[2] This theology, interestingly enough, did not arise in the first place in America but in Scotland and England in the first half of the nineteenth century, but it certainly flourished like a native plant when it was brought to America by J. N. Darby and then promulgated at length by D. L. Moody of Chicago, among others. In fact the first American Christian bestseller after the Civil War, *Jesus is Coming*, was written right here in Chicago by an entrepreneur named W. E. Dubois (1878), trumpeting the rapture theology and the imminent but invisible return of Christ.

Dispensational theology was and is synthetic in nature, by which I mean it has a propensity to glue together otherwise disparate texts in order to create a picture of a deeply cherished theological idea—in this case the pre-tribulation or mid-tribulation rapture of the faithful out of the world when the maelstrom of final judgment begins to afflict a fallen and sinful world. Bits from Revelation are welded onto bits from the teaching of Jesus, but it is fair to say that while such texts provide the superstructure of such notions, the real engine and chassis of this vehicle comes from a certain interpretation of 1 Thessalonians 4, which is where we will concentrate our attention.

The linchpin text for a rapture theology is of course 1 Thess 4:13–5:11[3] which reads in part:

---

2. See Witherington, *The Problem with Evangelical Theology* (Waco: Baylor University Press, 2005). See the two chapters entitled "On Dispensing with Dispensationalism."

3. For an in-depth treatment of other "rapture" texts including the "left behind" texts from Matt 24 and parallels see Witherington, *The Problem with Evangelical Theology*.

> For this I say to you in/on the word of the Lord that we the living, those who are left around until the parousia of the Lord will not forestall those who have fallen asleep, for the Lord himself with a summons, with the voice of the archangel, and with the trumpet of God will come down from heaven and the dead in Christ will rise first; then we the living, those left around, together with them shall be caught up in the clouds unto the public welcoming of the Lord in the air and so we will always be with the Lord. So console one another with these words. But concerning the times and seasons brothers, you have no need for me to write to you, for you yourselves know accurately that the day of the Lord as a thief in the night, thus it shall come.

To understand this text one must realize that the Parousia is not something different from the second coming or the coming of the thief in the night or the glorious appearing of Christ. These are all alternate ways of describing the same dramatic event. The public nature of the event is stressed. It involves a public herald (in this case an angel) and a trumpet blast announcing to all that Christ is coming. The imagery here presupposed is drawn from the notion of a royal visit to a city, with the cry of command going up to the watchman on the walled city as we see in the royal entrance liturgy in Psalm 24. Our text then says that the dead in Christ will rise and go to meet Christ in the air and will be joined by the living in Christ.

The location of this rendezvous is not heaven but the earth's atmosphere. More importantly, the place where the gathering goes after meeting is down to earth to reign, not up to heaven to escape a tribulation. This is perfectly clear from the use of the royal visitation language in 1 Thessalonians 4. The greeting committee goes out to meet the Lord where he is and then welcomes him back into the walled city. Though Paul does not spell this out in detail, the allusion is so clear that it could hardly have been missed by the Thessalonians who had had such royal visitations in the past, indeed whose city was named for the sister of Alexander the Great himself. In other words there is no concept of the "rapture" in the NT, if by rapture one means something more than a meeting of Christ in the air at the second coming. There is no "beam me up Scotty" theology in the NT. Indeed, if one actually studies this text in the larger context of 1 Thessalonians it becomes clear that the Thessalonians had already suffered, and some had apparently died for their faith. The anxiety being responded to here was not whether they had been martyred (and others might be) but whether the dead in Christ would miss out on the return of Christ, which Paul reassures they will not.

## The Social and Literary Context of 1 Thessalonians 4–5

There is more to the social and rhetorical context of this text than at first meets the eye. Notice first the connection in 1 Thess 4:13 between grieving and being like the remainder of humanity that has no hope. *It is the inevitability of death which robs persons of their sense of hope or security.* Notice also the use of the present subjunctive verb which implies the cessation of something. The Thessalonians are grieving for those Christians they have already lost, and Paul wants them to stop grieving for them.

Grieving is for those without hope, and it is the natural reaction for those who have no positive view of the afterlife. Notice as well the implication of the phrase "the rest of humanity who have no hope." Paul is suggesting that outside of Christ there is no hope of life beyond death. Paul was certainly no universalist or pluralist when it came to the matter of salvation, but it was not just that pagans had no hope of a positive afterlife. According to 1 Thess 1:10 and 5:9 (cf. Rom 1:18–32; 11:7; Eph 2:3) they faced the judgment of God both in the present and in the future. Things look bleak for pagans from Paul's viewpoint.

On the opposite end of the spectrum, *Paul is assuming that for Christians an increase in hope will cause an increase in holiness.* They will be in earnest about Christian behavior because they know what is coming. He is also assuming that a proper knowledge of the fate of the Christian dead should put a stop to hopeless grieving. In 4:13 *kathōs kai* really cannot be translated "to the same extent as the pagans." Paul is here urging a cessation of grieving altogether, the grieving which was already ongoing.

Although grammatically awkward, in the second half of v. 14 Paul is showing what follows from believing Jesus died and rose. This belief has a consequence for what we should believe about the fate of the Christian dead. The structure of the Greek as we have it favors linking the phrase "through Jesus" with "those who have fallen asleep." But, what does it mean to have fallen asleep through Jesus? Does it mean what Acts 7:29 suggests, that Jesus will receive the spirit of the Christian when she dies? Possibly this is so, but it is not probable.

It is possible that *dia* ("through") has the force of *en* here, in which case Paul is speaking about dying *in* the Lord—i.e., dying as a Christian (1 Cor 15:18). In fact, the aorist participle *koimethenta* favors this interpretation since it refers to the moment, not the condition of death: they died in the Lord. It is only deceased Christians that Jesus will bring with him or bring back from the dead when he returns at the

Parousia.[4] This may mean they will be brought with Jesus from heaven, but it may simply mean they will be brought back from the dead and so raised when Jesus returns, as texts like 1 Cor 6:14 and 2 Cor 4:14 suggest. Paul assumes that the concern in Thessalonica was not about resurrection per se but about the relationship of the Christian dead to the Parousia and whether they would participate in the greeting party in the air, when Jesus returned and they would be with him forever. In no case is Paul assuring his audience that they have an escape clause so that they may expect to avoid persecution and the fate of those who have already died in the Lord, unless of course they happen to live until the Lord returns.

Verse 15 has been a flashpoint in the discussion of Pauline eschatology at least since the time of A. Schweitzer. Here, it is said, we have proof positive that Paul believed that he would definitely live to see the Parousia of Jesus. Unfortunately, these sorts of discussions have tended to overlook at least a couple of key factors: Paul did not know in advance when he would die[5] and he argues that the second coming will happen at an unexpected time, like a thief in the night. It could be sooner, it could be later, and in either case the *indeterminancy* of the timing is what fuels exhortations that one must always be prepared and alert. It needs to be stressed that since Paul did not know the specific timing of either his death or the return of Christ, and does not claim to know such things, he could *not* have said "We who are dead and not left around to see the parousia of the Lord."

In short, Paul did not know that he would *not* be alive when Jesus returns, and so the only category in which he can logically place himself and his contemporary Christians is the category of the "living."[6] What these verses surely imply is that Paul thought it *possible* that he might be alive when Jesus returned. Paul, as E. Best has stressed, until he was much older and near death, always had both possibilities before him, both the possibility of living until the Parousia and the possibility of dying first and rising at the Parousia when Jesus returned.[7] The reason we do not

---

4. As in 1 Cor 15 Paul operates with a concept of the resurrection of the righteous. In 1 Cor 15 he can talk about Christ being the first fruits and those in Christ the latter fruits of the resurrection. This is in part because for Paul resurrection means for the believer full conformity to the image of Christ, something the dead outside Christ will not receive when Christ returns. See the discussion in Witherington, *Jesus, Paul, and the End of the World* (Downers Grove, IL: InterVarsity, 1992).

5. One thing this text probably does suggest is that Paul was in good health at this juncture and did not anticipate his imminent demise.

6. See the more detailed discussion in Witherington, *Jesus, Paul, and the End of the World*.

7. See E. Best, *First and Second Thessalonians*, (London: A. & C. Clark, 1972), 195–96. Paul's imagery of the thief implies a denial of knowing with that sort of precision.

hear the language of possible survival until the Parousia in the later Pauline letters is because one of the two unknown factors, the timing of Paul's death, was becoming more likely to precede the Parousia. We should not speak of Paul's changing his view about the second coming or his considering it *delayed* in the later Paulines for the very good reason that the term "delay" implies that one knows with some precision when it was supposed to happen so that when it does not happen one could speak of it as being "late." Paul's imagery of the thief implies a denial of knowing with that sort of precision. Here it could be argued Paul combines a saying of Jesus with his own reflections on Dan 7:13–14 and 12:2–3.

Paul saw himself as both a prophetic interpreter of the sayings of the historical Jesus and of the OT and also as someone who received direct messages from the risen Lord himself. In 1 Thess 4:15–5:7 Paul draws on the Jesus tradition found in Matthew 24, but in vv. 16–17 he also draws on both his own reading of Daniel and prophetic insight that he himself had been given by the risen Lord. The following chart shows the various parallels:

| Theme | 1 Thessalonians | Matthew |
| --- | --- | --- |
| Christ returns | 4:16 | 24:30 |
| from heaven | 4:16 | 24:30 |
| accompanied by angels | 4:16 | 24:31 |
| with a trumpet of God | 4:16 | 24:31 |
| believers gathered to Christ | 4:17 | 24:31, 40–41 |
| in clouds | 4:17 | 24:30 |
| time unknown | 5:1–2 | 24:36 |
| coming like a thief | 5:2, 4 | 24:43 |
| unbelievers unaware of coming judgment | 5:3 | 24:37–39 |
| judgment like a mother's birthpangs | 5:3 | 24:8 |
| believers not deceived | 5:4–5 | 24:43 |
| believers to be watchful | 5:6 | 24:37–39 |
| warning vs. drunkenness[8] | 5:7 | 24:49 |

---

8. Here I am following D. Wenham, *Paul: Follower of Jesus or Founder of Christianity?* (Grand Rapids: Eerdmans, 1995), 303–14 who should be consulted at length on the whole matter of Paul's use of the Jesus traditions. See his "Paul and the Synoptic Apocalypse," in *Gospel Perspectives* (ed. R. T.

These parallels should not be minimized, and they make it likely that Paul is drawing on the general sense, trajectory, and imagery of some of that Synoptic material. They also make clear an important point. Paul did not think there is some difference between the Parousia and the second coming (or glorious appearing). Indeed, as in Matt 24 all of this material is referring to one event, the coming of the Son of Man on the clouds. Notice that the parallels with Matt 24 continue in 1 Thess 5:1–11. This is because Paul does not think he is describing some different event in 1 Thess 5:1–11 than he was in 1 Thess 4:13–18. We can say with even more assurance that the rhetorical function here of citing a "word of the Lord" is to console and reassure the audience about the fate of their deceased Thessalonian brothers and sisters and their equal participation in the Parousia event.[9]

At this juncture something needs to be said about the background of the Danielic material. Daniel 7:13–14 is, of course, part of the famous oracle about "the one like a Son of Man" (*bar 'ĕnāš*). Though it has been debated as to whether this figure goes up into the clouds and heaven to meet the Ancient of Days or comes with the clouds to meet the Almighty on earth for the day of judgment, in light of v. 14 Paul's view must surely be the latter. It is the kingdoms "under heaven" that are handed over to the Son of Man and to the saints, and we are told all rulers will worship and obey this figure. It is surely not envisioned that these non-Jewish kingdoms and rulers are in heaven or are ruled from heaven. The rule, like the final judgment, takes place on earth. Notice as well the statement that the Son of Man comes with the clouds of heaven, an image of clouds coming down from above, not clouds rising up from the earth with someone ascending with them. Theophanies were described as involving this very sort of motion with clouds involved, and a theophany by definition always takes place on earth. This background material is important for another reason. Daniel 7 is about this Son of Man ruling on earth over those who had oppressed God's people. It is not about rescuing God's people out of this world into heaven for an interim period of time. The Son of Man language and imagery taken over from Daniel 7 in the sayings of Jesus in Matthew 24 and here by Paul in 1 Thessalonians provide further proof that 1 Thess 4:13–20 is not about a rapture.

The phrase "we the living, those who are left around/remain" is important for it means Paul envisions that Christians will still be living on planet earth when Jesus

---

France and D. Wenham; Sheffield: JSOT, 1981), 345–75.

9. This reassurance may have been particularly needed by any in Thessalonica who knew teaching such as that found in *4 Ezra* 13:24 which states that those who survive to the end are more blessed than those who die before it.

returns. It also may suggest that he thinks *the majority* of Christians will be dead when Christ returns.[10] But, could the return Paul envisions be said to be a secret or invisible one? Do we have some sort of theology of a pre-tribulation rapture with Jesus not actually coming to earth? The details of the text as well as the use of the language of the royal visit to a city surely rule such a view out.

It has been rightly stressed by G. Beale that we should probably take vv. 14–15 together, with v. 15 providing the reason why believers can be confident about the resurrection of the deceased Christians, namely that Jesus himself spoke of this matter and affirmed this truth.[11] We should also not neglect what Paul says in v. 15b, namely that the living shall not have precedence or any advantage over those who have fallen asleep when it comes to participating in the Parousia event. All believers will be on the same footing when Jesus returns.

As v. 16 makes quite clear, Paul connects the resurrection of believers who are dead with the Parousia and with the meeting of Christ in the air. Clearly it is the Parousia which precipitates these other two events. Notice that there is no mention of the resurrection of unbelievers at this juncture. Paul takes that to be a separate event and one that occurs on a different occasion (contrast *4 Ezra* 4:1–5). Verse 16 makes it as clear as one could want that we are dealing with a public event, announced not only by a loud command as on a battle field[12] and the voice of the archangel (see Jude 9; *1 En.* 20:1–7; *4 Ezra* 4:36) but also by the trumpet call of God, though these may be three ways of referring to the same thing.

The images conjured up are martial, as if Jesus were summoning his army. Notice that in 2 Thess 1:7 we also find angels playing a role in the second coming (cf. Mark 13:24–27). Only audible factors are mentioned in 1 Thess 4:16. The meeting place is said to take place in the clouds or in the air, not in heaven. Notice that Paul considers the dead in Christ to be persons who can be "awakened" or "addressed." It is quite likely that Paul is drawing on the Day of the Lord traditions, which refer to a trumpet blast announcing the event (cf. Isa 27:13; Joel 2:1; Zech 9:14; *4 Ezra* 6:23; *Sib. Or.* 4:174; 1 Cor 15:52).

It was also the case that a royal visit to a city would be announced by a herald (see Ps 24:7–10) and might well also be announced by a trumpet blast meant to alert those in the city that the king was coming. This imagery is pursued further in v. 17

---

10. When one talks about a remainder, the implication seems to be that a minority of the total number is referred to. See I. H. Marshall, *1 and 2 Thessalonians* (Vancouver: Regent College, 2002), 127.

11. G. Beale, *1 and 2 Thessalonians* (Downers Grove, Ill.: InterVarsity, 2003), 135.

12. Cf. Prov 30:27 LXX; Thucydides *Hist.* 2.92.

with the use of the term *apantēsin*. Notice for example what Cicero says of Julius Caesar's victory tour through Italy in 49 BC: "Just imagine what a meeting/royal welcome (*apantēseis*) he is receiving from the towns, what honors are paid to him" (*Ad. Att.* 8.16.2) and compare 16.11.6 of Augustus: "the municipalities are showing the boy remarkable favor.... Wonderful *apantēsis* and encouragement"). This word then refers to the action of the greeting committee who goes forth from the city to meet the royal person or dignitary before he arrives at the city gate to pay an official visit. The greeting committee will then escort the dignitary back into town on the final part of his journey. "These analogies (especially in association with the term *parousia*) suggest the possibility that the Lord is pictured here as escorted the remainder of the journey to earth by his people—both those newly raised from the dead and those remaining alive."[13]

John Chrysostom picked up these nuances quite clearly. He says "For when a king drives into a city, those who are honorable go out to meet him; but the condemned await the judge within. And upon the coming of an affectionate father, his children indeed, and those who are worthy to be his children, are taken out in a chariot, that they may see him and kiss him; but the housekeepers who have offended him remain within." (*Hom. 8 on 1 Thess*).[14] Paul's Thessalonian audience may have missed some of the allusions to the OT, but they would not have missed the language used here about a royal visit, indeed an imperial visit (cf. also Acts 28:15). They would remember the visit of Pompey and later Octavian and others in the days when Thessalonica could even be talked about by Pompey as the capital in exile. There is more to be said along these lines as Paul keeps using such loaded language in 1 Thessalonians 5. K. Donfried sums things up nicely:

> If 1 Thessalonians is at all representative of his original preaching then we certainly do find elements which could be understood or misunderstood in a distinctly political sense. In 2:12 God, according to the Apostle, calls the Thessalonian Christians "into his own kingdom"; in 5:3 there is a frontal attack on the *Pax et Securitas* program of the early Principate; and in the verses just preceding this attack one finds three heavily loaded political terms: *parousia, apantēsis,* and *kyrios. Parousia* is related to "the 'visit' of the king, or some other official." When used as court language *parousia* refers to the arrival of Caesar, a king or an official. *Apantēsis* refers to the citizens

---

13. F. F. Bruce, *1 and 2 Thessalonians* (Waco: Word, 1982), 103.

14. Notice as well that the going out to meet the dignitary is a great honor and is part of a public event, and note the implication that this authority figure will deal with the dishonorable when he returns inside the city or home.

meeting a dignitary who is about to visit the city. These two terms are used in this way by Josephus (*Ant.* XI.327ff.) and also similarly referred to by such Greek writers as Chrysostom. The term *kyrios,* especially when used in the same context as the two preceding terms, also has a definite political sense. People in the eastern Mediterranean applied the term *kyrios* to the Roman emperors from Augustus on . . . All of this, coupled with the use of *euaggelion* and its possible association with the eastern ruler cult suggests that Paul and his associates could easily be understood as violating "the decrees of Caesar" in the most blatant manner.[15]

Donfried then goes on to suggest that the dead in Christ in Thessalonica were victims of the persecutions alluded to elsewhere in this letter, which is certainly possible. In Acts 7:60 Stephen is stoned and then "he fell asleep" (*ekoimēthē*). This language in the context of persecution could refer to one who suffered death through persecution. We may need to take seriously that the charge Paul and his co-workers had violated the decrees of Caesar (see Acts 17:7) would have had severe repercussions not only for Paul and his co-workers but also for his converts. Some lost their lives. No wonder Paul was so concerned about them.

However, Paul in 1 Thessalonians is not backing down from his anti-imperial rhetoric, or better said, his co-opting of imperial rhetoric and applying it to Jesus. It cannot be an accident that the word *parousia* shows up four times in 1 Thessalonians (2:19; 3:13; 4:15; 5:23), twice in 2 Thessalonians (2:1, 8), and only once elsewhere in Paul (1 Cor 15:23). The borrowing of imperial rhetoric is especially apparent in the Thessalonian correspondence.[16] H. Koester has helpfully pointed out that the problem in Thessalonica is certainly not the delay of the Parousia, but rather concern about the fate of the Thessalonian Christian dead, concern exacerbated by persecution and possibly even martyrdom. Will the dead Christians join the living in the great welcoming of the return of their Lord?[17] Paul's answer is an emphatic yes, but in the course of giving that assurance and making some remarkable christological and eschatological assertions Paul is also busily deconstructing the extant pagan

---

15. K. P. Donfried, "The Imperial Cults and Political Conflict in 1 Thessalonians," in *Paul and Empire* (ed. R. A. Horsley; Harrisburg: Trinity, 1997), 215-223, here 217.

16. One has to wonder whether Paul was reflecting on the crackdown of Claudius on Jews and Christians in Rome in A.D. 49 and its aftermath as Claudius' reign deteriorated into bad government in his last years (i.e., A.D. 49-54), a crackdown which gave officials and others in a city like Thessalonica a license to treat Paul and his co-workers and converts as they apparently did.

17. H. Koester, "Imperial Ideology and Paul's Eschatology in 1 Thessalonians," in *Paul and Empire* (ed. R. A. Horsley; Harrisburg: Trinity, 1997), 158-66, see 158-59 especially.

value system so his converts will not lapse back into allegiance to it. N. T. Wright puts it this way:

> Paul's opposition to Caesar and adherence to a very high, very Jewish Christology were part of the same thing. Jesus was Lord—*kyrios*, with all its Septuagintal overtones—and Caesar was not.... [N]either the recognition that Paul's main target was paganism, and the Caesar-cult in particular, nor the equal recognition that he remained a thoroughly Jewish thinker, should blind us for a moment to the fact that Paul still held a thorough and stern critique of non-messianic Judaism.... [I]f Paul's answer to Caesar's empire is the empire of Jesus, what does this say about this new empire, living under the rule of its new Lord? ... [T]his counter-empire can never be merely critical, never merely subversive. It claims to be the reality of which Caesar's empire is the parody. It claims to be modeling the genuine humanness, not least the justice and peace, and the unity across traditional racial and cultural barriers, of which Caesar's empire boasted.[18]

Notice that it is particularly in Paul's more eschatological sections of his letters that the imperial cult language shows up. This is because the imperial cult was an eschatological institution itself, suggesting that a human being, namely the Emperor, was divine and was walking around on the earth bringing the final form of peace and security to earth (see Virgil's *Aeneid*), a thought fully embraced in the eastern part of the Empire.[19] Paul came into the same segment of the empire suggesting there was another God walking on the earth offering a kingdom, and this one had even come back from the dead. In such an environment this was an explosive message with considerable political implications. This message qualified as a subversive one, violating Caesar's decrees.

It should be clear from the beginning of v. 16 that Christ is said to come *down* out of heaven and meets his followers somewhere else, in this case in the atmosphere where there are clouds. There is likely an echo of Micah 1:3 here: "For behold the Lord is coming forth out of his place, and will come down and tread upon the high places of the earth." Clouds are regularly said to accompany a theophany, when God comes down to the human level, not when humans are taken up into the presence of God in heaven (see Exod 19:16; 40:34; 1 Kgs 8:10–11; Ps 97:2). Trumpet blasts also

---

18. N. T. Wright, "Paul's Gospel and Caesar's Empire," in *Paul and Politics* (ed. R. A. Horsley; Harrisburg: Trinity, 2000), 160–83, here 182–83.

19. There is now a fascinating study by D. R. Wallace entitled *The Gospel of God: Romans as Paul's Aeneid* (Eugene, OR: Pickwick, 2008) which argues that in Romans Paul is co-opting the rhetoric of the *Aeneid* to tell a counter story called the gospel of God.

accompany theophanies (Exod 19:16; Isa 27:13; Joel 2:1; Zech 9:14).[20] The meeting does not take place in heaven, so there is no discussion of rapture into heaven even here.[21]

Paul then adds as the ultimate reassurance about the dead in Christ that they will rise *first*, after which according to v. 17 the living Christians will be snatched up in a bodily condition (cf. Rev 12:5; Acts 8:39; Wis 4:11)[22] together with them in the clouds to meet the Lord in the air and be with the Lord forever.[23] Far from the deceased Christians being left out of the Parousia party, they will be first to be involved. It will be the ultimate family reunion with the King. There may be echoes here of the promises made sometimes in Greco-Roman contexts and epitaphs that the deceased would be with the "heroes," perhaps even in the Elysian fields. How much better to be with the Lord himself than just the heroes?

Paul does not tell us here what he thinks happens next after the reunion in the air. That information is conveyed in 1 Corinthians 15, and in both these texts nothing is said or suggested about non-believers participating in this resurrection. Paul separates what will happen to believers and what will happen to non-believers when Christ returns. Note the reference to future wrath in 1 Thess 5:9. What Paul most wants to convey about what happens at the Parousia is that the dead will not only not be left out or be disadvantaged, they will in fact take precedence. In a culture where pecking order was important, it would have reversed normal expectations to suggest that the dead had an advantage over the living.

---

20. See Marshall, *1 and 2 Thessalonians*, 129. The clear implication is that the Parousia of Christ is the coming of God to earth.

21. The term rapture does not appear in the NT. It comes from the Latin term *raptus*, which is a rendering of the Greek here, for *raptus* in Latin means "snatched." The idea is present in *4 Ezra* 6:26 and 14:9 and also in Gen 5:24 LXX, where it is used of Enoch being taken up into heaven. The word itself, however, whether in Greek or Latin does not carry the connotation of "into heaven," as the texts which speak of death doing the snatching or the land of the dead being the place to which one was snatched make clear.

22. Interestingly and ironically this verb is used in Plutarch, *Letter to Apollonius* 111C–D, 117B and Lucian, *Funerals* 13 to refer to the action of death itself. Inscriptions as well refer to fate snatching away loved ones into the realm of the dead (IG II.1062a.3; 11477.9; IV.620.2; V.733.12). *Fourth Ezra* 5:42 is interesting for it says "just as for those who are last there is no delay, so for those who are first there is no haste." Paul is using funerary language, another little clue that the rhetoric here is epideictic in character.

23. The classical distinction between the pure ether of heaven and the atmosphere which has clouds in it is preserved here (see e.g., Homer, *Iliad* 8.558; 17.371; and we find it also in Christian writers, Athenagoras, *Leg.* 5 and *Eph.* 2.2). *Eis aera* here denotes that the Lord will descend into the immediate region of the earth, where he will be met by believers.

First Thessalonians 4:18 involves an exhortation to encourage and comfort each other with these eschatological promises, the very sort of rhetoric that would be appropriate in an epideictic attempt to help the bereaved (cf. 1 Thess 5:11). With hope in the *Parousia* and coming resurrection they could expect to see their departed Thessalonian Christian friends again, but also they could expect a reunion with all the believers and with Jesus. Notice finally that the Thessalonians were actively to convey this consolation to each other (cf. *P. Oxy.* 115: *paregoreite oun eautous*). It was not just a matter of hearing and heeding what Paul said. They were to participate in their own healing.

## It Takes a Thief

The second division of the eschatological parenesis in 1 Thessalonians 4–5 begins at 5:1. The use of *peri de* as well as the use of the term "brothers" makes evident that Paul sees this as a new topic or a new angle on a previously discussed topic, and here it is clearly one which is related to what has just been said about the *Parousia*. In 1 Thessalonians 5 the rhetorical function of the eschatological material is a bit different. Rather than consolation through new information, this segment is more about exhortation based on the eschatological knowledge the audience *already* has. This section seems to have three divisions, the markers of each involve the word *de* ("but"): "but concerning" in 5:1, "but you" in 5:4, "but we" in 5:8. Paul will deal in turn with three related topics in these sections: the sudden and for some unexpected coming of the day of the Lord when unbelievers will be judged (5:1–3), the preparation of believers for that day (5:4–7), and the necessary faithfulness of God's people, which is the basis for encouraging one another (5:8–11). The structure of this material is carefully framed with the section ending with an inference to be drawn in v. 11 from what has just been said.

It is helpful to compare what is said in this whole passage with Rom 13:11–14. There are obvious similarities in the use of the language about waking and sleeping and sobriety. If there is debate about which of these passages conveys more of a sense that the eschatological clock is ticking and the end may be nearer than one thinks, it is surely the Romans passage, which just goes to show that no easy evolutionary development schema will work when analyzing Pauline eschatology. Romans was surely written after 2 Corinthians, and yet Paul is still talking about the return of Christ, and how the day of the Lord is possibly imminent.

The attempt to take 1 Thess 5:1–11 as if it were referring to events *after* the catching up of believers into the air, rather than seeing 1 Thess 4:13–18 and 5:1–11 as both talking about the Parousia in different ways, must be said to be special pleading. Both of these passages deal with one and only Parousia/return of Christ from slightly different angles and with differing rhetorical functions, both commending the same sort of behavior of Christians in light of the eschatological events. The exhortations in 1 Thess 5:1-11 would be pointless if in fact believers were not envisioned as still on earth until the Day of the Lord. Notice the repetition of the phrase "with the Lord" in 4:17 and 5:10 and the similar endings directed toward the immediate audience in 4:18 and 5:11. Both the context and the content of these passages indicate that Paul is speaking in both of the one and only second coming.[24] What is not usually appreciated is that while the former passage examines the second coming from the angle of coming rescue of believers the latter passage examines the same event from the perspective of judgment on unbelievers.[25]

The phrase *chronoi kai kairoi* in 5:1 is an important one found elsewhere in early Jewish and early Christian literature (Acts 1:7; 1 Pet 1:11; Ign. *Pol.* 3; cf. Neh 10:34; 13:31; Dan 2:21; Wis 8:8; Eccl 3:1; and Demosthenes, *Olynth*. 3 para. 32). It is too simple to say that *chronos* refers to a longer period of time and *kairos* a shorter one. *Chronos* is the general term for time, whether a long or short period is involved, and refers to the date of something if a particular event is in mind. *Kairos* can refer to place or time and has the sense of the fit measure, the appropriate or propitious moment or the right place. In reference to time it surely refers to the right moment. In short, *chronos* refers more to the quantity of time, while *kairos* refers to the quality of time, or of other things, and sense the propitious moment is usually a brief one, it often does refer to a short length of time, though this is incidental to its real thrust. The gist of the phrase here then is that the audience has no need to be informed about how much time must elapse before the big event happens or what significant occurrences will mark or punctuate that crucial occasion.[26] Paul refuses to set up timetables for this event because he cannot do so.[27] The timing has not been re-

---

24. See T. Howard, "The Literary Unity of 1 Thessalonians 4.13–5.11," *Grace Theological Journal* 9 (1988): 163-90, rebutting the Dispensational reading of these texts.

25. Rightly noted by C. Wanamaker, *1 and 2 Thessalonians* (Grand Rapids: Eerdmans, 1992), 177-78.

26. It is of course possible since this is epideictic rhetoric that Paul is using these terms as virtual synonyms, and so we would have an example of pleonasm or fullness and redundancy of expression. See Marshall, *1 and 2 Thessalonians*, 132. However, throughout the history of Greek usage, including in modern times, these two words when juxtaposed had distinct meanings. Today *chronos* refers to the year, *kairos* to the time.

27. We may point out that Paul is capable of talking about events that must precede the Parousia,

vealed. Indeed, what had been revealed is that no one knows the timing of this event, not even Jesus during his ministry (Mark 13:32). All the pointless speculation about the timing of the rapture or the return of Christ is an exercise in futility because the former event is not going to happen, and we are told that the latter event will happen at a hitherto undisclosed time.

Verse 2 then tells us nothing about when Jesus will come, but rather *how*—in a sudden and unexpected manner.[28] Paul is describing a sudden intrusion into human history which will catch many unaware and unprepared. The controlling metaphor "thief in the night" goes back to the Jesus tradition (cf. Matt 24:43; Luke 12:38–39; 1 Thess 5:2; 2 Pet 3:10; Rev 3:3; 16:15) and stresses both the suddenness and unexpectedness of the event but also its unknown timing. It also has an aura of threat or unwelcomeness to it, at least for the unprepared.[29] Strictly speaking it is the Day of the Lord, rather than Jesus, that is said to come like a thief, although it is used of Jesus in Rev 3:3 and 16:15.

Paul uses several related phrases to refer to this coming event—the day (1 Thess 5:4; 1 Cor 3:13; Rom 2:5; cf. 13:12), that day (2 Thess 1:10), the Day of the Lord (1 Thess 5:2; 2 Thess 2:2; 1 Cor 5:5), the Day of our Lord Jesus Christ (1 Cor 1:8), the Day of the Lord Jesus (2 Cor 1:14), the Day of Christ Jesus (Phil 1:6), or simply the Day of Christ (Phil 1:10; 2:16). Paul has adopted and adapted the Day of the Lord traditions from the OT and applied them to Christ, for now it is Christ who will bring the final redemption and judgment to earth.[30] If one compares 1 Thess 4:14–17 and 1 Thess 5:2 it becomes clear that "the day" is the same as "the Day of the Lord" which in turn is the same as the Parousia. It is in no way surprising that when the phrase "Day of the Lord" is used by Paul, judgment is most frequently spoken of since it is this phrase which in the Hebrew Scriptures and LXX was used most often

---

as a way of making clear that the end is not yet at hand, but he does not speak of these events as sign markers or events which trigger the return of Christ and so must be closely juxtaposed in time with the Parousia.

28. The Greek phrase *en taxei* can either be used adjectively or adverbially. It can mean "soon," but it can also mean "suddenly." Too often scholars have simply ignored the possibility of translating the phrase "suddenly" (literally "in quickness"), overlooking the fact that the controlling metaphor when it came to discussion of the coming of the Lord/Son of Man was "thief in the night," a metaphor which suggests a sudden break-in at an unexpected time.

29. See Marshall, *1 and 2 Thessalonians*, 133–34.

30. Of course he is probably not the first one to make this transfer. It seems to go back to Jesus and what he says about the coming of the Son of Man for judgment (Mark 14:62).

to speak of coming judgment (cf. Rom 2:5).[31] Zephaniah 1:15-18; 2:2-3, and 3:8 (cf. Amos 5:18-20; Obad 15; Joel 1:15; 2:1-2, 31-32; Zech 14:1-21) stress the idea that the Day of the Lord is a day of God's judgment, though in Obadiah and Zechariah it is also a day of deliverance. Paul says with emphasis that his audience knows very well about this matter. There is a note of irony here. The audience knows very well that the timing of the Parousia has not been revealed and so is unknown and unpredictable.[32] In addition, Paul says that this day will come like an event at night![33] If this is not a use of metaphor and simile, nothing is.

Verse 3 begins with the phrase "when they say peace and security." It has sometimes been conjectured that Paul is drawing on an OT phrase here, perhaps Jer 6:14 or Ezek 13:10. The latter text condemns false prophets for crying "peace" when there is no peace, but it says nothing about security specifically, though the comments about the whitewashed wall may imply such a concern. Jeremiah 6:14 is of the very same ilk, criticizing false prophets for crying "peace, peace" when there is no peace. Clearly Paul's phrase is not a direct quote of an OT phrase, and if his audience is mainly former pagans, as 1 Thess 1 clearly indicates, they could not be expected to recognize such an allusion anyway. "When *they* say . . ." is also a very odd way to refer to the OT prophets, but it makes perfect sense if Paul is quoting a cliché or proverb familiar in his audience's world. As A. Malherbe notes, the diction is not Pauline; Paul does not use either *legōsin* or *eirēnē* in quite the same sense elsewhere, and he does not use *asphaleia* at all elsewhere.[34] There is some likelihood that at least the second half of this sentence is echoing the Jesus tradition, specifically material found in Luke 21:34-36, but again that material does not account for the combined use of "peace and security," and Paul would hardly introduce a word of Jesus by "when *they* say," which suggests outsiders not insiders.

In fact, there were inscriptions up all over the Empire attributing to Rome and to its army the bringing of peace and security to one region after another. For example, in Syria we have the inscription which reads "The Lord Marcus Flavius Bonus, the most illustrious Comes and Dux of the first legion, has ruled over us in peace and given constant 'peace and security' to travelers and to the people"

---

31. See the discussion in Witherington, *Jesus, Paul and the End of the World*, 163-65.

32. Wanamaker, *1 and 2 Thessalonians*, 178-79. The term *akribōs* occurs only here and in Eph 5:15 in Paul and refers to investigating something with great care and so knowing beyond reasonable doubt. See Josephus, *Ag. Ap.* 2:175.

33. A. Malherbe, *The Letters to the Thessalonians* (New York: Doubleday, 2000), 290.

34. See Wanamaker, *1 and 2 Thessalonians*, 180.

(OGIS 613). Velleius Paterculus says "On that day there sprang up once more in parents the assurance of safety of their property, and in all men the assurance of safety, order, peace, and tranquility" (II.103.5). It is added that "The Pax Augusta which has spread to the regions of the east and of the west, and to the bounds of the north and the south, preserves every corner of the world safe/secure from the fear of banditry" (II.126.3). Tacitus speaks of the time after the year of the three Emperors as a time when security was restored, and then he adds that the "security of peace" includes work without anxiety in the fields and in the homes (*Hist.* 2.21.2; 2.12.1). Not to be plundered by robbers either at home or on journeys is "peace and security" (Josephus, *Ant.* 14:158–60, 247).

A variant of this "peace and security" slogan was that of "peace and concord." We find this in inscriptions dating back to 139 B.C. referring to a pact between Rome and the cities of Asia "preserving mutual goodwill with peace and all concord and friendship" (*SIG* 685:14–15).[35] Paul must have thought "What foolish slogans and vain hopes when the Day of the Lord is coming." Paul is critiquing the slogans and propaganda about the *Pax Romana*. It is on those who offer this rhetoric that destruction will come, which may suggest that Paul foresaw the same future for Rome and its empire and those who cooperated with it as John of Patmos did in Rev 6–19.[36] Paul does not want his audience to be beguiled by such rhetoric, especially after Paul has been expelled and they have suffered persecution from those who are supposedly the bringers of "peace and security." It is the imperial propaganda and prophecies to which Paul is offering a rebuttal. Paul is rebutting the ancient equivalent of homeland security political rhetoric with his own theological rhetoric.

What is predicted for those who offer this slogan is sudden destruction, which comes upon them much like a birth pang suddenly seizes a pregnant woman unexpectedly (cf. Ps 48:6; Isa 26:17; 66:8; Jer 30:6–7; Mic 4:9; 4 *Ezra* 16:35–39; *1 En.* 62:1–6). The wording is closely parallel to Luke 21:34–36.[37] Paul stresses the fact that there can be no escape from this coming destruction for "them." Paul is not a crusader against the Empire in the sense of someone leading a social movement for reform. Rather he is a believer that God in Christ will intervene once and for all and right the wrongs that he and his audience have been experiencing because of their

---

35. For more of this sort of evidence see the detailed discussion in K. Wengst, *Pax Romana and the Peace of Jesus Christ* (Philadelphia: Fortress, 1987), 19–26, and in regard to our text, 77–78.

36. On Revelation see Witherington, *Revelation* (Cambridge: Cambridge University Press, 2003), ad loc.

37. See Marshall, *1 and 2 Thessalonians* 134–35.

witness. God in Christ is the one who will bring justice and peace and security once and for all, not the emperor with his slogans. Paul will say more on this theme in 2 Thess 2. The rhetorical effect of what Paul has done is to create a sense of urgency in regard to heeding the exhortations. "Paul in no way seeks to decrease, let alone defuse, the eschatological pressure felt by the Thessalonians."[38] And this brings us to a major conclusion: *rather than offering theological comfort food promising an escape from extreme suffering or death, Paul ramps up the eschatological pressure on the audience to remain faithful and be prepared to suffer and if need be die, before the Lord returns, implying in effect "blessed are those who die in the Lord henceforth."*

In 1 Thess 5:4–5 we have a clear contrast between believers and unbelievers. Using the darkness and light metaphors Paul in essence says that his converts are neither in the state of darkness nor is the darkness the source of their existence.[39] They should not be surprised by the coming of the Day of the Lord, even if it arrives at an unexpected time. "Unpredictable events have different effects on those who are unprepared for them and those who are ready for them."[40] Believers are children of the day, children of light (cf. Luke 16:8; John 12:38; Eph 5:8). The self-descriptive language of the in-group is much like that we find at Qumran (1QS III, 13–IV, 26; 1QM I, 1–3). A saying of Euripides helps us understand the force of the imagery: "Night is the time for thieves, daylight is the time for truth." (*Iph. taur.* 1025–26). Verse 5 is interesting because it calls the audience both children of light and children of the day. Here we see the two poles of Paul's eschatology. The light had already dawned in Christ, and his converts were already children of light, transformed into new creatures,[41] but they awaited the day.

Provisionally they are also called children of the day, reassuring them they will be participants when Jesus returns.[42] Notice that Paul says that "all" his audience are children of light and children of the day. Paul does not hold to a concept of an invisible elect within the church. He assumes his whole audience believes in Jesus and so is among the elect and will be children of the day. Before they arrive at that day there

---

38. Best, *First and Second Thessalonians*, 208.

39. In his helpful response to this essay Andy Johnson rightly pointed out that the saints here are seen as visible, and there is no hint in 1 Thessalonians of an invisible elect within the visible church. Rather the whole church is addressed throughout, and the whole church is warned of the real possibility and dangers of apostasy under pressure and persecution. The rhetoric calls for steadfastness and perseverance precisely because the audience might well do otherwise.

40. Marshall, *1 and 2 Thessalonians*, 136.

41. Best, *First and Second Thessalonians*, 210.

42. See Beale, *1 and 2 Thessalonians*, 144–45.

is much to prepare for and much to persevere through. They must remember that they are no longer of the night nor of darkness. They are not in a benighted condition, and they should not be caught out by the coming of the day.

Knowledge is power, but it can also be used for motivation, and in v. 6 Paul turns to his exhortation based on what the Thessalonians know about the eschatological situation. With *ara oun* ("so then") as a marker that he is turning to a logical conclusion or a moral consequence of what he has just said, Paul draws an ethical conclusion about how Christian behavior should differ from that of "the rest." It is interesting that Paul uses the metaphor not only of being awake and sober but of wearing certain clothes, or as we might say, keeping our day clothes on, to describe the state of preparedness of Christians for the Parousia.[43]

The exhortation here probably owes something to Mark 13:34–37 (cf. also Matt 24:42–43), and in any case Paul is not saying what Clement of Alexandria later said, namely "we should sleep half-awake" (*Christ the Educator* 2.9.79). No, Paul is calling for his converts to remain awake, alert, and to remain sober (cf. Eph 5:14). Malherbe insightfully notes that while in those Synoptic texts alertness is mainly grounded in the fact that there is ignorance of the timing of the second coming, here it is mainly grounded in one's Christian identity—a Christian is of the light and enlightened and as such should always remain morally and spiritually alert.[44] Paul is urging both intellectual and moral preparation and readiness for the Parousia. The opposite of this is being morally and spiritually asleep or unconscious. It is interesting that Plutarch the moralist also urges his audience to be awake and sober and contrasts this with being asleep or drunk using these same terms (*To an Uneducated Ruler* 781D). Christians are held to the standard of God's twenty-four hours of daytime.

Verse 8 states the consequences of being daytime people. We must be awake and sober and put on the appropriate clothing to deal with the "slings and arrows of outrageous fortune." Notice the reference to the famous triad faith, hope, and love (cf. 1 Thess 1:3; 1 Cor 13). Here we have the breastplate of faith and love, and the helmet is said to be the hope of salvation, seen as something to be experienced in the future, an imagery further developed in Eph 6:14–17. In both texts there is an indebtedness to Isa 59:17 where God wears the helmet of salvation on his head.

The terminology is probably chosen carefully. The most vulnerable part of a person in a life-threatening situation is the head. One can survive wounds to almost any other part of the body, but a deep wound to the head is usually mortal. The

---

43. See Beale, *1 and 2 Thessalonians*, 149.
44. Malherbe, *The Letters to the Thessalonians*, 295.

Scriptures therefore speak of the helmet of *soteria*, a term which can mean rescue, help, healing, or saving in a mundane or profound sense. In this case it is the helmet of the *hope* of salvation. What protects the believer against a mortal blow to one's faith is to some degree the hope of salvation. If one has no hope or trust that God will one day make things right, then one's faith is fragile and can be overwhelmed by the problems and the injustices of the present. This hope not only protects the person in the present, it gives them courage in the face of the coming judgment of God, knowing that one will be saved or rescued from that maelstrom.[45]

Verse 9 reassures the converts that God did not appoint them to suffer judgment and wrath in the future but rather to receive salvation through "our Lord Jesus Christ." This is not a promise of escape before Christ returns but rather of vindication when he does and thus avoidance of the judgment which comes after his return. The sentence begins with *hoti* ("because"). The converts are to put on the armor *because* God did not appoint them for wrath. Their destiny is different from those referred to as sleeping or drunk in v. 3.[46] Of course destinies and destinations can change. Those in darkness may finally see the light, and those in the light may make shipwreck of their faith. One reason Paul insists on speaking of salvation as something to be obtained[47] *in the future* is precisely because Christian behavior before one dies or Jesus returns can affect the outcome. One is not eternally secure until one is securely in eternity.

Salvation is a gift whether one is talking about initial or final salvation, but when one is referring to the latter, it is a gift given to those who have persevered, have put on the armor, have stayed alert, have remained faithful and true, and the like. The word *etheto* in v. 9 as elsewhere indicates God's soteriological purpose. God appoints or destines believers for final salvation (cf. 1 Pet 2:8). This passage is somewhat like Rom 8:28–29, and in both cases the language of destining is used to reassure Christians, those who love God, about their future. *The subject is not about destining or electing some to be believers.* Finally notice that salvation is obtained through the Lord Jesus. He is the medium or agent of salvation, and if one is not

---

45. Notice the reference in Gal 5:5 to waiting for the hope of righteousness. The consummation of everything for the believer comes when Christ returns and they are transformed into his likeness. This is clearly not a reference to Christ's righteousness, but to the believers' which they will not fully obtain or reflect until the return of Christ and their bodily transformation.

46. See Malherbe, *The Letters to the Thessalonians*, 298.

47. The word *peripoiēsis* is rare and often refers to a possession (Eph 1:14; 1 Pet 2:9), but in 2 Thess 2:14 and Heb 10:39 it refers to obtaining.

connected to him, one cannot obtain final salvation. It is his work on the cross that makes possible the giving of the gift of salvation.

The idea is that God has provided the believer with the necessary "equipment" so that by putting on the armor, staying awake and alert, and persevering they may obtain the gift of final salvation. Paul "does not suggest that God's plan is fulfilled independently of the action of [human beings] . . . Paul's exhortations to vigilance would be nonsensical if vigilance was the product of some inward causation in the believer by God or if there was no possibility of disobeying the exhortation."[48]

G. Beale has rightly noticed the clear parallels between 1 Thess 4:14–18 and 5:10–11. Both sections conclude with essentially the same remark.[49] This makes quite clear that Paul is not addressing sequential events in 1 Thess 4:14–18 and 5:1–11. Verse 11 rounds out this entire section with the same words found at 4:18, except that here Paul amplifies them with the exhortation to build each other up, preparing for what he will say in 1 Thess 5:12–22, and then he concludes with the reassurance "just as also you are doing." Confirmation that we have been on the right track all along in our interpretation of 1 Thess 4–5 comes when one examines 2 Thess 2 where it is perfectly clear that Christians are to expect only one return of Christ to gather the saints, and it comes after the tribulation.[50]

## The Implications of Paul's Discourse for Contemporary Rhetoric about Peace, Security, and Salvation

Rhetoric can, of course, take many forms. Spiritual terms can be used to refer to political ends and aims, and political ends and aims can be used to refer to spiritual or even supernatural matters. In our own day when all sorts of false gospels about peace and security are abroad in the land, 1 Thessalonians 4–5 has much to teach us, as it cuts in various directions against such false gospels. Let us consider first the false peace and security of the rapture gospel.

One of the real weaknesses in the dispensational approach is that on the one hand with texts such as 1 Thessalonians 4–5 and 2 Thess 2:1 Dispensationalists want *parousia* to refer to the secret rapture of the church, while on the other hand they usually concede that *parousia* refers to the Second Coming in this very same ar-

---

48. Marshall, *1 and 2 Thessalonians*, 139–40.

49. The parallels include references to Jesus' death in 4:14 and 5:10, the phrase "together with" in 4:16 and 5:10, and, of course, the identical closing exhortation "Encourage one another." See Beale, *1 and 2 Thessalonians*, 155.

50. See C. Hill, *In God's Time*, (Grand Rapids: Eerdmans, 2002), 205.

gument at 2 Thess 2:8. But, Paul always uses the term *parousia* consistently when speaking of Jesus to refer to the second coming, an all too visible event. The further proof of this comes, not only because of the general use of this term to refer to a public event, but also because in this very context in vv. 8–9 we note how *parousia* is used in parallel with the verb "revealed" to refer to the very public coming of the lawless one.

In 2 Thess 2:1–2 Paul reminds his audience about the Parousia and the gathering of the believers to Christ at his coming, the subjects addressed in 1 Thess 5 and 4 respectively. We should compare the use of the term *episynagogēs* ("gathering") to the use of the verbal form of the word in Mark 13:27 and Matt 24:31, where it refers to the gathering together of the believers at the coming of the Son of Man. In 2 Macc 2:7 it refers to the regathering of Jews into the temporal kingdom after the Babylonian exile.[51] In 2 Thess 2:1 Paul is alluding to 1 Thess 4:17 and is speaking of the same event as he spoke of there, the second coming.

It is truly remarkable that it was 2 Thess 2:1–2 that caused J. N. Darby to become convinced of a rapture of the saints before the Day of the Lord, which in turn led to the attempt to distinguish what is referred to here from the discussion in 1 Thessalonians 5 about the return of Christ. Unfortunately for Darby's position, the subject of 1 Thessalonians 5 is the Day of the Lord, and that very same subject is discussed in 2 Thess 2:1–2, as the second of these verses makes perfectly evident.[52]

What is the upshot of this reading of 1 Thessalonians 4–5, 2 Thessalonians 2, and the other related texts sometimes thought to refer to a rapture? The upshot is that unless by "rapture" one merely means being taken up into the air to welcome Christ and return with him to earth, there is no theology of the rapture to be found in the NT anywhere, never mind the term itself. If this is so, what then are the implications? If there is no rapture, much of the dispensational system falls down like a house of cards.

For one thing it means that the church of the last generation will go through the fire, just as every other generation of Christians has had to do. This is why Jesus' word of comfort in Mark 13 is not that we will be spared the tribulation but that God has shortened the time of it for the sake of the elect people of God, which clearly refers to the followers of Jesus (Mark 13:20). Notice what Rev 12:1–6 in fact promises. The woman, who represents the people of God, is not raptured out of the world when the devil pursues her; rather, she is protected from any spiritual harm

---

51. See also Beale's critique, *1 and 2 Thessalonians*, 198.
52. See Bruce, *1 and 2 Thessalonians*, 163.

while remaining in the world. Such is the lot of the people of God in every generation until the Lord returns. There will be no "beam me up Scotty" effect for the last generation of Christians. Rather, there will be suffering and martyrdom just as there was in the time when John wrote his Revelation. What was true then will also be true in the end.

What exactly is the Parousia and why was this term chosen to refer to the return of Christ? What difference, if any, does the literal meaning of this word make? It makes a considerable difference to the interpretation of this event.

It has been argued for instance that *parousia* refers merely to "presence" in 1 Thessalonians and that what is envisioned is not a descent but rather an unveiling, with a removal of the barrier between earth and heaven, like the raising of a curtain.[53] The Greek text of 1 Thess 4:16, however, speaks of Jesus coming down from heaven. As for the meaning of *parousia*, Paul can use the term to mean "presence" (2 Cor 10:10; Phil 2:12) in a non-eschatological context, but he can also use it to mean "coming" in a non-eschatological context (1 Cor 16:17; 2 Cor 7:6–7). The question is how the term is used in an eschatological context like 1 Thessalonians 4.

We must bear in mind that the word already in the Hellenistic period had special associations concerning the arrival of significant persons. When coupled here with the language of coming down, it is hardly likely to mean anything else. In fact, most commentators say that every time this word appears in an eschatological context it means "coming" or "arrival," and they have the majority of the evidence on their side. As Best says, the word in its primary sense has a sense of movement anyway.[54] A good example of the usage in a Hellenistic context in connection with an arrival and a greeting of a royal figure can be found in Josephus, *Ant.* 11:26–28 where a priest is awaiting the *parousia* of Alexander in order to go out and meet (*hypantēsis*) him.

We must also keep in view that everywhere else in the NT the term is used in the eschatological sense of the coming or arrival of the Lord/Son of Man (Matt 24:27–39; James 5:7; 2 Pet 1:16; 3:4; 1 John 2:28). E. Best concludes, "The secular significance of *parousia* reinforces the conception of a coming of Christ which is a public event, in which he returns from 'outside' history to end history and which therefore eliminates any idea of a gradual development of events within history which themselves share the End."[55]

---

53. Beale, *1 and 2 Thessalonians*, 138–40.

54. See the excursus of Best, *First and Second Thessalonians*, 349–54.

55. Best, 354.

It is also true to say that no one spoke of a "Second Coming" before Justin Martyr (*Dial.* 14:8; 40:4; 118:4) in the second century AD, and it is well to remember that the word *parousia* just means "arrival" or "coming." It does not carry the connotation of "return," and it is never used of the Incarnation before Ignatius, *Phil.* 9:2. Lastly, it seems clear that the concept enshrined in this term is found in the Aramaic prayer *marana tha*, "come O, Lord" (1 Cor 16:22). We must conclude then that the translation "presence" in 1 Thessalonians 4–5 or elsewhere suits neither the eschatological context nor the history of the use of the term when speaking of "lords" or royal figures, and Paul always uses the term *parousia* in 1 Thessalonians in connection with the term "lord" (2:19; 3:13; 4:15; 5:23).[56]

The theological comfort food of the rapture theology, which lets Christians off the hook when it comes to embracing the gospel message about crossbearing, suffering, and even martyrdom can only be called an offering of the wrong sort of peace, security, and salvation to those looking for all these things. This whole text makes evident that the general theology of eternal security is not what Paul is offering in place of such a rapture theology either. In Paul's view there are three tenses to salvation: I have been saved, I am being saved, and I shall be saved, and until one gets through all three stages, the situation is, in a word, tense. Apostasy is possible, and Paul warns Christians, not pagans, against this at length in 1 and 2 Thessalonians. Paul's view is that one is not eternally secure until one is securely in eternity. But, Paul, while stressing that Christians must persevere in order to obtain final salvation, also promises that God is there keeping them on the right track and protecting them along the way, so long as they are trusting and believing in God.

Paul's message also has ramifications for other sorts of so-called gospels offering false security and salvation. It cuts against the notion that a human government could provide us with lasting peace, for example, through war. Peace through war is as much of an oxymoron as the phrase Microsoft Works. This "peace and national security through war" is what the Roman Empire's rhetoric asserted, and it is what other superpowers assert still. But, alas, as Paul says, politicians will say "peace and security, peace and security," but there is no peace and security to be found in the plottings and machinations of human beings. This happens only with the Prince of Peace. *Pax Romana* in fact meant not peace but rather the pacification and silencing of the enemies, which as collateral damage always involved the silencing of the lambs, the slaughtering of the innocents. Such is the nature of war. The only thing fear-based policies and practices such as Homeland Security accomplishes in the

---

56. Malherbe, *The Letters to the Thessalonians*, 273.

long run is ramping up the anxiety and insecurity in the homeland. It is a constant reminder that we do not have that sort of absolute security from harm.

There is more. Paul, like other early Christians such as John of Patmos, believed that justice should always be left in the hands of God and that in particular the justice issue would be resolved only when Christ returns. There is a reason why so many of the early Christians believed that embracing the gospel of the returning Jesus Christ, the gospel of suffering love, meant embracing nonviolence, turning the other cheek, loving one's enemies, and the like. We can see Paul clearly working out the implications of this in his paraenesis in 1 Thess 4–5 and Rom 12–14. When early Christians quoted the phrase "'Vengeance is mine, I will repay,' says the Lord," this was not said because they were vindictive, like the man muttering "They will get theirs." It was said to remind them that justice should always be left in the hands of God and that the Christian should patiently await the eschatological resolution of such matters when Christ returns and brings in the great and terrible Day of the Lord. I suspect that it is precisely because of the loss of such a clearly theocentric eschatology in our day and age that other eschatologies, whether spiritual or political, have been substituted. The longing for security and peace is deep in the human heart, and rather than embrace no hope, false hopes, false eschatologies, and idolatries will be substituted. Those who refuse to drink from the springs of living water will readily turn to the contemporary Kool-aid—Homeland Security.

Lastly, Paul reminds his Thessalonian converts who had already suffered much and probably had endured some martyrdoms, that nevertheless they should not live as people without hope. They could not give way to fear-based thinking but rather had to engage in faith-based thinking of a christological and eschatological sort. They were not to live as people who kept grieving, even for the Christian dead. For not only would their day come when *the* Day came and justice would finally be done on the earth, even more they would receive their life back again at resurrection. In the end it is God's yes to life in resurrection that silences all the fear-based thinking or the dread of death, all the false-security-based thinking based on the fear of losing control. God's yes in resurrection offers the peace that passes understanding. When a nation submits itself to fear-based thinking based in a false and idolatrous gospel of "peace and security," it is a clear sign that it is no longer "one nation, under God, indivisible with liberty and justice for all."

We conclude with a paraphrase of Jeremiah's warning not to rely on the inviolability doctrine saying "This is the temple of the Lord, this is the temple of the Lord." Similarly, Christians should not rely on an inviolability doctrine saying "I am the temple of the Lord, or I am eternally secure, or I am sealed in the Spirit, or I will escape final tribulation." Instead of placing their trust in and looking for succor and security from a faulty theological idea, they should place their trust in the God who raises the dead and sing "Trust and obey, for there's no other way..." instead of "Trust in our theology."

# RESPONSE TO WITHERINGTON

## Andy Johnson

In his paper Ben Witherington has given a careful exegetical discussion of 1 Thess 4:13–5:11.[1] The main burden of his detailed exegesis *in the context of this symposium* is to argue against a popular premillenial Dispensationalist interpretation of the passage, especially its attempt to argue for a "secret rapture" in 4:13–18 and the attempt by some of its adherents to argue that the Day of the Lord in 5:1–11 is not simultaneous with the Parousia in 4:13–18. Such rapture theology is in his view "comfort food . . . an escape clause should things go bump in the night on planet earth . . . offering false peace and security." I could not agree more that rapture theology and any security that might come along with it are false. Unfortunately, for my role as respondent, I also agree with most of the exegetical detail he marshals against it, and our differences are not particularly relevant to our purposes here.

In the context of a symposium on the idolatry of security, his words and analysis imply that the sort of security offered by rapture theology is not only false but also somehow idolatrous. He never actually says this, nor does he show how such theology is necessarily idolatrous. That impression, however, was created for me in two steps. First, he describes the background of the "homeland security" rhetoric of the *Pax Romana* in obviously idolatrous terms and then connects that to the contemporary fear based politics of "homeland security." Second, given that most folk I know who hold to popular forms of premillenial Dispensationalism also tend to support such "homeland security" politics, I tacitly associated the idolatry of the "homeland security" rhetoric of the *Pax Romana* with rapture theology. But, at the very least, any association of the two deserves more clarification.

I wonder if it is not better to say that the whole web of interrelated assumptions in which the idea of a secret rapture is embedded tends toward an idolatrous form of security. Many in the United States who hold to *popular* forms of premillenial Dispensationalism[2] (and some conservative evangelicals who do not) identify the

---

1. Much of the material is from his recent commentary on 1 & 2 Thessalonians (Ben Witherington, *1 and 2 Thessalonians: A Socio-Rhetorical Commentary* [Grand Rapids: Eerdmans, 2006], 125–58).

2. What follows does not characterize all who hold to a form of premillenial Dispensationalism. I

United States as "a Christian nation," or better, a nation that "needs to get back to God," i.e., to being "the Christian nation" it once was. In this case the nation becomes the visible social body to which it makes theological sense to commit one's self. This is reinforced by the ecclesiological assumption that the "true Church" is not the visible/institutional one but rather an invisible/spiritual reality that will be revealed by the rapture. It is composed of a collection of individuals who, via an inner/spiritual "transaction," exchange their *sincere* faith (understood as *belief and inner trust*)[3] for the security of sharing in what is usually a sort of immaterial/spiritual salvation (in spite of the fact that actual bodies are raptured). Granted, one must not only make this transaction but must also "abide" in order to be secure in their salvation, but "abiding" tends to be focused more on individuals' (commendable to be sure) private practices of piety that seem to have little connection to larger issues of societal justice.[4] As Walter Moberly points out, premillenial Dispensationalism's *uncritical* support of Zionism is a good example of this. He is correct that the reason they are able to claim faithfulness to Scripture for such a stance is that they ignore the "conditional and response-seeking nature of much biblical prophecy" as well as passages stressing God's desire for the *public* practice of justice in society. But, it is the secondary assumption he identifies that closes the idolatrous loop so to speak, namely, that God will grant blessing/security to America because of its no-questions-asked support of Zionism. Turning a blind eye to its injustices and associating God with it amounts to what Dan Carroll calls creating "a false YHWH . . . the most insidious idol of all." Ironically, in the absence of a visible church that takes up public space, one might say that it is the visible social body of "America" that turns out to be the *public* reflection of the character of this version of God.

Things, of course, were different in Thessalonica. The audience of 1 Thessalonians was not necessarily in danger of creating a false version of Israel's God but of falling back into worship of gods and goddesses that sanctioned the shape of their society. The only place in the letter where Paul mentions idolatry is in 1:8-10 where it is connected with the *pistis* (faith) of his audience. The reason that Paul says he has no need to speak about their *pistis* (1:8c) is because (*gar*) it is being announced

---

also want to point out that even among those who do hold to popular premillenial Dispensationalism that many live lives that clearly embody faithfulness to God in spite of their views.

3. For this "transaction" view of faith, see the illustrative conversation in Tim LaHaye and Jerry B. Jenkins, *Left Behind: A Novel of the Earth's Last Days* (Wheaton, Ill.: Tyndale House, 1995), 200-1.

4. E.g., paying tithe, private prayer, Bible reading, avoiding such things as secretive lustful practices (again, see the illustrative conversation in LaHaye and Jenkins, *Left Behind*, 195-98).

by others outside Thessalonica in their report of the kind of entrance Paul and his companions had with them (v. 9). This entrance, and therefore the audience's *pistis* (faith), is further described[5] in what they are announcing, namely, "how you turned to God away from idols to be enslaved to the living and true God and to await his Son from heaven" (vv. 9–10, my translation). It is the totality of this phrase that defines their *pistis* (faith) in this context in terms of three verbs: "turned," "to be enslaved," and "to await." Since religion permeated every aspect of city life in this culture, a "turning to God away from idols" by a group of Gentiles that can be announced by others outside their city is not simply a reference to an individual's *inner* change of disposition (although it is certainly that) that then *results* in private practices of piety (although it may include such things). With the present infinitive *douleuein*, Paul portrays others as describing the state of this *ekklēsia* as one of *ongoing enslavement to God*, i.e., as a life pattern of loyalty and obedience toward God. It is not that their *pistis* (faith) "*results*" in turning from idols, etc., but that their faith [*pistis*] *is* the turning from the security of worshiping Rome's gods and goddesses to the apparent insecurity of obedience/fidelity[6] to the living God of Israel and awaiting the royal coming (*parousia*) of that God's Son from heaven.[7] A publicly visible rejection of idolatry's security and the display of singular obedience/loyalty to Israel's God are thus constitutive of faith (*pistis*).

Concomitantly, there is no hint in 1 Thessalonians that the "true church" is an "invisible/spiritual" collection of individuals to be distinguished from the visible church. Rather, analogous to eschatological Israel in Ezekiel 36–37, the audience is enabled by the giving of the Holy Spirit (1 Thess 4:8; cf. Ezek 36:26–27; 37:6) and the transformation of their imaginations/hearts (36:26) so that they are or become a *public* display of the (now crucified) Lord's character/holiness (1 Thess 3:12–13; 4:3). They do so before the eyes of the nations by means of their life together (Ezek 36:23b).[8] While this might be more implicit than explicit in 1 Thessalonians, the

---

5. Taking the *kai* at the beginning of v. 9b as explanatory ("that is") rather than as connective ("and").

6. *Pistis* has this sense of faithfulness/loyalty in 1:3, 8, 3:2, 5, 6, 7, 10 and possibly in 5:8.

7. This is a slightly modified sentence from Douglas Harink, *Paul Among the Postliberals* (Grand Rapids: Brazos, 2003), 36, n. 26.

8. "And the nations will know that I, myself, am the Lord *when I manifest my holiness by means of you [plural]* before their eyes" (my translation). I have fleshed out this connection between Ezekiel and 1 Thessalonians at greater length in "The Sanctification of the Imagination in 1 Thessalonians" in Kent E. Brower and Andy Johnson, eds., *Holiness and Ecclesiology in the New Testament* (Grand Rapids: Eerdmans, 2007), 275–92, esp. 276–79.

*ekklēsia* is indeed depicted quite explicitly as a publicly visible corporate body in the letter. As a result of their imitation of Paul, his companions, and the Lord, *their corporate life together, their ecclesial body as a whole* became a singular example (*typon*) to all those exercising believing allegiance in Macedonia and Achaia (1: 7). Hence, the publicly faithful way this audience conducted their corporate life together in the midst of tribulation functioned as a pattern to be imitated, a pattern of rejecting idolatry's security and displaying obedience/loyalty to Israel's God.

For non-Jews publicly to embody such a pattern in Thessalonica might indeed have been perceived as threatening the peace and "homeland security" of their city and possibly of the empire in which they lived. The inevitable result of such perceived disregard for the security of other city residents would have been "tribulations" (1 Thess 1:6; 2:14–15; 3:3–4) most probably in the form of social ostracism, verbal harassment, possible political sanctions, and perhaps even sporadic physical violence. Part and parcel of this would have been an ascription of public dishonor. Both individually and as a corporate body their lives would have been characterized by both insecurity and public dishonor precisely because they had rejected the "security" of idolatry. Here I want to push Witherington's depiction of the Parousia a bit further with regard to the issue of honor. To participate in the royal parade welcoming and honoring one crucified by the empire, one whom you had publicly acclaimed as Lord, would bring vindication not only to the Lord coming to receive his kingdom but to you as well (2:12; cf., 2 Thess 1:12a). In such a context, the import of the resurrection of the dead would not simply have been about the assurance of individual salvation but also about issues of *public honor*. Hence, the rhetoric of 1 Thess 4:13–5:11 funds and bolsters their perseverance in faith by affirming that those whose lives are/were riddled with publicly ascribed dishonor on account of their faith will be publicly vindicated (justified?) as they participate in the royal coming of their Lord. This is part and parcel of the salvation for which they are hoping (1:3; 5:8), a fully embodied[9] salvation that publicly restores their honor (the logic of 2 Thess 1:12; Rom 8:17; et al.). As such, it is quite consistent with the public nature of both faith (*pistis*) and the *ekklēsia* in 1 Thessalonians and sits uncomfortably with the notion of publicly dishonored persons disappearing into thin air "leaving everything material behind."[10]

---

9. Although Paul does not mention it here, on the basis of other Pauline texts one is warranted in imagining that the bodies of the dead and the living are transformed toward conformity with the body of the risen Christ (e.g., 1 Cor 15:42–48, Phil 3:20–21; Rom 8:17, 29).

10. LaHaye and Jenkins, *Left Behind*, 210–11.

I want to emphasize that it is not just premillenial Dispensationalism but much of North American evangelicalism that understands the nature of faith in "transaction" terms and makes the ecclesiological assumption that the "true" church is invisible. I conclude with a question for discussion: Is there something inherent in such conceptions that make premillenial Dispensationalism and much of North American evangelicalism more susceptible to creating false concepts of God that underwrite various forms of injustice in the name of "security," whether that be economic, social, or national/homeland security? To modify William Cavanaugh's language a bit, do such construals of faith (*pistis*) and the church make it difficult to even recognize when we are giving our souls to the (invisible) church and our bodies to the market and/or the state in exchange for "peace and security?"[11]

---

11. William T. Cavanaugh, *Torture and Eucharist: Theology, Politics, and the Body of Christ* (Oxford/ Malden, Mass.: Blackwell, 1998). While Cavanaugh's analysis is very specific to the Chilean context, there are structural similarities between the theology undergirding the official Roman Catholic stance toward Chilean "homeland security" throughout much of the Pinochet years and the broader theological commitments of premillenial Dispensationalism and many North American evangelicals.

# HOOFBEATS FULL OF GRACE?

## *Andy Johnson*

By singing "All Creatures of Our God and King" earlier in this service we have joined in the heavenly worship around the throne in Revelation 4 and 5. We have heard the heavenly anthem drowning all music but its own in "Crown Him with Many Crowns." When we move from that heavenly throne room to our sermon text, the music fades and the hoofbeats of horses seem to make the heavenly anthem barely audible. Hear the word of the Lord from Rev 6:1–8:

> Then I saw the Lamb open one of the seven seals, and I heard one of the four living creatures call out, as with a voice of thunder, "Come!" I looked, and there was a white horse! Its rider had a bow; a crown was given to him, and he came out conquering and to conquer. When he opened the second seal, I heard the second living creature call out, "Come!" And out came another horse, bright red; its rider was permitted to take peace from the earth, so that people would slaughter one another; and he was given a great sword. When he opened the third seal, I heard the third living creature call out, "Come!" I looked, and there was a black horse! Its rider held a pair of scales in his hand, and I heard what seemed to be a voice in the midst of the four living creatures saying, "A quart of wheat for a day's pay, and three quarts of barley for a day's pay, but do not damage the olive oil and the wine!" When he opened the fourth seal, I heard the voice of the fourth living creature call out, "Come!" I looked and there was a pale green horse! Its rider's name was Death, and Hades followed with him; they were given authority over a fourth of the earth, to kill with sword, famine, and pestilence, and by the wild animals of the earth. (NRSV)

When we hear these verses, no one needs to tell us that things on earth *are not* as they are in heaven. When the twenty-four elders stand before the glassy, calm sea, their singing is not interrupted with the sound of chaotic hoofbeats rumbling through the halls of heaven. I have to be honest. My natural reaction after hearing this passage is *not*: "Thanks be to God," especially since it is God who gives the riders their authority to do their damage in the first place.

Maybe it would be easier to respond with thanks if I could just believe that the four horsemen were only out to get the "inhabitants of the earth"—as John calls them later—after the church was raptured away safe and secure in heaven, but Revelation gives no hint of that. The visions were meant for the seven churches where the risen Christ walks and the Spirit has things to say. The visions were meant for us.

The Spirit has different things to say to different churches. I doubt any of us live in persecuted, poverty stricken churches like the one in Smyrna or the ones in Orissa. Most of us live in churches like the ones in Pergamum, Thyatira, and Laodicea, churches the risen Christ through the Spirit calls to repentance. We have been squeezed into the mold of our own society. We have complacently turned a blind eye to the injustices around us as long as we and those we love are secure. For us these visions are threatening and in them we recognize the daily realities of our own world writ apocalyptically large. We have an uneasy sense that they involve us as victims of harm. Further, if we listen carefully to what the Spirit is saying to churches like ours, we may begin to sense that they involve us as perpetrators of harm.

When the lamb opens the seals and the living creatures give the command, out come the riders dressed in the headlines and images with which we are all too familiar. We hear the headline, "Al Qaeda Claims Responsibility for Bombing," and out comes the rider on the white horse, a threat to all empires, reminding us that we cannot secure ourselves behind the borders of a nation. But, in Pergamum, Thyatira, and Laodicea we have certainly tried. To keep from being victims, we have purchased our "peace and security" at the price of turning a blind eye to our willingness to sacrifice others.

I will never forget one morning a couple of years ago when I was working in my study at home and read a story on MSN. After I read it, I could hardly work the rest of the day. It was a story about an Iraqi family who approached a United States military checkpoint in Iraq in a van. Inside the van was a driver who could not understand English and a young Iraqi mother with three or four of her children. Two of the children were about the same age as my two sons at that time, eight and six. When the van approached the checkpoint, the soldiers ordered the driver to halt, but the driver misunderstood and kept on going. At that point, the soldiers—perhaps understandably given the daily threats they faced—opened fire. The young Iraqi mother watched in anguish as two of her children, the two who were close in age to my sons, were riddled with bullets and died in her arms. The official line, of course, was that this whole train of events was indeed terribly tragic, but in the end we had to be prepared to accept some "collateral damage" to protect "our security," by which,

I suppose, they meant my security and that of my wife and two sons. The hoofbeats of the white horse get louder and louder shaking the ground under our feet, trying to shake us loose from our idolatry, and the Spirit says to those with ears to hear "Repent."

Other headlines and the red horse rides: "Violence in Darfur Worsens," "Dramatic Increase in Homicides in Kansas City." People are slaughtering one another everywhere, even in *my own* backyard. Those of us who live in Laodicea and Overland Park, Kansas, are reminded that we cannot secure ourselves from the violence within our own borders. We have certainly tried. To keep from being victims, we build more jails and put the bad guys in them, all the while complacently turning a blind eye to the injustice that feeds the violence just a few miles from our doorsteps. The hoofbeats of the red horse get louder and louder shaking the ground under our feet, trying to shake us loose from our idolatry, and the Spirit says to those with ears to hear "Repent."

Still other headlines and the black horse rides: "Wall Street Wobbles as Giants Fall," "Worst Financial Crisis Since the Great Depression." The fall of Lehman Brothers, the sale of Merrill Lynch, and the crisis at AIG may have something to do with Wall Street bears, but I suspect it has more do with a black horse.

Financial chaos runs rampant as chief executive officers make decisions based solely on greed, and average workers lose their jobs and their life savings. I recently heard a heart-wrenching story on National Public Radio describing the plight of an average middle-class family caught in the mortgage crisis that ended with a haunting line like: "For now, she just waits, looking nervously out the window, wondering if today will be the day the sheriff shows up on *her* front porch bringing the eviction notice." This is someone *like me, like most of us* who live in Laodicea and North Park. We are reminded that we cannot secure ourselves from economic instability or even personal financial collapse. We certainly have tried, in the process complacently turning a blind eye to the economic injustice that funds our own prosperity, both domestically and abroad. Folk in the majority world have seen the black horse ride through their neighborhoods so many times that some call it by name: "Greed, North American Style." The hoofbeats of the black horse get louder and louder shaking the ground under our feet, trying to shake us loose from our idolatry, and the Spirit says to those with ears to hear "Repent."

Finally, out comes death riding the pale green horse cloaked in headlines like: "AIDS Epidemic in Africa Continues Unabated," "CDC Warns of Possible Global Pandemic." The arrival of death on this pale green horse with Hades close behind may be John's way of saying that the general of this grisly cavalry has now arrived. It is not surprising that violence, famine, and economic hardship bring with them deadly disease and death. Those of us who live in Laodicea and Excelsior, Minnesota, are reminded that we cannot secure ourselves from the disease and death that will no doubt come our way. We certainly have tried.

We spend billions on gym memberships and on unnecessary plastic surgery, all the while not saying much when poor children in the majority world and right down the street cannot get access to the most basic forms of health care. The hoofbeats of the pale green horse get louder and louder shaking the ground under our feet, trying to shake us loose from our idolatry, and the Spirit says to those with ears to hear "Repent."

These are hard words for those of us who live in churches like Laodicea, Pergamum, and Thyatira. We know that things on earth are not like they are in heaven where creation is rightly ordered in true peace and security as all creatures of their God and king give God proper honor. We know that things have to change for the kingdom of this world to become the kingdom of the Lord and of his Messiah. We know that *we* have to change, or better, *we know that the Spirit has to change us.*

The good news today is that the One who refuses to allow *Lo-Ammi* and *Lo-Ruhamah* to keep their names (Hos 1:1—2:1), even if he has to lead Israel into restorative judgment, will not abandon us. The Risen One who opens the seals continues to walk among his churches refusing to abandon us to our enslaving idolatries. If we are open to hearing what the Spirit is saying to the churches, we might recognize that God is somehow gracefully at work to shake people like us loose from the idolatries that enslave us *precisely because we cannot shake ourselves loose.*

If we heed the warnings and the Spirit delivers us from our misplaced grasping for security, we *might* lose our lives and everything we hold dear, but our future is in the same hands that open the seals. These are the hands of the one still marked by nail prints from the hoofbeats of the crucifixion. *With him* the last thing we hear will not be hoofbeats because his hands also hold the keys of death and Hades. The same hands that healed the deadly diseases of Peter's mother-in-law and many others in the Gospels are the hands that will finally throw death and Hades into the lake of fire. They are the hands of the one who "lives that death may die." No, the last thing we hear will not be hoofbeats but rather a glorious hymn sung by a creation rightly ordered around the Lord of life in true peace and security.

# SECURITY

## *William H. Willimon*

*Of course, the people don't want war but after all, it's the leaders of the country who determine the policy and it's always a simple matter to drag the people along, whether it's a democracy, a fascist dictatorship, a parliament, or a communist dictatorship. Voice or no voice the people can always be brought to the bidding of the leaders. That is easy. All you have to do is to tell them that they are being attacked and denounce the pacifists for a lack of patriotism and exposing the country to a greater danger.*
(Hermann Goering, Nuremburg)

In the last national election, for the first time in the last sixty years, women supported the war and increases in military spending at the same level as men. Earlier, American women could be counted upon to be reluctant militarists; 9/11 changed that.[1] The end of the gender gap related to war is striking. The major reason given for this change: women's concerns about security.

Luther said that for which you would sacrifice your daughter is properly your "god." That we, men and now women, would so readily sacrifice our sons and daughters for this war suggests a new idol. Once we killed for "liberty, equality, and fraternity," now it is "security." Once we had the integrity as a nation to call it the War Department, later the Department of Defense, now it has become "Homeland Security."

The United States is spending about $500 billion on security, a larger military budget than all other nations combined. The war with Iraq is expected to cost about $300 billion. The cost is staggering, particularly because we are borrowing from our grandchildren in order to pay for our children's war with no tax increases. Our war in Afghanistan costs just over one billion dollars per week.

Biblical scholar Richard Hays says this huge expenditure suggests that we are undertaking "a kind of programmatic commitment to salvation through violence and military force . . . We are a very fearful people and . . . we are putting our trust in

---

1. http://www.womensenews.org/article.cfm?aid=857.

swords and chariots and guns to somehow secure our well-being."[2] Or, as I might say it, we are attempting to accomplish through dollars and bombs that which Christians expect of God: security.

Jesus told a naughty little parable: What is God like? God is the thief who breaks into your house, just when you least expect, and rips off everything you have—not the nicest thing ever said about God, but when you are the Son of God, only you have a right to call God a thief.

Just for today let us agree that a major tenant of the Christian faith is this: none of us is going to get out of this alive. God is going to kill all of us in the end anyway.

Master horror storyteller Stephen King was hit by a speeding van while walking down a road one morning. He nearly died. When interviewed by National Pubic Radio's Terry Gross, King noted how many interesting books he had written since his recovery. Still, he said, "If someone had asked me, 'Would you like to live a boring life and retire at 55 or be hit by a van and have horrible pain but knock out a couple more good books? I would have taken the former in a heartbeat."

Christians call the van that hit King "God," which brings me to my text, Luke 12:13-20:

> Someone in the crowd said to him, "Teacher, tell my brother to divide the family inheritance with me." But Jesus said to him, "Friend, who set me to be a judge or arbitrator over you?" And Jesus said to them, "Take care! Be on guard against all kinds of greed; for one's life does not consist in the abundance of possessions." Then he told them a parable: "The land of a rich man produced abundantly. And he thought to himself, 'What should I do, for I have no place to store my crops?' Then he said, 'I will do this: I will pull down my barns and build larger ones, and there I will store all my grain and my goods. And I will say to my soul, 'Soul, you have ample goods laid up for many years; relax, eat, drink, be merry.' But God said to him, 'You fool! This very night your life is being demanded of you. And the things you have prepared, whose will they be?'"

A man makes an appeal to Jesus to work justice in a matter of a brother who does not want to divide the family inheritance with his sibling. An injustice has been committed, inheritance laws violated. Jesus refuses to arbitrate (v. 14), to side with the victim or the perpetrator, the cheater or cheated, to do or say anything in behalf of justice in this case. Jesus acts as if such concerns are trivial. Riches should not cause loss of sleep (Eccl 2:23).

---

2. Richard Hays, "U. S. Seeks Salvation through Violence," *Vital Theology* 2.1 (March 15, 2005).

He responds by telling a nasty story that assaults those who, in Luke's words, pile up riches "for themselves and who are not rich toward God,"[3] or as I might put it, those who seek security for themselves and are insecure with God. This episode begins a whole section in Luke on possessions (vv. 13–21), or is it more properly a section on anxiety? (vv. 22–34). The story is evoked here by a question from the crowd, a question that Jesus refuses to answer. Or is it more properly a question that Jesus reframes with his parable of the rich man? Is it a story against covetousness or against insecurity and improper security? Let us say that it is a story about security of goods in place of God, of not being "rich toward God" (v. 21). Paul would call it serving "the creature rather than the Creator" (Rom 1:25).

In the parable there is no condemnation of the rich man for graft, corruption, theft, etc. The man is not a criminal; he is a fool. He is blessed with beautiful, productive, bountiful land, all considered to be blessings from God. He makes prudent economic decisions by pulling down old barns and building new ones. He is in no way unjust, not wasteful.

He talks in monologue to himself ("I know what I will do, I will pull down my barns, I will say to myself, 'self, take ease,' I will. . ."). The irony is that this man who has such a well-developed, active sense of himself by the end of the story loses himself. He puts his trust in himself to save himself, and in the process his self is obliterated.

We say on our money, "In God we trust," but our military budget suggests that this is a lie.

Jesus' story is about security and our inept attempts to get it. Jesus is the one who calls our attempts to secure ourselves by ourselves "foolish" and then demands our life. I am claiming that built right into the heart of the Christian faith is the truth that we are not secure and never will be by our own efforts. (Is that what Paul means when he exhorted those who have things to live as if they did not [1 Cor 7:29–31], which perhaps he would paraphrase as "Let those who are secure live as if they were not"?)

Thus St. Jerome worked with a skull atop his writing desk. We once built churches in the middle of graveyards, but that was when we still had the theological resources to admit, at least on a yearly basis on Ash Wednesday, "From dirt you came and to dirt you shall return."

Remember that play (which became a movie with William Hurt), "Whose Life Is This Anyway?" You know the answer to the play's question, "By God, my life

---

3. Similar to logion 63 in Gospel of Thomas.

is *mine*!" The irony is that the dying doctor, who so raged against others taking charge of his life, was doing so precisely in that time when humans are dramatically confronted with the truth that our lives are definitely *not* and never have been our own—death. Death is the ultimate rip off, the ultimate reminder that our vaunted boasts about self-possession are delusions. In the end God is going to rip off everything that we thought we owned. In the end the One who so graciously gave life is also the one who so unexpectedly takes it. Nobody has a right to take anything from anyone without permission—unless he owns what he takes in the first place.

Recently at a conference on higher education a speaker, speaking on the moral development of students, said that she thought the purpose of higher education was to foster the "Art of self-possession by Students." We possess cars, houses, why not also ourselves? I thought that was an honest admission of the bankruptcy of much of American higher education. What we thought to be a four-year path towards wisdom is reduced to mere training in being more savvy consumers. You go to college to nurture the illusion that your life is your life to utilize as you please and that the purpose of your efforts is to secure your life against mortality.

The church at its best has always known this to be false faith. Church is where we go to be reminded that the life you live is not your own. In the church in which I grew up, we were sometimes urged to "commit your life to Christ." There was a youth service, the preacher preached, then we all stood and sang, "Take my life and let it be, consecrated, Lord to thee." In other words we admitted with this God that there is no decision to "commit your life to Christ." God does not accept your life; he takes it, since it is God's to begin with.

I made a call to a pastor whom I had just appointed to move to a church where the salary was seven thousand dollars less than the meager salary he was making at his present church. I called him to offer him condolence and said, "Although I think this church is a good match with your gifts, the cabinet and I do regret that we are having to ask you to take such a large cut in salary." The pastor thanked me for my concern, then he said, "Bishop, I want you to tell the cabinet not to worry. There is no way they can hurt me financially as bad as Jesus hurt me when he called me into this ministry. I was pulling down eighty-five thousand a year when Jesus grabbed me and made me go to seminary. Tell the cabinet that there's nothing they can do to hurt me as bad as Jesus has already hurt me."

The Bible says, "It is a fearful thing to fall into the hands of the living God" (Heb 10:31). Presumably it is not a fearful thing to fall into the hands of dead god. A dead god is otherwise known as an idol, a work of human spirituality and imagination, a "god" who is but our own sweet concoction, as Flannery O'Connor would say. This no-god is not fearful at all since it is an idol that is created through our own wish-projection to serve our selfish needs. But, to have one's life grabbed, commandeered, ripped off by a living God, that is a fearful thing.

It takes guts to admit at the end, when all is said and done, that it is a lie that our lives are our possessions to give. It takes grace to admit that our lives are God's gifts to take. Death tells the truth about that widespread deceit and conceit, which perhaps explains why we go to such extraordinary lengths, when we can afford it, to extend our lives through technology. Immortality fantasies are the downfall of modern medicine and the lie as well.

It is a fearful thing to commend our spirits to God because, well, who knows what God will do with our lives? If you have commended your life to God on a Sunday morning only to be shocked and dismayed by what God commanded you to do on a Monday morning, you know what I mean. Our only reassurance from God is the promise that God will never allow anything worse to happen to us than God allowed to happen to his only Son. There, does that make you feel better?

I think most of us, or maybe this is just me, spend most of our lives attempting to get our lives out of God's hands and into our own. We achieve, work, build and hoard, work out at the gym, and watch our cholesterol. For most of us, if God wants my life, then God will have to damn well come out and get it. And truth to tell, by the end one way or another God does. We die.

In an earlier day, long ago, we Wesleyans once proudly pointed to the instances of "Happy Death" among us, those deaths in which the Christian, being so perfected in love, so close to God, slipped into death with a joy that comes from a short journey from life through death to God. I fear that we have very few "Happy Deaths" today because most of us, in death, make a very long and arduous trip from total self-absorption in this life to a most anguished and reluctant total self-loss in the next.

One way you can tell a true God from a home made idol is that idols tend to promise us continuity, immortality, and security, being mirrors of our ideal selves. Israel was forced to leave the security of a well functioning economy in Egypt and live with the freedom that God pushed her into in the uncertain wilderness. We so hope to establish ourselves by ourselves in certainty and security, through our military hardware, our pension systems, and our burglar alarms. Israel learned that the major threat to her security was not the Canaanites but rather the Lord. The prophets had to tell her that all attempts at "security" tend to be efforts to establish ourselves by ourselves, i.e., *idolatry*. But, Israel existed only by God's act: ". . . it is because the Lord loves you" (Deut 7:7–8). Israel had no foundation, no means of existence, no secure reason for being Israel today or tomorrow, except as an undeserved, unearned, gracious act of God. Israel had to learn to worship her Lord even when circumstances (the exodus, the exile) did not warrant such confidence in God's creative love. Abraham, the father of the faith of Israel, had to venture out to he knew not where if he would walk with this God and be open to the promises of this God (Heb 11:1) Only God knew where Abraham was being taken. Abraham and Sarah had to let go and let God lead. Of course, the ultimate letting go, the ultimate exodus and the final exile, the greatest of all insecurity is the annihilation that comes with death. So when Christians speak of cross and resurrection, we are saying something akin to what Israel said when she remembered exodus. We were nothing; then we were something because of God, and we very well could be nothing again without God. Our only security is that much evaded insecurity that is called fidelity to a living God, or, as Jesus put it at the end, "Father, into thy hands I commit my Spirit."

The prophets told us not to put our trust in chariots. When we admired the apparently eternal temple in all its glory, Jesus was at his most prophetic in telling us, "It shall all be cast down, destroyed, stone-on-stone." There was something about this Savior that thought nothing of demanding that folk abandon the security of home, marriage, family, and a good paying job in fishing and follow him down a narrow path with no place to rest and lay our head. John the Baptizer had warned us, "I just want to half-drown you but One comes after me, who is greater than I, who shall burn you, consume you, cut you down to the root."

Paul says that we, the baptized, are to live in such a way that "united with him in a death like his, we shall be united in a resurrection like his" (Rom 6:5). That is our hope. We have a choice, whether vainly to attempt to preserve ourselves by ourselves or instead to die like Jesus, commending ourselves and all those whom we love in death to the Lord, the Giver of Life. (Forgive me for thinking it sad that Christians, who ought to be just dying to commend ourselves to God, fight so valiantly, so expensively to enable those whom we love, commending them to the gods of technology, sucking oxygen and Medicare long after their apportioned lives have run their course, anything to avoid commending our spirits and theirs to God.)

So in commending his life to the Father, Jesus' last word is a take charge, direct, strangely confident word: "Father, into thy hands I commend my spirit."

I think of Christian discipleship as a lifetime of training in learning to live with the destabilization and insecurity that came upon us now that the Word has become flesh and moved in with us. Our task is to let go and allow the cross to be our only sign of security. "My peace I give to you," he says, "*not* as the world gives peace give I peace unto you."

We have labored sometimes to change the conflicts that cause people to make war. Christians believe that we must also change the people in the conflicts. Sanctification is the source of true pacification. Peace is not the result of our earnest efforts to improve the world and our situation in it; in fact, such idealistic efforts are usually the cause of our wars rather than their cure. Peace is a gift that only God can give.

I began with a quote from Hermann Goering. Let me end with a quote from a man of similar political disposition, Aristotle: "People make war in order to have peace" (*Nichomachean Ethics*, 10.1177b, 5–6).

# PROTECTING GOD
Psalm 91, Luke 4:1–14

## *Brent Laytham*

Late on the morning of September 11, 2001, eyewitnesses say that they saw the most horrible thing in a series of horrors. From the top of the World Trade Center people began to jump. We will never know why. We can certainly imagine their terror and despair. Perhaps someone madly hoped to survive the fall, but that is not likely. Nor is it likely that any of them quoted Psalm 91 and expected the protecting angels to bear them up. In the weeks since our minds have turned regularly to the question of the protecting God. Some ask why God did not protect the people; others seek to protect God from such charges—protecting God.

In Luke's temptation story the climax is this same question of the protecting God. We read it today, out of lectionary sequence, but paired with Psalm 91. The psalm does not ask about the protecting God; it asserts most forcefully a God of deliverance and refuge, of safety and rescue—the protecting God.

I confess that I have usually preferred Matthew's version of the temptation to Luke's. Matthew appears to move logically from the smallest temptation to the greatest, but for us today Luke's order speaks more directly. It intentionally moves from the wilderness to Jerusalem, from desert to temple, from periphery to center. In quoting Ps 91:11 Luke adds that the angels are promised "to protect you." There is the question behind the question: standing on the symbol of God's presence, reminded of the promise of God's protection, yet in that place where he will suffer and die, what can Jesus expect from God?

In commenting on Psalm 91 John Calvin called the devil "a sufficiently acute theologian" (*Commentary on Psalm 91*, p. 486). Calvin meant that the devil had grasped the promise of a protecting God in Psalm 91. Its message is summarized by contemporary commentators with words like security, protection, and providence. They are also quite clear that the Israelites heard these words, not as a promise of special protection for God's messiah, but as a general claim for God's people. So, our horizons merge. The quest of ancient Israelites, the question of the diabolical deceiver, and the current crisis of the American suburbanite is for security in the midst of trial and tribulation, danger and terror.

Now the problem with security is that it easily, almost automatically, becomes an idol. Either the situation of security we seek, or the securing God we supplicate, becomes a substitute for the living God. This is true both at personal and social levels.

Liberation theologians have regularly pointed out the way that national security is nearly always an idol, an idol we serve, an idol to which we sacrifice our children and the children of our enemies. Archbishop Oscar Romero wrote a letter in 1979 to Jimmy Carter asking him to stop sending money and arms to El Salvador. "They are used to kill us," he wrote. These were prophetic words, for a year later Romero was killed while celebrating the mass, killed for speaking out against the kidnapping, torture, and murder of the Salvadoran people. Carter did not stop the money, nor did Reagan after him, because they were convinced that the security of the United States depended on maintaining the San Salvadoran government.

Safety, peace of mind, security—we all want them, but may we have them, and at what price? As Christians, we can never embrace a security that trusts in force and fear. Rather, we are called to dwell "in the protection of the Most High" (Ps 91:1). We are called to find our refuge in the protecting God.

The psalm suggests that security lies in a relation with God that "dwells," that "stays," that "clings," one that in NT terms abides. This is suggested by the psalm's images of "refuge," "fortress," and a protecting mother bird, but my theology students will not be surprised if I ask us to look more closely at the pronouns. Someone, perhaps a priest, addresses the worshippers in the singular—you, not you all. The promise is to you, to "thou." It is a reminder or even an invitation for you to call this Most High God, this Almighty God, *my* refuge, *my* fortress, *my* God. This is an invitation, not just to *trust* God, but to *entrust* yourself to God. Later God speaks, saying, "I [God] will protect those who know my name" (v. 14 NRSV).

What is that name we must know? Of course, this could be the ancient fascination with the power of naming, or it could be the covenantal motif of the graciously revealed divine name. Let us seek our answer in Luke, at the baptism of Jesus. There God spoke in the first person. "You are my Son . . ." (3:22). Karl Barth says that God cannot say, "I am your God without saying you are my people." That flows in both directions. God cannot say to Jesus "You are my Son" without saying at the same time "I am your Father." God cannot say to us "You are mine" without saying "I am yours." This means that whatever divine name the psalmist had in mind with the claim "I will protect those who know my name," God has definitively attached to that name the first person singular possessive pronoun "my": my refuge, my fortress, my God.

Of course, in that way lies the danger of presumption, which is precisely where this third temptation comes in. At a trivial level the third temptation is to presume upon this relation with God, to assume that God will or must protect us from every danger. Old fables about guardian angels walk that path. (However, note that there are no ministering angels at the end of Luke's account.) Over the centuries Jews and Christians have worn bits of this psalm in amulets that were believed to be a kind of magical protection for those who wore them.

At a deeper level, though, this third temptation probes the meaning of security and tests the totality of our trust. If my God will protect me, the question is from what? If God is my refuge, what security may I expect?

The psalmist promises that if we cling to the protecting God, we will have "no fear." I suppose the "no fear" bravado of the Gen-Xers was already fading before September 11, but I wonder now whether it has been permanently erased. Either way, from AIDS to global warming to recession, "no fear" has been a social pretense and a false profession. The psalmist promises that those who "abide in the shadow of the Almighty" will abide in a realm without fear. Daytime or darkness, midnight or noon, there is no fear "under the wings" of the Most High. In a series of images the psalm appears to promise protection from natural evil (pestilence and diseases), from human violence (the arrow that flies at daytime), and even from supernatural affliction (the terror of the night). It is easy to hear Paul's claim in Rom 8 as an echo of Psalm 91: "For I am convinced that neither death, nor life, nor angels, nor rulers, nor things present, nor things to come, nor powers, nor height, nor depth, nor anything else in all creation will be able to separate us from the love of God in Christ Jesus our Lord" (8:38–39).

Yet, there is a difference. The psalmist says, "A thousand may fall at your side, ten thousand at your right hand, but it will not come near you." Apparently this is a claim that the protecting God secures us *from* every danger and threat. Paul, on the other hand, reminds us that "God did not withhold his own Son, but gave him up" (8:32). Certainly he could just as well have said "God did not protect his own Son, but handed him over to death." While the psalmist knows no other way to state poetically the all-encompassing protection of God, we now know narratively a different way to think about it. It is not an almighty protection *from* every threat and fear and danger, but an unfailing presence *in* every affliction. Security, then, is not protection *from* but protection *in*. Protection in every hardship, or distress, or persecution, or famine, or nakedness, or peril, or sword, protection in every terrorist attack, every economic recession, every cancer and car wreck and divorce.

This brings us back to Jesus. Luke Timothy Johnson reminds us that Luke's Christian readers ". . . learn something of their own path from the conscious decision of the 'Lord Christ' to choose another than a violent way to be Messiah, who rejected power over nature to serve his appetite, over humans for the sake of glory, over God for his own survival, in favor of the 'path of peace' (1:79; 2:14, 29; Acts 10:36!) . . ."[1] In these temptations Christ conquers the attempt to secure his future through violence precisely by taking refuge in the Almighty. Thus he comes forth from the wilderness triumphant, full of the *power* of the Holy Spirit, a power which does not seek protection from, but finds security in, the presence of God. We see that same power in Luke's account of the crucifixion. Here there is no cry of dereliction: "My God, My God, why have you forsaken me." Instead, Jesus entrusts himself to the protecting God: "Father, into your hands I commit my Spirit."

We are called to entrust ourselves to the Almighty God revealed in Jesus Christ. "Fear not, I am with you; O, be not dismayed, for I am your God and will still give you aid; I'll strengthen you, help you, and cause you to stand, upheld by my gracious omnipotent hand."[2] The omnipotent hand of God is the open bleeding hand of Jesus Christ. Let us dwell always and only in that security. Thanks be to God.

---

1. *The Gospel of Luke* (SP 3; Collegeville, Minn.: Liturgical, 1991), 77.
2. Stanza two of "How Firm a Foundation."

# ANNOTATED BIBLIOGRAPHY

Bader-Saye, S. *Following Jesus in a Culture of Fear*. Grand Rapids: Brazos, 2007. This book explores the ways in which fear pervades the lives of people who live in a post 9/11 culture dominated by fear. A focus on fear naturally leads people away from following Christian ethical imperatives. Bader-Saye calls Christians to take the risks that are necessary to live out these Christian virtues and encourages a return to the image of God as a providing parent as a counter against the fears which are prevalent in the culture.

Baldwin, David A. "The Concept of Security." *Review of International Studies* 23 (1997): 5–26. Baldwin argues that the meaning of "security" has been eroded because it has been broadened beyond all useful application. He seeks to eliminate extraneous meanings to get back to a true and meaningful understanding of the concept of security.

Barclay, J. M. G. "Manna and the Circulation of Grace: A Study of 2 Corinthians 8.1–15." Pages 409–26 in *The Word Leaps the Gap: Essays on Scripture and Theology in Honor of Richard B. Hays*. Edited by J. R. Wagner, C. K. Rowe, and A. K. Grieb. Grand Rapids: Eerdmans, 2008. Barclay examines the exodus themes behind this text from 2 Corinthians and emphasizes the idea of God's grace being conveyed from God to humanity and from one human to another in a system of mutual sharing. This essay argues the concept of the grace of God is in "surplus," meaning that no one must grasp it or hoard it but rather should accept the richness in this gift by the giving of one's self for others.

Barton, S. C., ed. *Idolatry: False Worship in the Bible, Early Judaism and Christianity*. London and New York: T. & T. Clark, 2007. This book is a collection of essays concerning various aspects of idolatry. Among other things the essays treat idolatry in the OT, in the writings of Josephus, the connection between idolatry and the laws about sex and food, and the connection between idolatry and modern capitalism. This book provides a broad spectrum of ways to think about and understand the issues associated with idolatry.

Beale, G. K. *We Become What We Worship: A Biblical Theology of Idolatry*. Downers Grove, Ill.: InterVarsity, 2008. This book asserts that people reflect the image of what they revere or idolize, with idolatry being defined in part as that to which one clings for ultimate security. Texts are treated from various sections of the canon to indicate that this assertion is biblically accurate and attention is also given to modern applications.

Beck, Ulrich. *World Risk Society*. Cambridge: Polity, 1999. The author explores and systematizes the changes taking place in the cultural switch from an enlightenment-based modernity to what he calls a "second modernity." This sociological analysis of the modern situation involving poverty, globalization, and politics helps readers understand what it means to live in a world risk society and how to approach the changes.

Bindé, Jérôme. "Toward an Ethics of the Future." *Public Culture* 12 (2000): 51–72. Bindé discusses our relation to time in the modern world and its impact on economic, social, political, and ecological issues. He discusses the "tyranny of emergency" as a distorted relation to time that diminishes our ability to pursue "collective aims."

Booth, Ken. "Security and Emancipation," *Review of International Studies* 17 (1991): 313–26. Booth, a proponent of "critical security studies," argues that security needs to be reconceptualized in terms of emancipation, and that "emancipation, not power or order, produces true security."

Brueggemann, Walter. *Isaiah 1–39*. Louisville: Westminster John Knox, 1998. Brueggemann draws attention to the ways in which Isaiah represents a radical call to trust God in times of crisis. Isaiah has a complicated portrait of divine sovereignty which both assures and challenges our security.

———. *The Prophetic Imagination*. 2d ed. Minneapolis: Fortress, 2001. Brueggemann explores better than most the tensions between the ideology of those in power and the prophetic critique. Although his perspective can be a bit too neat in its dichotomies, this is a classic study that deserves attention.

Buzan, Barry, Ole Waever, and Jaap de Wilde. *Security: A New Framework for Analysis*. Boulder, Colo.: Lynne Rienner, 1998. This Copenhagen School's approach to security studies receives its fullest exposition here. The concept of securitization outlined by Waever is applied to the various "sectors" of analysis previously developed by Buzan. The "new security" scholars' rationale for broadening the security agenda is thus articulated on the basis of a substantial reworking of the meaning of security itself.

Calvin, John. The sovereignty of God over all things is central to Calvin's entire theological project. Therefore, his understanding of the Christian life is consistently imbued with consideration of God's providential governance and its effects. Security in this view is completely dependent upon God, though the reality of what trusting God for our security entails is nuanced in complicated ways as Calvin applies these themes to the Christian life in both its personal and political dimensions. Though Calvin only occasionally speaks directly of "security," the following texts offer additional elaboration of the theological points where the impact of his thought is most relevant:

———. "Against the Libertines." In *Treatises Against the Anabaptists and Against the Libertines*. Edited and translated by Benjamin Wirt Farley. Grand Rapids: Baker, 1982 [1545]. Calvin contrasts the Libertine Sect with orthodox Christian beliefs. He refutes such Libertine beliefs as pantheism, Gnosticism, and their understanding of Christian liberty.

———. "Defence of the Secret Providence of God." In *Calvin's Calvinism*. Translated by Henry Cole. Grand Rapids: Eerdmans, 1950 [1558]. In this work Calvin defends his doctrines of predestination, election, and persevering grace.

———. *Commentary on the Book of the Prophet Isaiah*. Translated by William Pringle. 4 vols. Grand Rapids: Eerdmans, 1948 [1550]. Most pertinent to the discussion of security are the treatments of Isa 7–8, 28, and 35–43.

———. *A Commentary on Genesis*. Translated and edited by John King. Edinburgh: Banner of Truth Trust, 1965. The treatment of the story of Joseph and his brothers (Gen 37, 42–45, esp. 45:7–8) offers some of Calvin's most significant teaching on God's providential rule of history.

———. *Commentaries on the Epistle of Paul the Apostle to the Romans*. Translated and edited by John Owen. Grand Rapids: Eerdmans, 1947 [1540]. Most pertinent will be the treatments of Rom 8–11.

———. *Sermons from Job*. Translated by Leroy Nixon. Grand Rapids: Eerdmans, 1952. Calvin's late revisions of the material on providence in the *Institutes* was influenced by the intensive study of Job which gave rise to these sermons; here the relation of divine and human causality, including God's work through evil and sin, is treated with great attention to the difficulties of the subject.

———. *Institutes of the Christian Religion*. Edited by J. T. McNeill. Translated by Ford Lewis Battles. 2 vols. Library of Christian Classics, vols. 20 and 21. Philadelphia: Westminster, 1960 [several editions from 1536 to 1559]. Although the entirety of Calvin's summation of the faith involves the explication of divine sovereignty in all its various aspects and effect, the following selections may be of particular interest for questions of security: Calvin's direct treatment of providence (Book I, ch. xvi–xviii); the manner in which God works through human beings (Book II, ch. iv); and the effects of divine sovereignty on the Christian life (Book III, ch. vii–x) and civil society (Book IV, ch. xx).

Carroll R., M. Daniel. "'For So You Love To Do': Probing Popular Religion in the Book of Amos." Pages 168–89 in *Rethinking Contexts, Rereading Texts: Contributions from the Social Sciences to Biblical Interpretation*. Edited by M. Daniel Carroll R. Journal for the Study of the Old Testament: Supplement Series 299. Sheffield: Sheffield Academic, 2000. This study explores the nature of popular religion and how it functions to legitimize and sanction aspects of culture, society, and politics. It examines in some detail the material in the book of Amos and uses cultural anthropology to assist in the analysis.

Church of Norway Commission on International Affairs (Council of Ecumenical and International Relations). "Vulnerability and Security." December 2000; English translation, February 2002. Available online at http://www.kirken.no/english/engelsk.cfm?artid=5850. This very interesting document produced by the Church of Norway argues that discussions of security must begin with a consideration of human vulnerability. Vulnerability, the authors contend, is not the opposite of security; it is not something that must be abolished or overcome in order for security to be achieved, but rather it provides the basis for the mutual dependence and empathetic relationships upon which true security relies. Although primarily ethical and political, some aspects of theological anthropology are included.

Der Derian, James. "The Value of Security: Hobbes, Marx, Nietzsche and Baudrillard." Pages 24–45 in *On Security*. Edited by Ronnie D. Lipschutz. New York: Columbia Univeristy Press, 1995. This essay focuses on decentering security as a normalizing influence and instead constructing a security based on appreciation and articulation. The author presents discussions about four realist forms of security and the thinkers associated with them: Hobbes and epistemic realism, Marx and social realism, Nietzsche and interpretive realism, and Baudrillard and hyperrealism.

Dunn, J. D. G. *The Theology of Paul the Apostle*. Edinburgh: T. & T. Clark, 1998. Although this is a book much more general than the topic at hand, it provides a framework for understanding Paul's contribution and the chapter on the church is especially pertinent.

Furedi, Frank. *Culture of Fear: Risk-Taking and the Morality of Low Expectations*. Rev. ed. New York: Continuum, 2002; *Paranoid Parenting: Why Ignoring the Experts May be Best for Your Child*. Chicago: Review, 2002; and *Politics of Fear: Beyond Left and Right*. New York: Continuum, 2005. In these three books Furedi, a sociologist at the University of Kent, argues that Western cultures, notably Great Britain and the United States, have allowed "risk management" to become our moral and political touchstone. We create ever expanding categories of people, places, and things that are "at risk," which in turn creates a sense of fatalism and impotence.

Glassner, Barry. *The Culture of Fear: Why Americans are Afraid of the Wrong Things*. New York: Basic, 1999. Glassner, a sociologist at University of Southern California, discusses the misguided, culturally produced, fears that haunt many Americans and suggests that these fears keep us from acting on the real and legitimate threats we face such as hunger, poor schools, and inadequate health care.

Gorman, Michael J. *Cruciformity: Paul's Narrative Spirituality of the Cross*. Grand Rapids: Eerdmans, 2001. Rather than focusing on Paul's theology, Gorman chooses to explore Paul's experiences of faith and spirituality. This book provides a different way of understanding Paul and serves as a reminder that all spirituality must be formed by the understanding of the crucified and resurrected Christ.

Goudzwaard, Bob. *Idols of Our Time*. Downers Grove, Ill.: InterVarsity, 1984. Gourdzwaard's premise is that the current period is an age in which our ideologies possess us. He discusses the ideologies of revolution, nation, prosperity, and security and names these idols for what they are, explains them, and points toward solutions.

Halbertal, M., and A. Margalit. *Idolatry*. Cambridge, Mass.: Harvard University Press, 1992. This book explores the nature and meaning of idolatry and how arguments on this topic have shaped the course of Western history. While Islam and Christianity are considered, the primary focus is on Judaism. Halbertal and Margalit also explore the arguments which religious traditions have used against each other and then offer insights into the logic and lack of logic these arguments employ.

Harak, Simon. *Virtuous Passions: The Formation of Christian Character*. Eugene, Ore.: Wipf and Stock, 2002 [reprint of Paulist, 1993, publication]. Harak discusses how we make moral judgments about our passions, including fear, which we generally experience as "coming upon us" in a morally neutral way. He discusses the formation of the passions in relation to the life of virtue and character in Thomas Aquinas and Ignatius of Loyola.

Harvey, A. E. *Renewal Through Suffering*. Edinburgh: T. & T. Clark, 1996. This study of 2 Corinthians sees Paul's treatment of death as the means to understanding some of the most difficult passages in the epistle. The author believes that there was a traumatic event in Paul's life which fundamentally affected his understanding of suffering and influenced what and how he taught on these matters.

Hess, Richard S. *Israelite Religions: An Archaeological and Biblical Survey*. Grand Rapids: Baker, 2007. This work provides a very helpful survey of the extensive epigraphic and iconographic data concerning holy sites, rituals, and the various deities that all were part of the religious life of ancient Israel.

Hobbes, Thomas. *Leviathan*. London and New York: 1914 [1651 originally]. Hobbes' classic text on the structure of civil society presents the natural state of humanity as one of chaos and war and argues that peace and security are attainable for the commonwealth only when the "natural passions of men" are restrained by submission to the rule of an absolute monarch through a social contract.

Horrell, D. G. *Solidarity and Difference: A Contemporary Reading of Paul's Ethics*. London: T. & T. Clark, 2005. Horrell believes Paul's ethic focuses on a community that lives in solidarity while also allowing for differences in ethical practices. He makes use of modern views of ethical theory and sociology and examines Paul's role as a moral thinker.

Jewett, Robert and John Shelton Lawrence. *Captain America and the Crusade against Evil: The Dilemma of Zealous Nationalism*. Grand Rapids: Eerdmans, 2003. This is a biting critique of civil religion in the United States, its origins, and its recent manifestations. While not everyone will agree with the analysis and judgments, this volume will provoke fruitful reflection on the idols generated by the confusion of religion and politics.

Jones, Richard Wyn. *Security, Strategy, and Critical Theory*. Boulder, Colo.: Lynne Rienner, 1999. Jones, a leading proponent of "critical security studies," turns to critical theory to provide the backbone for his emancipatory critique of traditional security discourse. In this book he analyzes the work of several leading thinkers in the Frankfurt School (including Horkheimer, Adorno, and Habermas) and seeks to appropriate their insights for the question of security.

Krause, Keith, and Michael C. Williams, eds. *Critical Security Studies*. Minneapolis: University of Minnesota Press, 1997. "Critical security studies" is the name given to a wide-ranging school of thought whose proponents have sought to place actual people at the center of security discourse. Individuals, rather than states and their interests, are the objects of security, and interstate war is only one of many threats they face. This collection of essays presents diverse viewpoints.

Lipschutz, Ronnie D, ed. *On Security*. New York: Columbia University Press, 1995. Lipschutz's opening and closing essays ("On Security" and "Negotiating the Boundaries of Difference and Security and Millennium's End") frame the questions and establish the contexts for contemporary security research.

Long, A. A. *Epictetus: A Stoic and Socratic Guide to Life*. Oxford: Clarendon, 2002. The translations of the philosophy of Epictetus and the introductions and commentaries both introduce Epictetus and provide perspective on his works. This book shows how ancient philosophy can be practically applied to modern issues of ethics and theology.

McConville, J. G. *God and Earthly Power: An Old Testament Political Theology, Genesis–Kings*. Library of Hebrew Bible/Old Testament Studies 454. London: T. & T. Clark, 2006. This is an investigation of how the OT envisions a politics pleasing to God in contrast to the reigning ideologies of the ancient world. This work is exegetically sophisticated and is informed by current discussions in various pertinent disciplines within biblical studies.

Meadors, Edward P. *Idolatry and the Hardening of the Heart*. London: T. & T. Clark, 2006. God's action of hardening the hearts of some people in the biblical text is understood as a disciplinary action for the sin of idolatry. Both OT and NT texts are treated, and the answer to the issue is found in the new covenant of Jesus Christ.

Míguez Bonino, José. *Toward a Christian Political Ethics*. Philadelphia: Fortress, 1983. This is an important treatment of the relationship between the Christian faith and political realities from a Latin American liberationist perspective. One of the chapters is dedicated to exposing the idolatry of the national security doctrine of the dictatorships in Latin America.

Moberly, R. W. L. *Prophecy and Discernment*. Cambridge: Cambridge University Press, 2006. Moberly exegetes texts from both testaments to learn how to discern authentic prophecy and how we may appropriate these texts today.

Moltmann, Jürgen. "Control is Good—Trust is Better: Freedom and Security in a 'Free World.'" *Theology Today* 62 (2006): 465–75. Moltmann treats the issues of control that pervade societies obsessed with their own security. In such situations of over control, security becomes increasingly expensive, and no one tells the truth because they can only say what they believe the person in authority wants to hear. For freedom really to be possible a society must be based on trust rather than control. This trust must begin with trusting in God, the only truly trustworthy being, and recognizing that God trusts us.

———. *Theology of Hope*. New York: Harper and Row, 1967. This book is more an antidote to the idolatry of security. Moltmann sees Christian hope as grounded securely in the past event of the resurrection of Jesus Christ. On his approach theology is based on hope, rather than being about hope.

Morgenthau, Hans. *Politics Among Nations: The Struggle for Power and Peace*. New York: Alfred P. Knopf, 1948. This classic text of twentieth century realism defines security in terms of military relations between states. It takes a pessimistic view of human nature and sees self-interest as the primary motivation of actors on the international stage, which results inevitably in competition and conflict.

Müller-Fahrenholz, Geiko. *America's Battle for God: A European Christian Looks at Civil Religion*. Grand Rapids: Eerdmans, 2007. The value of this volume is that it represents a perspective from outside the United States on the cultural and political captivity of American religion. The author is a sympathetic critic, who has a considerable experience in the United States.

Neal, Ryan A. *Theology as Hope: On the Ground and Implications of Jürgen Moltmann's Doctrine of Hope*. Princeton Theological Monograph Series 99. Eugene, Ore.: Pickwick, 2009. This book explores the development of Moltmann's theology of hope to understand its character, composition, and progression. Neal shows Moltmann's doctrine is grounded in the crucifixion and resurrection of Christ and draws out the implications of this doctrine of hope for other theological doctrines.

Nichols, Stephen J. *Jesus Made in America: A Cultural History from the Puritans to the Passion of Christ*. Downers Grove, Ill.: InterVarsity, 2008. This work uses eight different categories to survey the many different constructions of Jesus in American history. This informed critique unmasks many of the idols called Jesus that have been worshiped in the United States since the Colonial Period.

Niebuhr, Reinhold. *Moral Man and Immoral Society*. New York: Charles Scribner's Sons, 1932. Niebuhr argues that groups (including states) have less ability to transcend self-interest than individuals, which makes power the arbiter and conflict the endemic feature of social and political life. This was a significant element of the "Christian realism" that influenced the security policy and public consciousness of post-World War II America.

———. *Love and Justice: Selections from the Shorter Writings of Reinhold Niebuhr*. Edited by D. B. Robertson. Glouchester, Mass.: Peter Smith, 1957. This book explains the "realism" of Niebuhr's Christian realism in terms of the unattainability—the "impossible possibility"—of agape love and the form which love then takes in a sinful world, i.e., justice.

———. *The Nature and Destiny of Man*. 2 vols. New York: Charles Scribner's Sons, 1943. In this work of theological anthropology Niebuhr posits anxiety—or insecurity—as the precondition of sin and understands sin as the result of the self's struggle to secure itself at the expense of others.

Overholt, Thomas W. *The Threat of Falsehood: A Study in the Theology of the Book of Jeremiah*. Studies in Biblical Theology. Second Series 16. London: SCM, 1970. Overholt evaluates the false conceptions of security which appear in the book of Jeremiah when the Israelites developed an idolatrous conception of security based on the temple as a symbol of a guarantee of national security. This false conception of security prevents the people from repenting, allows false prophets to emerge, and leads into idolatry.

Provan, Ian. "To Highlight All Our Idols: Worshipping God in Nietzche's World," *Ex Auditu* 15 (1999): 19–38. This was originally presented as a paper at the North Park Theological Symposium on the theme of idolatry. It is a quite helpful study of the nature of idolatry in the OT that engages what the author considers to be the idols of the present age.

Robin, Corey. *Fear: The History of a Political Idea*. Oxford: Oxford University Press, 2004. Robin, associate professor of political science at Brooklyn College and the Graduate Center of the City University of New York, writes as a political theorist about the ways in which fear has shaped modern political life. In Part I he explores such figures as Hobbes, Montesquieu, Tocqueville, Arendt, and Shklar before addressing "Fear, American Style" in Part II.

Sanders, John. *The God Who Risks: A Theology of Providence*. Downers Grove, Ill.: InterVarsity, 1998. This book presents an "open" or "relational" theism that argues against traditional notions of divine omnipotence and foreknowledge. Such a view sees God as limiting God's self and, therefore, to some extent vulnerable to creation. This has radical consequences for traditional notions of providence and raises important questions regarding the meaning and possibility of security

Sauter, Richard. *What Dare We Hope? Reconsidering Eschatology*. Harrisburg, Penn.: Trinity Press International, 1999. Sauter focuses on present hope rather than on eschatology as a doctrine of the future or of "last things," which has implications for understanding security.

Savage, T. B. *Power Through Weakness: Paul's Understanding of the Christian Ministry in 2 Corinthians*. Cambridge: Cambridge University Press, 1996. Paul's counter-intuitive theology is discussed as it relates to glory, shame, and the cross to provide understanding of the meaning of power through weakness, which obviously changes how one views security.

Seiple, Robert A. and Dennis R. Hoover, eds. *Religion and Security: The New Nexus in International Relations*. Lanham: Rowman and Littlefield, 2004. While acknowledging the ways in which religion and religious extremism are often implicated in violence, the authors of these essays move beyond this "negative" association to explore the potential of religion(s) for the promotion of peace and security. Central arguments include the claims that religious freedom and pluralism are necessary for political stability and that faith-based perspectives must be brought into the conversation in diplomatic and foreign policy circles.

Tickner, J. Ann. *Gender in International Relations: Feminist Perspectives on Achieving International Security*. New York: Columbia University Press, 1992. This classic text uncovers the biases in the methods, categories, and conceptual frameworks employed within International Relations theory which have traditionally silenced or marginalized the place and perspective of women in world politics. Tickner rereads the major issues in the field—including war, security, and the state—through the lens of gender.

Uniting Church in Australia, National Assembly. "No Security Without Justice." 2004. PDF available for download at http://www.unitingjustice.org.au/issues/democracy/democracy-resources-papers.html. This policy statement is another example of a church-based attempt to address issues of security from a faith perspective and in the public square.

United Nations Development Program (UNDP). *Human Development Report 1994: New Dimensions of Human Security* (New York: Oxford University Press). Also available online at http://hdr.undp.org/en/reports/global/hdr1994/. This significant policy document introduced the concept of "human security" and advocated a shift in emphasis and resources away from the Cold War preoccupation with nuclear catastrophe and towards the real threats faced daily by the majority of the world's population: "In the final analysis, human security is a child who did not die, a disease that did not spread, a job that was not cut, an ethnic tension that did not explode in violence, a dissident who was not silenced. Human security is not a concern with weapons—it is a concern with human life and dignity."

Von Balthasar, Hans Urs. *The Christian and Anxiety*. Translated by Dennis D. Martin and Michael J. Miller. San Francisco: Ignatius, 2000. Balthasar explores the ways in which Christ has overcome fear and anxiety on our behalf but suggests also that Christians, in imitation of Christ, take up the anxiety of the world as our own. He writes, in one memorable line, "Only a Christian who does not allow himself to be infected by modern humanity's neurotic anxiety . . . has any hope of exercising a Christian influence on this age. He will not haughtily turn away from the anxiety of his fellow men and fellow Christians but will show them how to extricate themselves from their fruitless withdrawal into themselves and will point out the paths by which they can step out into the open, into faith's daring" (p. 88).

Waever, Ole. "Securitization and Desecuritization." Pages 46–48 in *On Security*. Edited by Ronnie D. Lipschutz. New York: Columbia University Press, 1995. In this article Waever first set forth his speech-act conceptualization of security and introduced the notion of "securitization" which would become foundational to the work of the Copenhagen School. This theoretical framework allows for security to be analyzed in terms of the process by which an issue is raised to the level of a security threat (i.e., "securitized") and granted an urgency which legitimizes responses that exceed the normal bounds of political activity.

Walker, R. B. J. *Inside/Outside: International Relations as Political Theory*. Cambridge: Cambridge University Press, 1993. Walker analyzes the relationships between modern political theory and twentieth-century theories of international relationships and takes into account the issues around modernity and post-modernity, political identity, and the limitations of modern political theory.

Waltz, Kenneth. *Theory of International Politics*. Reading, Mass.: Addison-Wesley, 1979. This is the benchmark text of "neo-realism." Like the realists Waltz prioritizes the state and military in his analysis of international security, but rather than grounding his account in human nature (as did the "righteous realists," such as Morgenthau and Niebuhr), he sees the structure of the international system as determining the power and activities of the states within it. The Cold War emphasis on the balance of power was substantially dependent on Waltz's conception of "international anarchy," ideas which dominated international relations for decades and remain highly influential in security theory and policy today.

Welch, Sharon. *Real Peace, Real Security: The Challenges of Global Citizenship*. Minneapolis: Fortress, 2008. This book explains the arguments surrounding military policies which can prevent conflicts, and it reframes the concepts of security and peace. Welch is a Christian ethicist whose attention to this topic may signal a growing interest in its relevance for scholars and practitioners in the Christian tradition.

Williams, Rowan, *The Truce of God*. Grand Rapids: Eerdmans, 2005 [orig. 1983]. Williams, the Archbishop of Canterbury, looks at the way our fears corrupt our imagination, making us less able to pursue true peace. Williams comments, "The revelation of truth in Jesus both establishes our vulnerability—we grasp the force and depth of our self-protectiveness and liability to violence—and creates a centre of light against which we may judge ourselves and through which we may grow in discrimination. Thus Jesus is indeed grace as well as truth; and the community created by him is characterized by both things" (p. 122).

———. *Writing in the Dust: After September 11*. Grand Rapids: Eerdmans, 2002. Williams reflects on the 9/11 attacks and suggests possible ways of responding to such acts of terror that do not give ground to fear-based reflexive self-protection. "There may be something like a dreadful innocence about the first surge of anger; there is no innocence about the deployment of images to try and revive it" (p. 19).

Wright, Christopher J. H. *The Mission of God: Unlocking the Bible's Grand Narrative*. Downers Grove, Ill.: InterVarsity, 2006. The argument of this volume is that the Bible should be read missiologically. It is a testament to God's mission to redeem humanity and offers an invitation for God's people to participate in that mission. A significant section of the book deals with the nature and uniqueness of the God of the Bible and presents an extensive and very helpful discussion on idolatry, especially in relationship to the OT (pp. 136–88).

# NORTH PARK THEOLOGICAL SEMINARY
## SYMPOSIUM ON THE THEOLOGICAL INTERPRETATION OF SCRIPTURE

SEPTEMBER 25–27, 2008

*THE IDOLATRY OF SECURITY*

## PRESENTERS

**PROFESSOR SCOTT BADER-SAYE**
University of Scranton, Theological Ethics

**PROFESSOR JOHN BARCLAY**
University of Durham, New Testament

**PROFESSOR M. DANIEL CARROLL RODAS**
Denver Seminary, Old Testament

**JILL CARLSON COLWELL**
Yale Divinity School, Ph. D. Candidate, Theology

**PROFESSOR C. ANDREW JOHNSON**
Nazarene Theological Seminary, New Testament

**PROFESSOR WALTER MOBERLY**
University of Durham, Old Testament

**PROFESSOR SUJIN PAK**
Duke Divinity School, History

**PROFESSOR BEN WITHERINGTON III**
Asbury Theological Seminary, New Testament

**PROFESSOR RANDALL C. ZACHMAN**
University of Notre Dame, History

## RESPONDENTS

**AMY E. BLACK**
    Wheaton College, Political Science

**DARRELL COSDEN**
    Judson College, Theology

**JO ANN DEASY**
    Northwestern University, Ph. D. Candidate, Congregational Studies

**ROBERT D. HAAK**
    Augustana College, Old Testament

**ROBERT L. HUBBARD, JR.**
    North Park Theological Seminary, Old Testament

**C. ANDREW JOHNSON**
    Nazarene Theological Seminary, New Testament

**KYLE J. A. SMALL**
    Luther Seminary, Ph.D. Candidate, Ethics

**JOEL WILLITTS**
    North Park University, New Testament

EX AUDITU

Volumes Available

Ex Auditu Vol. 1 (1985) consists of selected articles presenting the issues inherent in the theological interpretation of Scripture.

Ex Auditu Vol. 2 (1986) discusses the theme: "Church and State Relationship." In addition there are two lead articles, one by Peter Stuhlmacher on "EX AUDITU and the Theological Interpretation of Holy Scripture," and the second by Ben F. Meyer on "The Primacy of Consent and the Uses of Suspicion."

| Ex Auditu Vol. 3 | (1987) | "Creation." |
| Ex Auditu Vol. 4 | (1988) | "The Church and Israel (Romans 9-11)." |
| Ex Auditu Vol. 5 | (1989) | "What is Salvation?" |
| Ex Auditu Vol. 6 | (1990) | "Prophetic and/or Apocalyptic Eschatology." |
| Ex Auditu Vol. 7 | (1991) | "Christology and Incarnation" |
| Ex Auditu Vol. 8 | (1992) | "Worship." |
| Ex Auditu Vol. 9 | (1993) | "Resurrection." |
| Ex Auditu Vol. 10 | (1994) | "The Church." |
| Ex Auditu Vol. 11 | (1995) | "Biblical Law and Liberty." |
| Ex Auditu Vol. 12 | (1996) | "Holy Spirit." |
| Ex Auditu Vol. 13 | (1997) | "What is a Human?" |
| Ex Auditu Vol. 14 | (1998) | "The Theological Significance of the Earthly Jesus." |
| Ex Auditu Vol. 15 | (1999) | "Idolatry and the Understanding of God." |
| Ex Auditu Vol. 16 | (2000) | "The Task of Interpreting Scripture Theologically." |
| Ex Auditu Vol. 17 | (2001) | "Biblical Ethics." |
| Ex Auditu Vol. 18 | (2002) | "Spiritual Formation." |
| Ex Auditu Vol. 19 | (2003) | "The Authority and Function of Scripture." |
| Ex Auditu Vol. 20 | (2004) | "Judgment." |
| Ex Auditu Vol. 21 | (2005) | "Health and Healing." |
| Ex Auditu Vol. 22 | (2006) | "Justice." |
| Ex Auditu Vol. 23 | (2007) | "Christianity's Engagement with Culture." |
| Ex Auditu Vol. 24 | (2008) | "The Idolatry of Security." |

Pickwick Publications
An imprint of Wipf & Stock Publishers
199 West 8th Avenue, Ste. 3
Eugene OR 97401

www.ingramcontent.com/pod-product-compliance
Lightning Source LLC
Chambersburg PA
CBHW081351230426
43667CB00017B/2796